I0824149

PRAISE FOR *RUN RIGHT*

"For generations, conservatives have defended our principles with passion. But too often, we've put principles before power—and lost both. *Run Right* by Cliff Maloney and Joshua Lisec fixes that with a clear, tactical playbook for organizing, door-knocking, and campaigning that actually wins races—so conservative principles can become public policy. If you're a Republican candidate running for any office, get copies for every staffer and volunteer on your team."

—Jack Posobiec, *New York Times* bestselling author and host of *Human Events Daily*

"*Run Right* does something rare—it respects the grassroots enough to tell them the truth about what works. Doors, data, discipline, and post-campaign planning . . . if your operation is missing any of those, this book will show you how to fix it."

—Tiffany Justice, vice president at Heritage Action

"Finally, the Right has the campaign manual we have desperately needed! There is *no one* in politics who understands not only 'what time it is' but also how to actually *win* better than Cliff Maloney. That's because through his entire life, he has actually put in the work and produced the kind of results everyone else dreams of. You want to save your country from the radical Left? Start reading."

—Nick Freitas, former Virginia delegate

"Most consultant books are about buying TV ads; this one is about actually winning. From target universes to GOTV and ballot-chasing, *Run Right* finally gives the Right a serious, data-driven playbook for modern campaigns. How do I know this? Because Cliff Maloney ran the ground game that elected me as Knox County mayor."

—Glenn Jacobs, mayor and former WWE wrestler "Kane"

"I've watched a lot of people in politics overcomplicate things—and fail. Cliff Maloney does the opposite. He leads with humility, sharp strategy, and non-stop work, and he doesn't get distracted by the noise or ego that dominates this business. Cliff cares about results, because results matter to freedom. In a space filled with talkers and 'professionals,' he and his team are a rare bright spot. His back-to-basics approach is simple, disciplined, and—most importantly—it's winning elections."

—John Brunner, businessman and mentor

RUN RIGHT

A COMPLETE ELECTION PLAYBOOK TO WIN

CLIFF MALONEY
JOSHUA LISEC

FOREWORD BY TYLER BOWYER

Regnery books may be purchased in bulk at special discounts for sales promotion, corporate gifts, fund-raising, or educational purposes. Special editions can also be created to specifications. For details, contact the Special Sales Department, Regnery, 307 Fifth Avenue, 4th Floor, New York, NY 10016 or info@skyhorsepublishing.com.

Regnery® is an imprint of Skyhorse Publishing, Inc.®, a Delaware corporation.

Visit our website at www.regnery.com.
Please follow our publisher Tony Lyons on Instagram @tonylyonsisuncertain.

10 9 8 7 6 5 4 3 2 1

Library of Congress Cataloging-in-Publication Data is available on file.

Cover design by Jonha Scherzer

Print ISBN: 978-1-5107-8701-8
Ebook ISBN: 978-1-5107-8702-5

Printed in the United States of America

For Charlie

"Doors win wars."
— Cliff Maloney

CONTENTS

FOREWORD
BY TYLER BOWYER

Charlie Kirk was a political genius. He was concerned for his faith and his family above all else—in that order. But because his relationship with Christ, Erika, and their two children were his priority, Charlie cared about influencing the culture that ultimately determines political outcomes.

Charlie understood there is no such thing as an apolitical thought. In fact, he believed with all his heart that one of the greatest plagues of the younger generation is apathy. Apathetic hearts about politics are indicators of much more devastating fractures within society; indifference of faith, laziness on starting a family, passiveness in desire to create and contribute to society through business.

This is why Charlie cared so much about Gen Z, and it translated into caring about Americans of all different ages and backgrounds. He knew no matter what worldview a person was born into, he possessed the unique ability—as an American—to speak directly to the heart of each person who took the time to listen. This is why we fight at Turning Point USA and Turning Point Action. It's why we teamed up with Cliff Maloney of Citizens Alliance. "Doors win wars" is a mantra we have adopted with Cliff to reach those who will listen. Together, we worked to win Pennsylvania and every other swing state for Donald Trump to revive the faith of citizens in the strength and permanence of the U.S. Constitution and the hope that it will be preserved for generations to come.

Charlie thought highly of Joshua Lisec and endorsed a number of his books. Unfortunately, the library for activism on the right is nowhere near as comprehensive as Charlie wished it was. We often spoke of writing more to give conservative activists a clear picture of what needs to be done for the next generation to win. I am grateful we get to incorporate this first handbook for the Right to win elections, win on the issues, and win hearts and minds.

I and the entire Turning Point leadership team are proud to endorse *Run Right* by patriots Cliff Maloney and Joshua Lisec. This is essential reading for every citizen activist who wants to take our country back from the treacherous Left one election at a time.

PREFACE
BY CLIFF MALONEY

It was 1:22 a.m. Eastern Standard Time. November 6, 2024. The first networks had called the race. Because they had called Pennsylvania. As Pennsylvania went, so did the whole election.[1] PA was the play.

I was live with Charlie Kirk that night. When we reported the news, sharing it on air, Charlie hid his face and his wife Erika shielded him with the most joyous embrace any of us have ever seen before or since or will ever see.

With Charlie speechless and the other cohosts like Jack Posobiec locked in on the incoming results, we were about to have dead air. In broadcast and livestream terms, that's when the audience is watching and listening to . . . nothing. The commentators, announcers, or otherwise hosts are on, but nobody is saying anything.

So I let Pennsylvania take center stage. Because it just had. And I told the story of how Charlie Kirk and Tyler Bowyer personally asked me to drop everything and win Pennsylvania for Donald J. Trump—and with it, the Electoral College and thus the forty-seventh U.S. presidency.

"Charlie, let me give you credit from right here in Pennsylvania," I said. "You were the guy—you and Tyler [Bowyer]—who convinced me. You said, 'Cliff, stop door-knocking across the country, go back to your home state, own Pennsylvania. That will be the deciding factor.' I thought you guys were nuts. We knocked five hundred thousand doors, we delivered Pennsylvania, and now, we've got our country back."[2]

We got our country; we lost our Charlie.

Every voice on the American Right has given their best effort of a eulogy for Charlie after he was assassinated on September 10, 2025, not one full year after that glorious late November night.

Under Charlie Kirk, Turning Point Action and its sister organization focused on college campus organizing—Turning Point USA—became the central node of the entire non-establishment Right-wing network. And not just in America, but for the world. When we all heard he had passed, we all grieved like we'd just lost a president. Because we had. And since that day, all of us have asked ourselves publicly and privately one question.

Now what?

I don't have the answer; but I have *an* answer.

And that answer is this book.

Turning Point will survive and thrive long as a protector and propellor of and for all things good and Right. A reason Turning Point works is it's a "big tent," so to speak. And that tent includes my organization, Citizens Alliance, that ran the groundbreaking PA CHASE program. I founded the organization and serve as CEO. I'm not here to grift, I'm here to give. And what I am giving you, with this book, is the simple truth about how to run a campaign that wins.

The election of President Trump may be a crown jewel in the Citizens Alliance and Turning Point collaborative saga, but we've both had our share of successes—and trials and lessons learned.

Years before I became the "Godfather of door-knocking," according to Roger Stone, I was amped up by Dr. Ron Paul and TEA Party politics. Barack Obama had recently won reelection, I realized the country was skidding into the quagmire of Cultural Marxism, and something had to be done. So I looked to the Left, of all places: How do they claim and retain so much power over minds, hearts, wallets, and ballot boxes in America? Oh, right—the latter. They show up and vote up and down the ballot for their guys, their issues, and their values. They organize, they move, and they win, as a collective.

Now that we are without Charlie Kirk, and as we look ahead to the future post–President Trump, we realize that we may have won our country back. But the game is not over. And yet as the fracturing of the Right following Charlie's death revealed, many of our players are rage-quitting off the field. Charlie's memory deserves better.

I'm just a guy from the Philly suburbs who wants to help get patriots elected who love the United States of America and want what's best for her.

Since 2016, I've deployed door-knocking campaigns to knock on over nine million doors and secure 450 election wins. I haven't done this alone. My right-hand man Justin Greiss has worked alongside me for over a decade now. We've plotted, funded, and executed more door deployments than any other operatives on the right.

Without Justin, and the thousands of patriots we've deployed, the ground game on the right would be nonexistent. Together, we've set a new standard to match the Democrats' tactics and fight fire with fire. *No more excuses* is the motto Justin and I use to break barriers as blue-collar kids trying to crush the commies and restore the Republic.

I will continue to knock on doors until the day I can no longer walk, knock, or talk. Until then, I urge you to join me—if you have political aspirations, perhaps duty is now calling you. This may be the book for you.

In the aftermath of it all, I reached out to Joshua Lisec, the *New York Times* bestselling author and ghostwriter of something like 110 books at this point. It turns out providentially that he had intended to reach out to me—I just beat him to it. He shared about the book he'd been wanting to write for more than five years but had not found the right coauthor.

It was meant to be.

Perhaps your candidacy as a freedom-loving American patriot is, too.

We encourage you to read this book in full to see if making America great again as an elected leader is right for you.

For Charlie.

Cliff Maloney
December 17, 2025

INTRODUCTION

THE MOST INFLUENTIAL BOOK OF THE LAST THIRTY YEARS

Have you ever wondered?

Why do candidates with radically unpopular ideas win important elections? And why do such victories happen in districts where the citizens treasure traditional conservative values? How is it that Left-wing ideologues pull together movements to make their minority views the laws of our land?

We've wondered. And we'll come right back to these questions. Because we now want to volunteer the following anecdote. It begins like this:

Coauthor Joshua Lisec once tweeted the following.

> The most influential book of the last 30 years, bar none:
> The Organizer's Handbook by Marshall Ganz
> There is a good reason you've never heard of it:
> It works.[3]

That's the colloquial title; the work's official name is *Organizing: People, Power, Change*. How could the book have earned such an award from Joshua? It turns out that this question has the same answer as the barrage of curiosity that opened this very chapter. It's all about to come together.

You see, this little fifty-pager—more so, specifically, the ideas therein—changed American politics. It packages and presents the work of Harvard University's Dr. Marshall Ganz, an activist hailing from the Civil Rights Era but later a chief strategist for Barack Obama's wonderluck 2008 U.S. presidential campaign. The framework inside this e-book is widely credited with bequeathing the Left with one of the most formidable sociopolitical organization-machines in world history. Groups like MoveOn, Indivisible, and the climate outfits didn't appear out of nowhere. They're running the same operating system as the handbook. Results are obvious; they've been out-organizing the Right for years—flipping seats, building movements, and forming pipelines of professional organizers who keep the wins coming.

How? Here's how. Ganz's methodology transforms ordinary progressives into future leaders into elected zealots. Leftist energy becomes results. The few collectivize; their passion becomes policy. There is discipline. Order. Power. Volunteers stick around election after election, get trained, take on responsibility, pull others with them, cultivate emotions, and move their side to act and act big. The Left wages culture war to win, and the Organizer's Handbook is their metaphorical battle plan they run over and over again to create upset after upset, whether it's on "green" energy, socialized medicine, illegal immigration protections, anti-baby abortion laws, and the radical candidates who stand for them all.

Republicans have no such book. Conservatives have no such North Star. The America First movement has no such book. For years, this bothered Joshua. For years, Joshua rolodexed influencers to coauthor an "Organizer's Handbook for the Right." A single resource with all the fundamentals patriots need to know to organize, fundraise, campaign, and win—on issues, in culture, and with candidates.

Meanwhile, community organizing is basically trademarked, owned, and licensed by the Left. They've mastered the art of organic unification and collective action. That's why they can push radical progressive policies almost anywhere they want—they organize around a cause, rally behind a candidate, or force their issue until enough passionate people line up to win. It's what Marshall taught, and it works. Every single time.

But for the Right, there's been no real playbook. No handbook. No written, accessible set of instructions that's publicly available for any of us to pick, reference, and implement. Especially when it comes to elections.

One of the most common complaints we've heard from conservatives—whether running for local, state, or even federal office—is, very simply, **"I don't know what to do."** See, there's no clear process, no central set of resources, no proven guide, no ready-made tools. It's more of a "you just have to know someone" reliance on word of mouth—or Daddy's money. Many such cases.

And that's all true at the grassroots level as much as at higher levels of organizing. That said, the closest thing the Right has had to a grassroots community organizing operation is Turning Point Action—not even the Republican establishment or any of their consultants, affiliates, or satellites!

We need a complete playbook to win elections, and everybody knows it. For local and county offices. For the state house, state senate, and other state-wide races. Even for U.S. Congress—and above. We need this book.

The most natural and best fit to collaborate was unveiled amid the unprecedented success of Republicans in the U.S. presidential and federal elections of 2024. I (Joshua) first heard of Cliff Maloney as a Right-wing organizer-extraordinaire who would go on to manage the coalition that hand-delivered in pure white gloves the commonwealth of Pennsylvania—the bellwether state—to now-president, Donald Trump. "PA is the play," fellow organizer Jack Posobiec said over and over and over; other prominents including world's richest unlikely activist Elon Musk who went all in on Pennsylvania.

What he (Cliff) was able to do in Pennsylvania, he's done year after year in state after state. And not just chasing ballots, knocking on doors, and persuading voters face-to-face. But cultivating new talent. Converting activists into leaders. And converging conservative principles with America First policies into win after win after win.

An organizer's handbook for patriots is born.

It's for you. Yes, *you*. Here's what we suspect about you, personally. You're tired of losing. You're glad to see team America win big, as with President Donald J. Trump and several key congressional races with national attention in otherwise toss-up areas. But winning a battle once in four years is not total victory. You're sick of Republicans who complain about Leftist hypocrisy, then turn around and allow more of it. Push "principles before power," then surrender said power to the opposing party whose single unifying principle *is* power.

And you're worried about the future. What happens when President Trump is no longer in office to unite all of us across the country who want to make and keep America great? What do we do now that the greatest constitutional rights activist of our generation—Charlie Kirk—has been slain? We all watched as a Leftist assassinated Charlie in bitter-cold blood, rank-and-file Democrat voters nationwide celebrated, then progressive entertainers and media personalities blamed conservatives for "rhetoric" that karmically merits our best man's public murder.

There will be no unity. Only victory.

So if you want to get involved . . .

If you want to, like Charlie Kirk, quote for yourself that ubiquitous excerpt from Isaiah 6:8 . . .

Here am I; send me!

And if you want to win the election, the system, the Constitution, and the law . . .

This is the book for you.

It's time to stop arguing with trolls online and start readying yourself to run for something—or follow this book to support someone who does.

Let us who stand on the shoulders of giants and martyrs and the great men of history do the right thing. We don't have to wonder why radicals win when and where they hypothetically "shouldn't" and why Leftists decide moral standards for the rest of us. It's not that evil prevails in our instance because good men do nothing; it's that we the good men (and women) have so often done it alone. The Left goes far—too far—because they go together.

Now it's our turn. Everything we cover in this book is to ensure you have a viable plan to run right, win elected office, and change the country forever.

For Charlie.

PART I

POLITICS, POWER, AND PERSUASION

CHAPTER 1

HOW TO PLAY THE GAME OF POLITICS (AND NOT GET DESTROYED)

There's something you should know.
More than 90 percent of incumbents win reelection—even when congressional approval is below 20 percent.[4, 5, 6]

There's something we see over and over again when someone decides to run for office the first time. A given patriot gets fed up. Like Peter Finch's character Howard Beale in *Network* (1976), this citizen is mad as hell and will not take it anymore. Often the inciting incident is something that shouldn't have happened to a friend, a family member, or themselves—and yet it did. *How is this OK?!* Our hypothetical yet true-to-life aspiring candidate wonders in raging disbelief. Well, John Smith, it's not OK, but you only have the rights you yourself are willing to enforce or see enforced on your behalf. Federal and state constitutions, laws, and codes are generally well-intended, but justice moves at the speed of the DMV. In other situations, our political hopeful believes something rather obvious should happen, but it's not getting done—and for the same reason. *Someone should do something. Maybe . . . that someone should be me.*

That's the American way. Fine. I'll do it myself. 1776 to present. (Americans are willing to cross frozen rivers in the dark of Christmas morning to kill you in your sleep, after all.)

And so our future public service star talks to those same jilted family members and spiteful friends. Wouldn't it be nice if someone who actually cared actually had power? They hear praise and feel support. They do a little googling. Discipline swells to match the size of motivation. They're totally gonna do this thing. And then . . . they do! So they announce. Candidacy. It's real now. They put up a sharp video or a heartfelt post. They get a flurry of likes, comments, texts, and pats on the back. People at church, the range, or the school board meeting tell them, "We need someone like you in there. You've got my vote."

For a few weeks, it feels like a movement is brewing. True grassroots change. This is literally the future of MAGA.

But then the first hard questions hit. Our hero walks into county party headquarters or sits down in a back room with a couple of local insiders. Everyone smiles. Shakes hands. Business cards exchanged. Glad you're stepping up. Hey, is that an AOL email address? Am I in the wrong room or—

"So, how much money have you raised so far?"

What now?

"Who's on your finance committee?"

My what?

"How many volunteers are knocking doors?"

Doors?

"What's your early-vote plan?"

Early voting?

OK, so that's hard to believe but it's not. We've been around the game long enough, the both of us. And the blunt truth is that most first-time candidates don't have real answers to any of that. At least not from the start. Oh, sure, they'll eventually get them. Well into the campaign. When they're already behind but don't know it yet. Then they get smoked in the primary. Come in sixth. Or stumble into the general and fumble an R +11 district to a Communist.

Is this an exaggeration? Yes. Is it directionally accurate? Yes. Do you get the point? Also yes.

Our candidate may have a message and a pretty logo with a nice yard sign design and maybe a stump speech written by a college kid they know who's majoring in English. But they'll walk out of that meeting with less momentum than they brought in and a sinking feeling they can't quite name.

Fast forward to primary night. The outsider who "everyone said they liked" loses badly to an incumbent or a "safe" insider the base claims to be tired of. The signs all come back to the garage. The Facebook page goes quiet. The person who stepped out in faith spends the next six months asking the same thing you've probably asked watching election returns on TV:

How on earth did that person win again?

This pattern is no fluke. It's what happens when good people walk into a very specific kind of game without realizing what they're actually playing.

THE ACTUAL GAME

People get into politics thinking it'll be their "Mr. Smith Goes to Washington" moment, only to realize it is more like "House of Cards." The system you are about to step into is not designed to reward fairness, authenticity, or even noble motives and a righteous cause. It is made to reward only one thing: predictability. To keep the people already in power in power, unless something stronger pushes them out.

Incumbents usually almost always win.

The organized few beat the outraged many. Status quo-maxxing. Voters change nothing until the pain of admitting they elected the wrong person is worse than the pain of changing their vote.

Understand this system. It's where big dreams of great change give way to the sweaty nightmare of reality itself. The system rewards those who understand its incentives and punishes those who don't. We're not here to make you feel better about this. In fact, if you already feel bad . . . this book is not for you because politics is *definitely* not for you. We are here to make sure you understand the game some of you are about to play—for real, in the arena, with your name and your money and your future all on the line. We want you to win for the right side without losing your soul.

So before we talk about the concrete steps of how to file, where to run, or how to raise your first five grand, we have to debunk Disney politics and show you a private screening of how the real world really works. Let's do that now.

WHAT POLITICS IS NOT

Most people come into this process with a half-remembered high school civics idea of politics. It's something like . . .

- "Looking after the common good"
- "Serving your fellow man"
- "Blind allegiance to a party or to 'our' guy"
- "The art of compromise"

Those phrases sound about right, and yet they have very little to do with how power actually works. If one assumes politics is mostly about mostly good people trying hard to do mostly right things most of the time, you'll never understand why the worst people with the worst ideas keep winning elections by a mile. You'll be stuck thinking, *But that doesn't make sense*, as if common sense has anything to do with politics (lol, lmao even).

Politics does not run on making sense. It runs on power. Which leads us to the real definition.

THE REAL NATURE OF POLITICS

It goes like this, and you'll remember it.

Politics is the adjudication of power.

That's a fancy way of saying that **politics is the process by which we decide who rules whom, who gets what, and what happens to those who get in the way.**

Politics is one of the only true zero-sum games left in public life. For the uninitiated, positive-sum games allow multiple winners. Think entrepreneurship. Zero-sum games are the opposite. There once was a pie, now there's only one slice left, and first-come-first-served that one last piece. So when someone wins an election, someone else loses. When someone's worldview gains ground in law and policy, someone else's worldview gets pushed out. A single primary with multiple political parties plus independents can be *dozens* strong—and yet only one person emerges victorious. There's no silver or bronze medal. **Losers don't legislate.**

Put this way, and modern politics sucks. And it does. The true definition of politics is simple:

poly: many
ticks: blood-sucking parasites

And yet it's the best way known to mankind for all of recorded history and even prehistory going back to the first hominids. Because for most of our existence, we settled our disputes through:

- Raping and pillaging
- Enslaving then human sacrificing
- All of the above followed by ritual cannibalizing

Meme Credit: Bring Our Troops Home, Director of Operations Diego Rivera.

That is less than ideal. Even in much of the world today where everybody has iPhones, polyester clothing, and Marvel movies, elections are theater; the real exchanges of power come through coups, civil wars, sectarian terrorism, assassinations, and street violence.

Still today in the Philippines, more than 10,000 political assassinations (supporters of one party or another) are commonplace each election. And even political assassinations of political candidates remain prevalent. In 2024, Mexico saw thirty-four candidates killed in a single election year.

The arrangement that our Founding Fathers desired for us, for all its flaws, lets us settle political disputes peacefully. We have checks and balances between branches. We have competing levels of government—federal, state, local. And we have elections instead of coups, lawsuits instead of firing squads. All good news, relative to the above alternatives. It's why we're still standing as a country. Can you name one other country whose structure has gone largely unchanged since 1776? We think not. Maybe one or two. And their populations are sub-10 million. That's not even one Pennsylvania.

That said, let's not confuse a relatively peaceful system with a neutral one. We are still talking about who rules whom. Political power is zero sum. The rules are more civilized, but the stakes are the same. The strong do what they will; the weak suffer what they must. Winner takes all. The sooner you accept all this, the more briskly you'll understand the political arena.

REAL POWER VERSUS FAKE POWER

You may have seen the *Game of Thrones* meme about power. Knowledge is power? No. *Power* is power. Returning now to this chapter, if politics is the adjudication of power, and if power is . . . power . . . then . . . what is power?

> **Power**: The ability and opportunity to force people to act the way you want—and to incentivize or punish them when they don't.

That's a lot, and yet it's not. Ability means you can, hypothetically; opportunity means you can, practically. And you either give the carrot, or the stick. Sometimes both. That's power.

Notice how the American system, copied globally, gives power to the people.

Meme Credit: Bring Our Troops Home, Director of Operations Diego Rivera.

The people's power: The ability and opportunity to force politicians to act the way you want—and to replace them when they don't.

That's cool. But the inverse is not. If you can't make leaders vote differently and you can't credibly threaten their seat, you do not have power. You may have something that feels like power, but you don't have the thing that affects laws. Which brings us to **pseudopower**, which is **access**. Access is when:

- A Congressman calls you by your first name
- The Governor's office returns your calls
- You get into closed-door meetings
- You get invited to nice dinners and photo ops

It's flattering. It feels important. It looks good on social media. But by itself, access is not power. Access means you're being listened to. It does not mean the person across the table is afraid of losing an election if they ignore you. It does not mean they pay a price for breaking their word. It does not mean they will act.

We want you to burn this sentence into your brain before you ever run: ***Unless you are politically feared, you will not be politically respected.***

This goes for power to the people, and for power to you, should you aspire to actual political power and its adjudication. Now, that doesn't mean you scream and threaten people. As a citizen, it means you build the capacity to elect people who keep their word and unelect people who don't. And as one of those elected leaders, it means you'll treat your colleagues—in both parties—with the carrot and the stick as needed. *Speak softly and carry a big vegetable.*

See, if a politician is more afraid of their own party leadership, their donors, and their consultants than they are of crossing you and your people, you are going to lose the important fights—whether we're talking about a primary race or a piece of legislation. No nice and professional meeting fixes any of this. Power is power.

Pseudopower, Continued: Education Versus Mobilization

Naïve political hopefuls, aside from believing access means influence, often likewise believe that education matters. Education feels safe and normal. *If we could just educate people. . . . If we could just hand out pocket Constitutions and explain this. . . . If we could just print out thick binders full of stats. . . . If we could just deliver detailed policy explanations about what good policy will look like. . . . If people just knew what was going on, we could wake them up . . . If only the truth got out. . .*

Any version of the above reveals a political virginity. Education is romantic. Let us ask you: If you've ever tried to talk politics with friends or family members who disagree with you, how many of them changed their minds after a single conversation? After ten? Probably close to zero. If you can't reliably "educate" your own family (the people who love and care about you the most) into changing sides, why would you build your entire strategy on "educating" thousands of strangers about why they should vote for you?

But there's another problem. Even when education works, it rarely translates into action. You can have a majority of people who say they support a position in polls, and still have elections and then laws that go the exact and precise opposite direction (just ask Californians). Public policy is not made of public opinion. It is made by mobilized minorities who are organized, disciplined, and willing to show up over and over again. This doesn't mean education is useless. But the goal is not awareness. The goal is **mobilization**, which includes:

- Training people into highly effective activists
- Giving them concrete tasks with deadlines
- Building a culture where showing up is normal, not extraordinary
- Turning anger into numbers

Education is useful only to the extent that it produces mobilized people who will knock doors, give money, show up for you, and vote in every election to keep you in office. Mobilization includes education, but education does not automatically include mobilization. Remember that distinction, and you will be ahead of most candidates, most consultants, and most issue groups on our side. We are going for **tangible impact**, not intangible victory.

Intangible:

- "I got involved."
- "I did the right thing."
- "I made my voice heard."
- "I ran the best campaign I knew how."
- "I owned the libs on social media."

Intangible victories are political masturbation; it may feel good, but nothing is created.

Tangible:

- "I raised $5,000 in forty-eight hours."
- "We knocked on 500 doors this weekend."
- "I had 50 people out collecting ballots."
- "I moved voters 5 whole points in my favor."
- "I won. By only 0.5 percent. But I won. Power."

Anything that doesn't fit on a tangible impact list is wistful, wasteful commentary. Leave that to the influencers selling mugs, t-shirts, and content subscription memberships to people who need their conservative ragebait fix.

Politics is like the wilderness. It's rough out there. And lonely. Very lonely. The isolation is more than you versus a whole field of opposition. It's separation from the voters; and the voters, from you. Here specifically is what we mean by that.

ELECTORAL REALITY AND THE "3 PERCENT + 1" RULE

In most races, not every eligible voter shows up. Not even close. Think of your district as a **marketing funnel**:

100% - Everyone who lives there.
Maybe ~60 percent - People eligible to vote.
Maybe ~40 percent - People actually registered to vote.
Maybe ~20–30 percent - People who vote in a given election.
Half of that - People who vote in your primary.
A sliver beyond that - The margin that decides the winner.

The actual number of people who determine whether you win or lose is shockingly small. In many local and state races, a few hundred or a few thousand votes are the difference between "fringe outsider" and "Honorable So-and-so." Mayor JD Longo of Slippery Rock, PA, best known for emceeing both of President Trump's 2024 Butler, PA, rallies, won his 2025 reelection by just forty-three votes. Under fifty votes separated the reelection of "America's Mayor" and a radical left lunatic in the rural county Donald J. Trump was shot in…

What's your fifty? The **3 Percent + 1 Rule**. It goes like this: Roughly speaking, if you can identify and mobilize a small, committed minority of voters—just a few percent of the district—and you can get one more vote than the other side in that committed band, you can decide the outcome.

We are not telling you this so you'll think small; we're telling you so you'll think realistically. Fifty. You do not need to flip the whole culture. You do not need to "wake up America." You need to build an organized, disciplined operation around the statistical sliver of people who are reachable and movable in the election you are actually in.

This might be the only good news of the chapter. In light of the 3 Percent + 1 Rule, polls strike no fear, social media noise quiets down, and the fundraising race slows. Because you're focused, in your lane, thinking, *Who is the high-propensity voter in this election, what is their contact information, and how can I reach them?*

That is how races are really won.

Power.

CHAPTER 2

UNDERSTANDING POLITICIANS (BEFORE BECOMING ONE)

There's something you should know.
The average member of Congress spends up to 70 percent of their time fundraising—not doing the job they were elected to do.[7]

Politics is a dirty business. Don't wear white.

We want you to be ready. That means knowing who you're going to be competing against, playing with, and even . . . becoming. Yes, if you follow this book and do exactly as we say, you'll find that, odds are, you are set to become . . . *gasp* . . . a politician. We owe it to you to tell you what will motivate the person you're about to become.

Now, we want you to imagine a very specific scene. You're at a church potluck, a backyard barbecue, or maybe your kid's ballgame. It's a Heritage-American moment, and everyone is among friends. This is high-trust society. And so the talk drifts, as it always seems to now, to "those people" in office.

Then someone brings up a name everyone knows.

"Remember when he first ran?" one guy says. "He actually sounded like one of us. Said all the right things."

Heads nod.

"Yeah, but then he got down there and started voting just like the rest of them."

"You know, I actually know him. He used to text me back. Now I barely get a call back from some staffer reading a script."

"He swore he'd never vote for that kind of bill. Then he did. Twice."

Of course, nobody around the picnic table knows the exact conversations that happened in the statehouse. Or at the steakhouse bar and grill after a day's work. Or in the bar's restroom. Yes, the leaders of the free world decide our fate at the urinal.

Most people don't know that. All we know is what we see and hear. And what we see and hear is that the longer this guy's in office, the less he acts like the guy who campaigned on all those promises that are going unmet. And the more power he gets, the more he seems to care about the party and its leadership instead of the people standing around back home with plastic forks and kids tugging their sleeves. At some point, "that guy changed" is less the exception and more the rule.

Now, that's one way ordinary people—we lovingly call them "normies"—come to believe that politics is a dirty business. They watch normal, church-going, flag-waving neighbors step into office and become some kind of swamp creature.

But we want you to switch vantage points. This time, you're not the voter. Now you're on the inside, perhaps a junior staffer in your first real political job. You signed up for this because you believe in this person. They ran as a fighter, a reformer, a maverick, an outsider, a change agent, a swamp-drainer. You imagined days full of meaningful policy research work and authentic connection in constituent meetings. But instead . . . you're stuck in the boiler room. Cramped office. Cheap accessories. Spreadsheets of names. Your boss sits there for hours, AirPods in, working lists to raise campaign dollars. Call after call, it's the same.

"How are you? It's great to hear from you. . . . Yes, we're working hard on that. . . . Listen, we've got a tough race coming up and I could really use your help again. . . ."

Sometimes the calls are to big donors with private jets. Other times, they're to small business owners who hosted a fundraiser last cycle. Even to people who barely remember who this person is, but their name's on a "likely contributor" list.

That's depressing. You peep the daily schedule and see that between "call time" and evening fundraising events, your boss is spending as much—even more?—time chasing money as they are showing up for the people. You're the one who sees their mood swing when a donor hedges, when a lobbyist hints that support might dry up, when the party's campaign arm calls to say, "We're worried about your numbers."

Now, to be fair, nobody is handing over paper bags stuffed with cash (with the exception of Somali-ran daycare centers in Minnesota). Nobody is shouting out, "Dance, puppet!" But sitting in that little room, you can feel what really scares and motivates the person whose name is on the door.

This is another face of dirty business: the quiet, grinding shift from "do the right thing" to "do whatever it takes to stay in the game."

THE ROOM YOU NEVER SEE ON C-SPAN

Alright, now we want you to picture a place most voters never see at all—the closed-door party or caucus meeting. No cameras, no mics, no speeches. Imagine a long table, cold coffee, and the people who actually set the tone for our side. The leader runs through the week's agenda. Like routine bills, technical fixes, resolutions no one cares about. It's all handled pretty quickly. Then they get to a package that is radioactive back home. You know it. They know it. Everybody knows it.

Now, the leader doesn't rant. Doesn't threaten. Just explains calmly what "we" need to do.

"This one is complicated. There's a lot going on behind the scenes. Major donors like it. The big guy's office is watching this one. The press is circling. We need to look united and responsible. Our expectation is that the caucus will be together on this."

People around the table nod. Some stare at the paperwork. Some look bored. You catch a few fleeting glances sent your way. You ran against this sort of thing. You gave speeches about it. You printed mail about it. They're wondering whether you're going to make trouble.

After the meeting, one of the veterans catches you in the hallway. They're all smiles. They ask about your family. They crack a joke about how confusing the building is the first month.

Then their tone shifts just a bit.

"Look, I remember what it was like to be in your shoes," they say. "You come in fired up. You want to fix everything at once. But if you blow yourself up on one early vote, you're not going to be effective. You won't get anything done for your district. There will be better opportunities to do the right thing down the line. Don't make yourself a martyr your first term."

They pat your arm. "You're smart. You're going places. Don't throw it away because you don't like how something looks on paper."

They walk away, humming and checking their phone.

Notice "the dog that's not barking," as Scott Adams used to say—that's the effect of what you don't notice when a usually noisy guard dog suddenly ceases to bark. It's the unnoticed warning. The dog that's not barking.

Notice in this true-to-life hypothetical that nobody said, "Abandon your principles." What they said was, in no uncertain terms, "Be smart. . . . Be realistic. . . . Don't commit career suicide over one vote. *<wink>*"

OK, maybe there's no Hollywood-esque wink. Anyway, from the outside, all your people will see is the final tally and maybe a thirty-second clip on the news. But on the inside, you see something else entirely. You are witness to a culture in which survival and advancement are incentivized—with urgency and prejudice—and keeping your word to voters is disincentivized, if it stalls your momentum in accomplishing the former.

IF YOU DECIDE TO RUN, THIS IS THE WORLD YOU'RE WALKING INTO.

Another important thing about this world. Most of the people you'll meet there are not comic-book villains. Now many of them might be sociopaths, but they're not all geniuses. They are, for the most part, "normies." People who want to get along, get the job done, and get home in time to watch the game.

Anything "dirty" about politics, elected normies aren't bringing with them. It's a systemic issue, to use Left-wing lingo. Winner takes all, remember? Nothing matters to a given political party more than loyalty, and being "principled" is a lightyears-away distant second.

This explains why so many voters get blindsided. They imagine "politician" as their own species. Then they see their neighbor, their Sunday school teacher, their local business owner run and win. And they think, *This time will be different.* Then that neighbor, teacher, or business owner spends a year in the call room and the caucus meeting, and the system starts doing to them what it did to the last guy or gal.

That's politics. And the political system ensures that all politicians (the good guys and the bad guys alike) want three and only three things. Understand this, and you'll be able to predict their behavior with near-99 percent accuracy in office—and even your own behavior, should your turn come next.

WHAT POLITICIANS WANT

Here it is.

1. **Politicians want to get <u>elected</u>.**
2. **They want to get <u>reelected</u>.**
3. **They want to get <u>elected to a higher office</u>.**

That's it. Those three desires are humming in the background at all times like some kind of perpetual harmonic rhythm. And now, behavior that used to confuse suddenly makes sense. See, when these are the goals, what feels safest (to the politician) is not sharp conviction. What feels safest is the middle, a safe harbor. It's the zone of behavior (and voting) where they don't boat-rock, they don't offend, they don't stand out. And not no, but hell-no, do they want to do *anything* that tempts an adversary back home to attempt a primary fight.

So now, we can translate. A soft-pressure statement like, "Don't make this your hill to die on" really means: *This vote could put your seat at risk. Don't do it.*

"Be a team player" means, *Don't do anything that makes leadership's life harder or complicates our fundraising.*

And, "Wait for a better opportunity to do the right thing" means "*Do nothing now. Maybe someday, when it's safer, you can pretend to care again.*"

That's politics. Get elected, get reelected, get promoted. Threatening any of these three is where real power begins.

PLEASURE AND PAIN

There's another aspect to the game that is worth covering from the get-go. You will walk into the arena with your eyes wide open.

Because politicians do their damndest to adhere to those three goals, they become exceptionally sensitive to anything that seems to move them closer to or farther away from their prime objectives. Like all animals, politicians respond most strongly to two stimuli: **pleasure and pain**.

Pleasure, in non-Clintonian politics, is anything that clearly helps Representative Jane Doe get what she wants. Think eager to knock doors for her, a fundraising report with strong numbers, endorsements from people her voters trust, positive coverage in media her base actually reads or watches, and quiet assurances from leadership that she's in line for a committee slot if she just "plays this smart." Pleasure.

Then pain, naturally, is anything that nakedly threatens those goals. Like a serious primary challenger sniffing around, a donor network that suddenly stops returning calls, activists who don't just complain online but start working for the other candidate, and public scorecards and receipts getting passed around back home instead of buried in some obscure newsletter. She's in pain. And what does one do when in pain? One seeks to make it stop.

The greatest source of pain for a politician is demonstrable proof of angry voters.

You don't have to become cynical to acknowledge pleasure-pain political power play. We just want you to be honest. In a job where losing an election means your entire world changes overnight, pleasure and pain are not abstracts . . . they're like the daily weather.

As a candidate, and later as an officeholder, you're going to be at the intersection of **all** of this. You will feel that weather on your own skin. And you also will be in a position to shape it for others.

One of my favorite moments in the Pennsylvania Senate chamber is when a sitting member was being lobbied by the establishment to support a corrupt bill and this was her response:

"I cannot vote for this bill. I cannot afford to have Citizens Alliance mad at me and launch a primary to take me out."

This line, by itself, shows the impact of political pain and how the fear of pain-to-be can impact legislation in real time. The bill failed and we won.

If you never accept that pleasure and pain are part of the equation, you will misjudge how everyone around you thinks. You might assume that a heartfelt argument or a well-researched white paper is enough to change behavior in a building full of people wired to react to votes, cash, and threats.

And if you refuse to let those same levers ever be pulled on you—if you cannot tolerate the idea that your own supporters might turn up the heat when you drift, according to their vantage point back home—then you're already becoming exactly the kind of insulated insider you might believe you hate.

THE QUESTION THAT WILL KEEP YOU SANE

There's one question that will save you from a lot of manipulation if you make a habit of asking it now.

Whenever someone from the political class—a party official, a consultant, a lobbyist, a senior colleague—tells you how politics works or what you should do next, pause and ask yourself:

If I believe them and do as they say, how does it benefit them?

You don't have to ask it out loud. No need to be rude about it. Just trace the line in your own mind.

If you take their advice, does it keep their majority intact? Does it preserve their influence? Does it protect their client's interests? Does it avoid a hassle in their caucus? Does it make their fundraising easier?

Sometimes, their advice will genuinely line up with your promises and your voters' needs. Sometimes, it won't. So the point is not to assume everyone is lying to you; it's to never again treat insiders' political advice as if *manna* from heaven, perfect and pure.

Every once in a while, turn that same question back on yourself.

If I believe my own excuse for breaking this promise and do what feels easier instead, how does it benefit me?

If you can be that honest with yourself, you're already ahead of most of the people in those beige rooms with stale coffee and bad lighting.

WHEN THEY GET MAD BECAUSE YOU KEPT YOUR WORD

There's one more pre-politics lesson we want to teach you before you face the campaign race. We'll make quick work of that starting in Chapter 3. Now, read this: **If you actually keep your word as a politician, many important people are going to be very angry at you.**

If you refuse to drift quietly toward the safe middle, you will embarrass colleagues who have made a career out of saying one thing back home and doing another in the capital. You will irritate party operatives who just want clean vote counts and no surprises. You will annoy donors who thought their check came with invisible strings attached. You will. And you will mean well. But that won't matter. Your phone'll light up. Your inbox'll get full. People you barely know will tell you, "I'm hearing you're being difficult," or, "You're hurting the team." You'll look them up later. Then right at that moment, you feel your heart skip and stomach churn. *This person can make my life hell.*

At that moment, you'll be tempted to adjust. Just a little. Just a little adjusting. Negotiating. Being reasonable. None dare call it compromise. No, you're simply toning it down. Holding off the fight. Going along "just this once" so everyone calms down.

Sometimes, you will genuinely need to pick your battles. This much is true. Not every hill is worth dying on. But you need a simple rule to keep you from talking yourself into cowardice:

If people are angry at you because you broke your word and hurt your own voters, you should listen hard, repent, and fix it.

But if people are angry at you because you kept your word and their comfortable arrangements got disrupted, that anger is not proof you're wrong. Very often, it's confirmation you finally touched something that mattered.

You will feel pressure, subtle and not-so-subtle, to treat every raised voice from the political class as a sign that you need to retreat and apologize—or else they will cancel you. But if you cave every time, the system will train you to be tame. They will not respect you. You remember what we said about respect in politics.

So if instead you let pushback become your momentum—if it drives you back to your promises, back to your voters, back to the reasons you ran in the first place—it will be much harder for this world to turn you into just another product of the machine.

That said, we're not attributing total malice to all politicians or even to most. This is a zero-sum system they, too, have to contend with. They, too, have spouses, families, friends, business interests, and secret lovers (!). Maybe not all, but still. Most of the people you'll be competing against, playing with, and tempted to become are not monsters. They are ordinary people—dare we say normies!—who are also getting shaped by a system that rewards safety and punishes courage. And that very system teaches them, day after day, that the worst possible sin is to **lose.**

If you walk into said system naïve—thinking that your sincerity alone will protect you—you will be easy to handle. Easy to steer. And ten years from now, someone at a church potluck will say about you, "He used to be different." And you did. You were. But you aren't now.

If you walk in with your eyes open, knowing what goals and fears are humming in the background of every conversation, you have a chance to do something very few people manage: **Serve, rather than get served.**

Alright . . . now you've now seen the game and the players. In the next chapter, we're going to ask the question that all of this has been building toward.

Knowing how politics really works, and knowing what it will try to turn you into, what do you do next?

Let's find out.

PART II

18 STEPS TO RUN AND WIN ELECTIONS

CHAPTER 3

SO YOU'VE DECIDED TO RUN FOR OFFICE (NOW WHAT?)

> ***There's something you should know.***
> More than 20 percent of young adults consider running for office—yet only about 2 percent of Americans do actually run.[8, 9]

We've given you a little preview of what politics and power are really all about—and what they turn people into. So now that you know what you're getting into, we can talk about why it's worth it. For the right people. Which may be you.

But before we talk about filing forms and deadlines, strict budgets, and voter data, it's worth pausing to call bullshit on ourselves. Are you in it for the right reason? Reasons? Why do people like you run in the first place—and why do some of them actually win?

You're not the first "normal" person to look at the country and think, *Fine. I'll run myself.* The good news, of course, is that you don't have to go first and guinea-pig it. A lot of people who've actually won for the right reasons on the Right started where you are now—mad, motivated, and sick of being sold out. That's what this next section is all about. Purpose, personalized.

TOP TEN REASONS THE RIGHT RUNS (AND WINS)

You don't have to sound like a sharp speechwriter-consultant from DC to have a real shot at political glory. In fact, most winning Right-wing populist and America First candidates have sounded nothing like such polished insiders from the get-go. The game is tough and the fight will get dirty; to be blunt, you've got to have your shit together or you will get eaten alive by those who do. And by getting your act together, we mean a hot-iron purpose no haters and critics can touch, be they liberal journalists or envious competitors in the party or even family members trying to play crabs-in-the-barrel. In more friendly terms, we mean "start with why" à la Simon Sinek. You have to know why you're willing to run the gauntlet of politics. Perhaps you already do. And there is more than one reason. Good. In fact, here are ten of the most common reasons the Right runs—and wins—straight from the mouths of candidates who showed the way.

1. To Put Our Own People First

Our 45th and 47th U.S. President Donald J. Trump ran on two words. Well, far more than that. But it all boiled down to two.

> I am not running to be President of the World. I am running to be President of the United States of America. From now on, it's going to be America First.[10]

America First names the enemy—globalists like the Clintons who treat America like an ATM for their NGOs and other special interests. Trump's simply-stated purpose also names the mission—to reorder policy around Americans who've been ignored for decades.

2. To Crush the Left and Hunt RINOs

Rags-to-riches stories can still happen in America, but they're less and less common due to "the uniparty," a phenomenon where both Democrats and liberal Republicans—called RINOs, or *Republicans in name only*—make policy that benefits illegal immigrants, unproductive migrants, and unemployable urbanites, all at the expense of hard-working, God-fearing Americans, who've witnessed their high-trust society wasted away by crime and grime in a single generation.

One of those stories is that of our current vice president, JD Vance, author of *Hillbilly Elegy*, which unironically was selected as a critical book for NPR-Americans to understand why Trump won the first go-around.[11] It was during this extended book tour that Joshua Lisec first met JD; his remarks that day foreshadowed the anti-RINO sentiment of Vance's victorious U.S. Senate campaign in 2022, when he notably said:

> I'm sick of the left devastating and decimating the greatest country in the world, and I'm sick of the weak Republicans who refuse to stand and fight against it. That's why I'm running for the U.S. Senate.[12]

3. To Defend Freedom from "Woke"

Ron DeSantis has turned Florida into a brand—the Free State of Florida. Previously a toss-up purple state, Florida is now patriot-red thanks to the policy and persuasion of Governor DeSantis. In his 2022 victory speech, he reminded voters that "Florida is where woke goes to die."[13]

DeSantis saw what Florida could become. He understood the enemy in the way—"wokeness," which is shorthand for Cultural Marxism. (As Joshua and coauthor Jack Posobiec write in the *Unhumans* book, Communist ideology didn't find fertile ground in free-market America. Rather than dividing the haves against the have-nots, Soviet infiltrators and their sympathizers decided to turn a Cold War hot via ethnic, gender, racial, and other demographics. The Culture War began, and women turned on men, blacks on whites, gays on straights, and so on. Cultural Marxism. Woke. Kill it, Ron. Thank you.)

Right-wing winners run to defend an actual place—a state, a district, a town—from radical-Left-wing cultural and bureaucratic takeover that everyone else is too scared to confront.

4. To Stand in the Gap When Others Give Up

Representative Lauren Boebert talks about politics as a fight for the "heart and soul" of the country, which, of course, it is. That's why she fought, and it's how she won.

> "There is a battle for the heart and soul of our country that I intend on helping win," said Lauren Boebert. "I'm running for Congress to stand up for our conservative values, address our current representatives' failed promises, and put far-left Democrats back in their place."
>
> . . . Lauren earned national notoriety in September when she attended a rally held by then-presidential candidate Beto O'Rourke and told him, "Hell no, you won't take our guns."[14]

Three months later, Lauren declared her candidacy. Nationwide, she is known for (among other things) Second Amendment activism. Many have stepped up to that fight; many have stepped away and moved on. Left-wing totalitarians always, *always* seize the guns upon takeover. If we lose the Second, we lose the First. We needed a hero—a heroine—to step up. "Next man up," as Steve Bannon says.[15] Sometimes, it's a woman.

We on the Right run because we refuse to be the last generation that shrugs and says, "Oh well, I guess that's just how it is now."

5. To Stop Gun Control, Open Borders, Socialism, and More . . . Directly

While she has since fallen out of favor in Trumpworld, we give credit and thanks where due and owed to Representative Marjorie Taylor Greene. The very day we wrote this section of this chapter, Rep. Greene announced her resignation from Congress.

Power changes people, and people change power. That's no surprise to you now. Still, Marjorie is a woman with purpose, and that purpose got her attention, which gave her influence. If you, too, want influence, let's pay her mind.

> Greene stated, "I'm running to stop gun control, open borders, the Green New Deal, and socialism."
>
> Greene's campaign said, "Radical socialists want Americans on the same government-run healthcare plan with welfare recipients and illegal immigrants. Marjorie Greene is fighting against these radical socialists and will take the fight to Congress."[16]

We must run to block specific Left-wing priorities, not just "raise awareness" about them. If you're not crystal clear on what you're there to stop, the machine will gladly hand you a bipartisan compromise instead.

6. To Put DC Back in Its Place

Another former U.S. Congressional leader, Matt Gaetz, has wisdom for our cause. You'll appreciate how simple his pitch was at the outset. Voters resonated; so have the larger public.

> I'm not running for Congress because I want to go to Washington. I'm running for Congress because we can't trust Washington.
>
> Gaetz played politics; unfortunately, politics played him, too. Nevertheless, we appreciate the lesson: The Right runs to be an adversary of Washington, not its newest junior partner. If you're going to walk into that building—or your statehouse or courthouse or county seat—you need to know whether you're going there to be liked, or be feared. Still, we count Matt Gaetz as America's honorary congressman and a friend. His future is brighter than the past.

7. To Be a Proven Conservative When Your Region Needs One

Before his U.S. Congressional career, Representative Byron Donalds worked in banking, finance, and insurance. Personal financial discipline is correlated with conservative values, so that makes sense.[17] So when Donalds ran for Congress, he ran as a conservative doer.[18]

> I'm running for Congress not only because [Southwest Florida] needs a proven Conservative, but because together we can make a difference.[19]

Professionally, personally, and politically, he was indeed proven; Donalds served in the Florida legislature and had been active in the resistance movement against President Obama's executive overreach, called the TEA Party. The Right win when we back all-around conservatives who didn't show up yesterday.

8. To Pay Back the Country That Gave You Everything

Representative Anna Paulina Luna's "Ditch" ad reframed her run as a thank-you note to America. We want you to read the entire transcript. This is Exhibit A under public service (or at least it should be).

> My mom chose life over abortion and decided to have me. I'm Anna Paulina Luna, and I'm living proof: anything is possible in America. Growing up, my family struggled with substance abuse, we moved around a lot, and I even lived in a drug house. I survived a gang shooting and an armed robbery. But I never gave up. Because being born in America is like winning the lottery. I joined the Air Force and found hope, helped rescue my dad from drug abuse and homelessness, and made stopping human trafficking the mission of my life. Anywhere else on Earth, my story would have ended in a ditch. But America saved me—and that's why I'm running for Congress. If you want more of the same, you know who to vote for, but if you want someone who will serve our country instead of themselves, I'm Anna Paulina Luna, I approve this message, and I'm asking for your vote.[20]

Representative Thomas Massie harmonizes her, focusing specifically on his home state of Kentucky.

> Thomas Massie is the fifth generation of his family to call Kentucky home. 100 percent pro-life. Member of the NRA. Man of faith. Thomas Massie shares our Bluegrass values. While graduating from MIT, Massie built a company from scratch, creating jobs and balancing a budget.[21]

The Left runs on guilt; the Right wins on gratitude. If you believe the United States of America is the greatest country in human history by every single measure, you might be one of us. Only America gives people like Anna and Wesley the opportunity to chase—and catch—their dreams; only Americans like them give back.

9. To Provide Constitutional Wisdom (Not Political Science)

Senator Mike Lee's early pitch in Utah emphasized that he wasn't there to invent a new ideology; he was there to apply what he'd already been doing as a constitutional defender and conservative leader. Just read this bio; it's even true.

> Elected in 2010 as Utah's 16th Senator, Mike Lee has spent his career defending the fundamental liberties of all Americans and advocating for America's founding constitutional principles.
>
> Senator Lee acquired a deep respect for the Constitution early in life while watching his father, Rex E. Lee, serve as the Solicitor General under President Ronald Reagan. He attended most of his father's arguments before the U.S. Supreme Court, giving him a unique and up-close understanding of government.
>
> Lee graduated from Brigham Young University with a degree in Political Science, and served as BYU's Student Body President in his senior year. He graduated from BYU's Law School in 1997 and went on to serve as law clerk to Judge Dee Benson of the U.S. District Court for the District of Utah, and then with future Supreme Court Justice Judge Samuel A. Alito, Jr. on the U.S. Court of Appeals for the Third Circuit.
>
> Lee spent several years as an attorney with the law firm Sidley & Austin specializing in appellate and Supreme Court litigation, and then served as an Assistant U.S. Attorney in Salt Lake City arguing cases before the U.S. Court of Appeals for the Tenth Circuit.
>
> Lee served the state of Utah as Governor Jon Huntsman's General Counsel and was later honored to reunite with Justice Alito, now on the Supreme Court, for a one-year clerkship. He returned to private practice in 2007.
>
> Throughout his career, Lee earned a reputation as an outstanding practitioner of the law based on his sound judgment, abilities in the courtroom, and thorough understanding of the Constitution.[22]

We see this pattern again and again. Another is U.S. Senator Rand Paul, also of Kentucky. From his bio:

> After completing his residency in ophthalmology at Duke University Medical Center, Dr. Paul and Kelley moved to Bowling Green to start their family and begin his ophthalmology practice, where he was a successful eye surgeon for seventeen years before running for the U.S. Senate.
>
> Dr. Paul founded the Southern Kentucky Lions Eye Clinic, an organization that provides eye exams and surgery to needy families and individuals.
>
> As a Senator, Dr. Paul has given of his time and skill by performing pro-bono eye surgeries for patients across Kentucky as well as around the world. He has performed eye surgery as part of medical mission trips to Guatemala and Haiti, where he restored the vision of hundreds of people who were blind with cataracts.[23]

Few see constitutional conservatism the way Senator Paul does. As a father himself, he would appreciate our dadly humor.

This is how it is for we patriots. People who've already led—in business, the military, law, or organizing—deciding to move that fight inside the legislature, the courtroom, and even DC.

10. To Make Politics About Real Families (Not Career Paths)

Most Right-wing political advertisements bring up children, hometowns, and family. How we do anything is how we do everything. The GOP has become our nation's unofficial Parent Party. Democrats, meanwhile, are the party of abortion, anti-natalism, and veganism, i.e., end pre-born children's lives, keep human beings from reproducing, and put animal "rights" first. This is what they do.

Governor Ron DeSantis, in this 2022 speech, framed Florida in Heritage-American fashion:

> I'm running for Governor because I want Florida to be a place where my children will want to live when they grow up—a state of prosperity and promise. . . . I ask that you vote for RON DESANTIS so we can work toward a prosperous future.[24]

Built different. That's us. We run to win when because we're more worried about the world our kids will inherit than the power ladder rungs we'll get to climb.

★ ★ ★

If you're serious about running, you should be able to put your name into one—or more—of these reasons without lying to yourself.

- Are you running to put your people first?
- To defend the Constitution against all enemies, foreign and domestic?
- To punish weak Republicans and a destructive Left?
- To defend a specific place—your state, county, or town?
- To pay back what this country did for you so others can have a shot at their American dream, too?
- To keep a promise to your kids and grandkids?
- To defend your principles and core beliefs?

Whatever your answer is, that's your *why*, and you're sticking to it.

Now. For the rest of this chapter—and the rest of this book—you're going to learn how to translate your political purpose into the step-by-step process it takes to organize a coalition to support your campaign, run to win, and then, of course, win—with no step skipped.

That said, right about now is the point where a lot of would-be candidates stall out. They've got the fire in their gut, but they don't have a sequence. So they'll start doing things out of order—announcing before they've done any district analysis, raising money from family and friends before they know how much they need, or filing for the wrong office at the wrong time. By the time they realize it, they've wasted months and sunk the goodwill they're probably going to need to keep their head above water.

Politics can be muddy—dare we say swampy—but like any journey into unfamiliar wilderness, it's a lot less terrifying if someone hands you a map and a compass. This chapter was your compass; the rest of the book is your guide walking beside you, pointing out the trail and the sinkholes.

We're going to lay it all out for you in eighteen steps with real timelines. This is not just a book you read, it's a book you do; we want you *doing* as quickly as possible. Right from this week. Today even. You'll see what we mean.

ALL THE STEPS TO RUN AND WIN—WITH NO STEP SKIPPED

At the highest level, here's what you're looking at:

1. **Alert the right people you're interested in running — NOW.** Don't wait until filing week. As soon as you're seriously considering a run, you raise your hand so people who know what they're doing can start helping you. (We'll talk about this at the end of this chapter.)
2. **Analyze your district options — THIS WEEK.** In the next few days, you look at the actual map: which seats exist, what the numbers look like, and where you'd have a realistic shot instead of just a romantic one.
3. **Position yourself to win — THIS WEEK (including party registration).** If your route to office runs through a partisan primary, you make sure your registration and paperwork line up now, not after the deadline has passed and you've disqualified yourself.
4. **Determine your "why" and refine your message — ~6 MONTHS BEFORE FILING.** About half a year before you file, you get crystal clear on why you're running and how you'll explain it in plain language. You do not wait until after you've filed to figure out your message.
5. **File to run for office — 6 TO 12 MONTHS BEFORE ELECTION (OR AS SOON AS LEGAL).** Depending on your state and office, you'll have a filing window. Somewhere between a year and six months before Election Day, you stop "thinking about it" and become an actual candidate on paper.
6. **Determine your budget — AROUND 12 MONTHS OUT.** About a year before Election Day, you build a real budget. You figure out how many votes you need, how many times you need to reach those voters, and what that will cost you in dollars and time.
7. **Raise the money you need — STARTING 12 MONTHS OUT (OR WHEN LEGAL).** As soon as you're legally allowed, you start

raising money against that budget. Not in a panic at the end, but steadily over the year, using a plan built around your actual needs.

8. **Have a communication strategy — ABOUT 6 MONTHS BEFORE FILING.** Around six months before you file, you decide how you're going to tell your story: which platforms, what kind of content, what tone, how often. You stop treating comms like random posts and start treating it like a system.
9. **Gain allies and endorsements — STARTING ABOUT 6 MONTHS OUT (BEGIN NOW).** At least six months before filing, you're already putting in the work: showing up for others, building relationships, and earning the right to ask for endorsements later. The earlier you start, the better.
10. **Recruit volunteers — AROUND 6 MONTHS OUT.** About half a year before the election, you begin identifying, recruiting, and training volunteers. You don't wait until crunch time to find out you have nobody to knock doors.
11. **Design and buy literature — AROUND 5 MONTHS OUT.** Roughly five months before Election Day, you're designing, testing, and ordering your walk cards, mailers, and palm cards so they're ready when it's time to hit doors.
12. **Have your announcement and door-knocking party — 6 TO 3 MONTHS OUT.** Sometime between six and three months before the election, you officially "go public" in a way that launches the campaign: an announcement event that rolls right into real voter contact.
13. **Build and manage your team — BEGIN AROUND 6 MONTHS OUT.** Around six months before the election, you start solidifying roles: campaign manager (if you have one), finance lead, volunteer coordinator, data help. You stop being a one-man band.
14. **Purchase data and software for voters in the district — ABOUT 5 MONTHS OUT.** Around five months out, you buy the voter file and the tools you'll use to track doors, calls, and contacts. No more guessing who lives where or who actually votes.
15. **Create your target universe — ABOUT 5 MONTHS OUT.** At the same time, you carve out your "universe": the specific voters you need

to win—likely voters, persuadable voters, key segments—and focus your effort on them.

16. **Work your targeted list — FROM ABOUT 5 MONTHS OUT UNTIL ELECTION DAY.** Starting roughly five months before the election, you and your volunteers methodically work that list: doors, phones, texts, events. Not "spray and pray," but deliberate, tracked contact.
17. **Get out the vote (GOTV) — FINAL WEEK.** In the last week, you pivot from persuasion to turnout. You're reminding, nudging, and, where legal, helping your supporters actually cast ballots.
18. **Have a post-campaign plan — WITHIN 1 MONTH AFTER.** Within a month after the election—win or lose—you execute a plan: thanking volunteers and donors, deciding how you'll serve if you've won, and how you'll stay engaged if you haven't.

The rest of the book will walk you through these steps in the order you need them and at the depth you actually need to execute. Every subsequent chapter roughly corresponds to each of these eighteen steps, with some variations. For now, there's only one step you need to act on right now,

STEP 1: DON'T DO THIS ALONE

The first step in our process is simple, and almost nobody takes it as early as they should: **Tell the right people you're serious about running.**

If you're reading this and you're even thinking about running—in the next cycle or four years from now—your next move is *not* to quietly agonize in your own head for six more months. Your next move is to raise your hand and say, "I'm interested. I want to get trained. I don't want to wing this. I want to win."

That's where Citizens Alliance comes in, my (Cliff Maloney's) organization. Citizens Alliance exists for exactly the kind of person who is holding this book—serious, right-of-center, fed up with getting rolled, and willing to work. We're no DC think tank or a donor cocktail club. We're a network of organizers, trainers, and data nerds who care about one outcome: more real America First conservatives winning real races.

When you reach out to Citizens Alliance, one of two things will usually happen:

1. We can help you directly. In some places and races, we'll be able to walk with you ourselves—training you, helping you think through district choices, connecting you to tools and tactics that have actually worked in the field.

2. Or we connect you with a trusted partner organizer. In other places, the best thing we can do for you is introduce you to someone local—a regional organizer, a grassroots leader, a state-based partner group—who shares your values and knows your terrain. We don't just hand out random email addresses; we only point you to people we're willing to put our name behind.

Either way, the point is the same. You do not have to invent this from scratch.

In practice, **Step 1 looks like this**: You go to my (Cliff's) site (www.cliff-maloney.com) and find Citizens Alliance. Then you'll fill out the pledge and survey honestly—who you are, what you believe, what office you're considering, and what your rough timeline looks like.

You signal, clearly, to us, *I'm mad as hell . . .*

The people who win are the ones who learn from others' scars instead of collecting all their own. This chapter was where you decided you're not going to do this alone. The rest of the book is where we show you, step by step, how to run right—from picking the right race, to building your message, to raising money, to working your list, to finishing strong. Let's do it.

CHAPTER 4

ANALYZE DISTRICT OPTIONS (TO DISCERN WHEN AND WHERE YOU CAN ACTUALLY WIN)

There's something you should know.
Only 15 percent of U.S. Congressional races are competitive—the remaining 85 percent are all but virtually guaranteed to elect the Democratic or Republican candidate due to demographic and partisan makeup.[25]

Before you fall in love with an office, you need a heart-to-heart with the odds. In our experience, most first-time candidates and political aspirants don't. They pick a race the way they'd pick a car or a house:

- "I've always dreamed of being in Congress. Imagine calling me 'Representative . . .' Wow. That would be so cool."
- "State senate sounds important. I could do so much good from there."
- "City council is full of complete idiots. I can do way better."

That's the starting point, sadly, because many will discover, too late, the brutal math. It all adds up to wrong district, wrong race, wrong timing, wrong opponent, no shot.

Imagine spending up to two years of your life as a prop in someone else's story of inevitable victory. It "felt so right" but was structurally unwinnable. Maybe it was wrong partisan lean or entrenched incumbent. Maybe both. Maybe more. We've seen it all before. (One of the worst examples of this, Joshua witnessed firsthand; a candidate invested personally and ultimately fundraised several hundreds of thousands of dollars for a cruel and unusual primary campaign fight that ultimately proved razor-thin . . . but the general election went 57 percent to 43 percent the other way. A complete blowout, and in a heavily Left-wing city. And now that candidate's name will forever imply "waste of money." There are rarely second chances in politics when you botch the first.)

Now imagine everything goes differently. You swallow your pride, trust the numbers, and choose a race that doesn't look as glamorous . . . but the data says a challenger like you can actually win. Same energy, same fight, different outcome. Winning.

This chapter will help you become the second kind of candidate. Because **you are not simply choosing a race; you are choosing a battle you can win.**

THE TWO QUESTIONS

In this endeavor, we are going to teach you how to answer for yourself the two all-important starting-line questions:

1. ***Where* should you run?**
2. ***When* should you run?**

Everything else in your campaign plan hangs on getting those two right. Let's go.

WHERE: KNOW THE GROUND BEFORE YOU CHARGE

Now, when we say "where," we're not asking, "What office do you think would be cool?" We're asking . . .

- Which district?
- With which people?
- In what political environment?
- With what recent history and catalysts?

Stop thinking like a voter; start thinking like a political scientist. Let's dig up the details.

District Demographics: Who Actually Lives There?

Every district has a personality, and that personality is built out of numbers. At minimum, you should know:

- ***Who lives here?*** Age, race, income, education, church attendance, veteran population, union presence, industries, family structure. These shape what messages land and what fights matter.
- ***How many people live here?*** Total population and, more importantly, registered voters. A state house district with 28,000 registered voters is a different world from a congressional district with 500,000.
- ***How do they lean politically?*** Not just "it's red" or "it's blue." What's the actual partisan registration split? Are independents a big share? How have recent statewide races performed here?
- ***Urban, suburban, or rural?*** An urban seat with tight neighborhoods is door-knocking heaven. A sprawling rural district means more driving, more gas money, and a different field strategy.
- ***District basics?*** We'll show you an example below.

All this means you're not asking, *Do I like this area?* but rather, *Does this area, on paper, ever elect someone like me?* Tools like www.DavesRedistricting.org and www.Ballotpedia.org will give you a head start here. But you still have to think. There is nothing wrong with throwing these questions into the Grok AI to get you started.

District Basics: An Idaho Example

To see what a few real-world "district basics" look like, here's a snapshot from Idaho House races that Citizens Alliance have previously participated:

- Average winning GOP primary candidate raised: approximately $31,000
- Total seats: 105
- Average district size (total population): approximately 52,600
- Average district size (registered voters): approximately 28,000
- Total registered voters statewide: just under 1,000,000

This is the level of clarity you want for your own target. How many voters are you dealing with? How many votes typically decide the primary and general? What does a "financially competitive" campaign look like, in dollar terms? Questions like these are the hard part now, but with clarity comes confidence.

Past Elections: Has Anyone Like You Ever Won Here?

Next, you look backwards. Like so:

- ***Past general elections:*** How have the last few general elections gone in this district? What were the margins? Was your party winning 70 percent to 20 percent, or clawing out 51 to 49?
- ***Past primaries:*** Who wins our party's primary here, and by how much? Are insurgents ever successful, or does the machine crush them every time?
- ***Party-specific outcomes:*** Assuming you will be running as a Republican as that is the primary audience of this book, how have conservative GOP candidates performed in this specific district, not just the office you have in mind?
- ***Up- and down-ballot performance:*** How did your district vote for president, governor, senator, or statewide ballot issues in those same years? (The Left-wing screed that is www.dailykos.com is the best place to find out.)

You're trying to answer, *Is there a pattern here that someone like me can ride, or am I just fantasizing?* If you don't know with absolute certainty it's the former, it's the latter.

That said, both of us have been criticized for advising political pragmatism. We've been called naysayers, doubters, and haters. Look . . . if you see that last election brought the Democrat an easy 57 percent victory, the same seat's prior election saw a 58 percent Democratic vote share, and the one *before* that *also* had a 58 percent Dem winner . . . and you still think you have a shot? This is not the book for you. We suggest *Politics For Dummies*® instead.

Pro Tip: For the vast majority of races, we are going to recommend you run as a member of our nation's Right-wing party, the Republican party. To run as an independent or third party is to run uphill both ways. Don't do it—except in the extremely rare exception, which we will cover in Appendix A later on. For now, stay on track; for Republicans, don't turn back.

Catalyst for Change: Know Your Opponent

Good demographics and low past spending are helpful, but they are not enough, especially when you're taking on an **incumbent**. These, together, are to be taken as a sign that someone might be able to make a race of it. And that someone could be you; your job is to look for a catalyst:

Is the incumbent vulnerable? If so, why?

We can be a little more explicit.

Why, specifically, might the incumbent be beatable in this district, in this cycle, by you, personally?

You're looking for factors like:

- ***Fish-out-of-water demographics:*** The incumbent looks, sounds, or behaves like they belong to a different place entirely; their priorities don't match the district's lived reality.
- ***Unexpected shifts:*** A demographic or economic shift like new employers, major migration, or housing changes can change everything, especially if the incumbent seems out of touch or otherwise unprepared. Or perhaps the district keeps voting more conservative on ballot issues (e.g., pro-baby, pro-guns, pro-parental rights, anti-taxation) than the incumbent's voting record.
- ***Low work rate or visibility:*** They never knock doors. They never show up at key events. They skip contentious meetings. The base feels taken for granted.

- ***Vulnerable voting record:*** Perhaps they voted for tax hikes, lockdowns, gun control, radical school policy, corporate welfare, "green" boondoggles, or other hot-button issues that infuriated core Republicans in the district. A subtler variation of this is that the incumbent's scorecards from conservative groups are trending down, and select influencers are beginning to notice and complain.
- ***A major local issue your opponent is on the wrong side of:*** Think school curriculum, medical mandates, property taxes, crime, a plant closing, a land fight, transvestites in the girls' room, and so on.
- ***Personal or ethical baggage:*** Scandals, conflicts of interest, messy behavior, or simply being known as arrogant, rude, or dismissive to normal people.
- ***Weak fundraising or shallow support base:*** They've coasted in low-turnout races or uncontested primaries, raising just enough money to mail in the same old script.
- ***Visible distance from constituents:*** Party insiders love them, but nobody at the local gun club, homeschool co-op, or even their own home church can really remember the last time they saw them.
- ***Public sentiment:*** School board or local meetings are packed with angry parents and citizens, even when legislative races have been sleepy. This signals vulnerability and therefore opportunity.
- ***Grassroots organizing:*** If grassroots groups in the area (e.g., church networks, Second Amendment protection groups, pro-life ministries, homeschool communities, etc.) are more organized and fired up than they were a few cycles ago, we just might have a catalyst.

Sometimes you'll find one major glaring weakness from this list. Other times, you'll find examples of three or four smaller ones that add up to a real change-catalyst.

By the way, most of these apply not just to the incumbent but to the "race favorite" if the previous or current officeholder is terming out or retiring. Usually, to gain the appearance of advantage, someone with (a) name recognition and (b) an unhealthily sized ego will declare their intent to run. Apply the same challenge-vetting criteria as above to that individual, if the situation applies.

Even in "safe" districts for the incumbent or incoming favorite, something occasionally cracks. You're looking for catalysts—they've gone soft, lazy, invisible, or worst of all . . . liberal. Do your homework, and you just might be able to move a race from hopeless to real-shot.

Otherwise, without a catalyst for change, your campaign will likely amount to just a complaint against the guy or gal who's going to win 70 percent in the primary against you. Now, a word of caution in the clearest terms: If you choose to run against an incumbent, you not only need to convince the voters why they should hire you, but more importantly, why they should *fire* the politician they have been voting for. You are inherently showing the voters why they should have buyer's remorse, not always a cheerful task. All other demographic and district factors may be in your favor, but without this one vulnerability from the opposition, pass.

Pro Tip: Pay most attention to an opponent's walk versus their talk. If an incumbent or previous officeholder, compare how they talk at home versus how they vote in the capitol. If their voting record shows a clear drift away from the base, and your people are quietly seething, you may be looking at a real opening. But if their scorecards are rock-solid and voters genuinely like them, you may need a different office, a different district, or a different cycle.

Knowing where you could win is only half the equation. You also need to know when to step onto the field.

WHEN: TIMING CAN MAKE OR BREAK YOU

Enough *where*; time for *when*.

There is almost always a better or worse time to run. Your job is to eliminate every lazy excuse for "next time" and decide on a real cycle.

Know Your Dates, Get Legal

At minimum, you should create a list of:

- ***Filing for office deadlines*** (for both exploratory committees, where applicable, and formal primary/general election filing)
- ***Campaign finance deadlines*** (i.e., initial filings, periodic reports, pre- and post-election reports)

- ***Voter registration deadlines*** (when voters must be registered to participate in your primary and general)
- ***Election dates and early voting windows in your state***

If you miss any of these, it doesn't matter how good your message is . . . you're done before you've begun.

Now, this is also where you double-check things like:

- *Do you need to form an exploratory committee before you raise money?*
- *Are there thresholds where new campaign finance reporting requirements kick in?*
- *Does your state have special rules for runoffs or nonpartisan races?*

Put these dates in one place where you'll see them constantly. Then add your own goal deadlines on top; here are a few examples:

- *"By A date, I will decide which district and which cycle."*
- *"By B date, I will complete my district analysis and ballot qualification research."*
- *"By C date, I will have a draft budget, message, and initial team."*
- *"By X date, I will have raised at least this much."*
- *"By Y date, I will have my target universe identified."*
- *"By Z date, I'll have knocked on so many doors and made voter contacts."*

You'll learn more about these in short order, like budget, team, and what we mean by "target universe." It's all to come. For now, we want you in the habit of writing. dates. down. Put them on a calendar where they are firm and real. If these live only in your head, odds are, they'll die there.

But here is one to stop and explain so we don't miss the big picture . . . if you're very green to politics (and that's OK) you need to understand this before reading further.

A typical election has two rounds of voting. 1) A party primary, 2) A general election.

1. Primary elections are held between March and September of the election year and the idea is to nominate a member of your political party to face off in a general election. There are varying rules of primary elections which we will expound on later, but for now understand this. In a primary the voters must "pick a name" amongst their party, they cannot blindly vote on party lines . . . i.e., all candidates in the Republican primary are Republicans (or at least claim to be).
2. General elections are what regular Americans are universally aware of. Vote Republican, vote Democrat, vote third party, or write in Mickey Mouse.

And lastly, as an added bonus, if you live in one of these nine southern states you are going to need to plan for a "runoff" election. A runoff election is a secondary round of a primary election (and on rare occasion a general election) where if no candidate receives 50 percent + 1 of the total votes, then the top two candidates move to another round of the election a few weeks or months later. Here are the nine states with a current runoff system for state legislature:

- Alabama
- Arkansas
- Georgia
- Mississippi
- North Carolina
- Oklahoma
- South Carolina
- Texas

Incumbents Versus Open Seats

In the previous section, we introduced you to the incumbent situation, which very well may be the case for your district. We want to bring this up again, but in the context of *when* to plan your run.

Open seats (no incumbent running) are almost always easier to win. Challenging incumbents is harder, more expensive, and more personal. That doesn't mean you must always avoid incumbents. It does mean you're honest about what you're signing up for. Earlier, we called out the factors that can add up to a catalyst for running for change. But all things being unequal, you may want to hold off until the officeholder times out. Here's why.

The Incumbency Advantage

There are three major odds-changers in favor of an incumbent.

- ***Name recognition:*** Your opponent starts the race with a built-in head start. Voters have seen their name on the ballot, in the mail, in the news. You're trying to buy what they've built over years. Tough.
- ***Fundraising power (often 6:1[26]):*** Incumbents typically raise many times more than challengers—think six dollars to your one, unless you change the equation. Donors like to bet on perceived winners and people who already have power.
- ***Cyclical:*** Some cycles are friendlier to challengers (e.g., "wave" years where an up-ballot candidate brings out their shared base, "backlash" years where voters' ire gets channeled against powerful officeholders in the opposing party). Others are "hold-serve" years where incumbents have an even easier time; these occur when only high-propensity voters show up, who tend to be tried-and-true party regulars who largely prefer the status quo. You're not just running against other candidates; you're running against the political season—or if you're smart . . . with it.

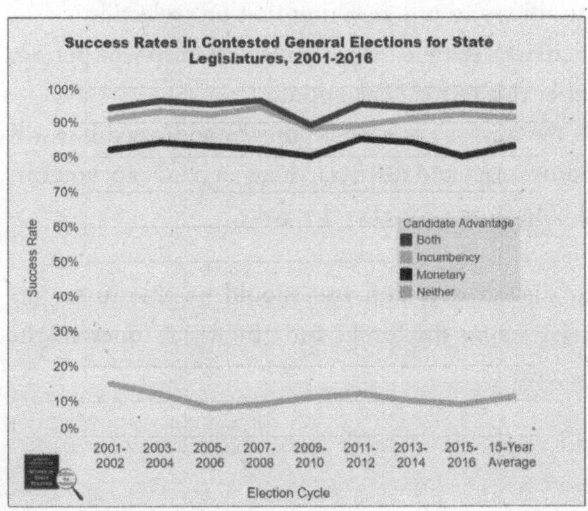

The lowest-resolution question to ask when considering the time and place of a run is, *Is this place conservative enough?* No. No. No. Ask yourself, *Do I really want to go head-to-head with all the structural advantages that come with an incumbent in this cycle?*

That's the question.

But what if there are signs of change? What if you could be first to see an incumbent's advantage is slipping, fading, crashing, or otherwise falling? What if you could get in the race first, lock up key endorsements, and buy voter mindshare before opponents have even filed to run? Here's how you can play that to win.

Signs a Seat May Be Opening

Here are some classic signals that an otherwise no-chance office is about to be timed for the taking—yours:

- ***Age of incumbent (around 70-plus):*** Not a guarantee, but it's where retirement rumors usually start for real.
- ***Incumbent's house for sale:*** Politicians like all people vote with their feet before they announce with their mouths.
- ***Scandal breaking:*** Ethical issues, messy personal stories, or conflicts of interest, even if survivable, will bleed support from a campaign.
- ***Shrinking margins of victory:*** If their win margins keep getting tighter each cycle, perhaps the district is sending a message—and you have ears to hear it.
- ***Pursuit of higher office:*** They're clearly more interested in the next rung on the ladder than the job they have now. Maybe they're going to run for a different office and put *zero* attention on reelection?
- ***Rumor mill:*** Local activists, staffers, or party insiders keep whispering, "I hear they're out after this term." Take notes.
- ***Term limits:*** This is the obvious one we've already addressed but still bears repeating. In some states and districts, there's a hard cap; you can see the open seat coming from several cycles away.

Align these facts with your district data and you should be able to see (a) which seats you should leave alone this cycle and (b) which ones might become prime targets in the next one.

Eligibility and Ballot Requirements

Before you fall in love with any plan, you must confirm: ***Are you even legally allowed to run for this office?*** We want you to check:

- Minimum age
- Citizenship requirements
- Whether you must live in the district and how that's defined
- How long you must have been a registered voter (and in which party, if it's partisan)
- Any special rules (petition signatures, filing fees, notarization, etc.)

This will all be spelled out in your state's election code and your Secretary of State (or equivalent) website. Do not skip this step or trust someone's memory. Laws and interpretations change.

Due diligence before a run from all angles—from demographics of the district to defenders of the office to details of eligibility—will protect you from a 57 percent general election blunder like Joshua witnessed. So now we turn inward to *your* personal timing.

Pro Tip: "Carpet-bagging is not a crime."™ — Patrick McGrady (Mayor of Aberdeen, Maryland)

All things considered, let's be honest about where you live now versus where your best opportunity may be. Patrick McGrady likes to irritate purists with that reference to carpet-bagging, which dates to the Reconstruction period of the American South when citizens of northern states moved southward to, among other things, run for office.

You can do the same. It is no mortal sin to run in a district that isn't your childhood neighborhood—if you understand the legal requirements and the political consequences. Every district and race has different rules on:

- Residency
- Time registered as a voter in the district
- Other ballot qualifications

If district and timing aren't aligning for the race you thought you'd run but you are otherwise "ready," your best move may be just that—***move!*** Run in a district where your current legal residence qualifies you, or soon enough will, even if it's not the place you've always thought about campaigning in, representing, or otherwise serving. Voters will care far more that you show up, do the work, and fight for them than whether your mailbox is one mile inside or outside a line a commission drew. Just don't fake a biography. Don't pull a Mitt Romney and pretend you have strong roots that you don't truly have. If you're new to a district, own it, and show why you chose them instead of anywhere else.

Questions to Consider: You Don't Have Unlimited Attempts

After you've thought about incumbents and openings, please reconsider and confirm that this is, in fact, the right time for you to even be doing this. Politics is dirty, and you'd better be dressed for it first. Write these down and answer honestly:

- ***Is this the right time in your life to run?*** Not "someday," not "when things calm down," but now. What will this do to your family, your work, your health? Can you realistically give this race the time and focus it deserves in this season of your life?
- ***Is there a catalyst?*** What is the concrete "why now?" for this race? If you can't point to a specific catalyst—an issue, a vote, a shift, a failure—then you may be trying to manufacture urgency that doesn't exist.
- ***Will you have a favorable matchup?*** Given what you now know about the district, the incumbency advantage, and the signs of an opening, is this actually a winnable pairing for you, specifically, against this opponent, in this cycle?
- ***Can you compete financially?*** Not, "Can I scrape together a few thousand?" but, "Can I get into the same ballpark as what it has taken to be financially competitive here in past cycles?" (More on this next.)

Bottom line: **You do not have an unlimited number of attempts.** Most people don't get to run serious campaigns five or six times. If you call your mother for a donation on your fourth attempt, even she may not support you. You might get one, maybe two real shots in your life where your energy, your family, your finances, and the political moment all line up. Act like this decision matters because it does.

If you can look those questions up and down and can honestly tell yourself, *Yes, this district, this cycle, this matchup, this catalyst,* then you're in position to proceed.

Welcome to the arena.

The arena wants your money.

Looking Back to Budget Smart

At this juncture of decision-making, you don't need a perfect forecast, but you do need to ballpark it. Fortunately, this is not hard to do. Have a peek at the last election and cycle . . . can you compete? Specifically, look at:

- Last cycle's campaign finance reports for your potential district
- How much the winning candidate raised and spent
- Whether they were financially competitive in both the primary and general elections
- Whether challengers who came close were underfunded or roughly matched

Use:

- Your state's campaign finance site (for example, in Idaho, it's sunshine.sos.idaho.gov)
- www.OpenSecrets.org and www.TransparencyUSA.org for a broader view of who gave what, and from where

Contribution limits or lack thereof may be a major factor in your race. All federal office limits are the same across the country. However, if you're running for state office these limits can vary wildly. A "wild west" state is one where there are no individual contribution limits. Therefore, you are typically looking at a more costly race per voter. If a business interest can give an incumbent candidate half a million dollars in one shot, you may be facing a much harder battle.

Examples of states where there are no individual contribution limits for state offices include: Alabama, Alaska, Indiana, Iowa, Mississippi, Nebraska, North Dakota, Oregon, Pennsylvania, Texas, Utah, and Virginia. Compare this wild west model to the strictest states Colorado ($200 cap per individual) and Maine ($475 cap per individual) and the incumbency advantage starts to diminish.[27]

Now, what you're trying to figure out is in this kind of race, in this kind of district, what does "financially competitive" actually mean? Is that a number you can realistically hit with your network, your effort, and your time?

If the average winning candidate for a similar seat in your state is raising $31,000 in a GOP primary (as in our Idaho example) but significantly more overall for the general election, that's the world you live in. You're not going to win a serious race on $2,500 and prayers.

ANALYZE DISTRICT OPTIONS: YOUR ACTION STEPS (12 MONTHS OR MORE BEFORE THE ELECTION)

This chapter is only useful to the cause if you read then do. Start here.

1. Always Independently Verify

Don't take our word—or anyone's—for what the rules are. Laws change. Maps change. Deadlines move.

Go to your:

- Secretary of State or equivalent election office
- State legislative or elections division website
- County election website

And independently confirm:

- Ballot qualifications
- Filing requirements
- Registration requirements
- Dates and deadlines

2. Fill In Your Ballot Qualifications

Start a simple table in your notebook or digital file:

State: ______________________________

Office You're Considering: ______________________

Minimum Age to Run: ______________________

Do You Have to Be a District Resident? If yes, how is that defined? ____
How Long Do You Have to Be a Registered Voter (and in which party)?
____

If you can't fill this out, you're not ready to announce anything.

3. Pick a District to Analyze—Right Now

Don't keep this theoretical. Pick one district and start plugging in numbers.

District name/number: ____________________
What is the population? ____________________
How many households are in the district? ____________________
When is your primary election date? ____________________
What election cycle are you aiming for? ____________________

Even if you later change your mind about the district or cycle, this exercise will teach you how to think.

4. Use the Right Tools

A few resources you should bookmark:

- **www.DavesRedistricting.org**: Demographic stats for districts and places.
- **www.DailyKos.com – Elections section**: Detailed election results and district diaries (yes, it's Left-wing; no, they don't lie about numbers).
- **www.Ballotpedia.org**: Elections, candidates, district maps, and past results in one place.
- **www.OpenSecrets.org & www.TransparencyUSA.org**: To find out how much is being raised, by whom, and from where. This gives you a realistic sense of the money environment.

These sites, plus your state's own election and finance portals, are how you stop guessing and start knowing.

From *Where* and *When* to *How to Win*

Alright, here's where we're at on your journey toward electoral exploits: **You've taken the first hard, unglamorous step that separates real candidates from daydreamers.** Meaning you've stopped thinking in abstract terms and started thinking in districts, dates, data, money, and opponents.

In the next chapter, we're going to assume you've narrowed down a realistic where and when, and you have a clear sense of who you're up against. From there, the question becomes:

How do you position yourself to win in that specific place, in that specific cycle, against those specific opponents?

So we'll walk you through how to move from "somebody who might run" to "the obvious choice" in your district—before you even file the paperwork.

CHAPTER 5

POSITION YOURSELF TO WIN (BIG)

> ***There's something you should know.***
> It's not just who you know—it's who knows you. More than 70 percent of mega-donors are male, 48 percent have been a CEO or held a similar role, and more than 12 percent are billionaires or are closely related to one.[28] If this does not describe your inner circle, you've got work to do.

Most people complain about politics. A smaller number ever think, *Maybe I should run*. Very few actually say, *I'm doing it.* But now comes the part that separates winners from *also-rans* (forgettable people who lose):

We must establish your credibility as a person—specifically, as a person people should want to vote for.

Good ideas for the office are good to have, as is anger at the system. But in politics, the message and the messenger are one. Everyday people in your district need to be taking one quick look at you and be going:

- "I've seen him around."
- "She shows up."
- "He helps."
- "He listens."

- "I trust him with my kids' future more than the guy who's there now."

Understand? Politics is personal; politics is personality. And creating yours for the voyeurism that is a campaign is no small task, no good luck, and no overnight success. You must present yourself into the candidate who personally has the best odds in the race. This will include not just who you know, but as we pre-sold you at the outset of this chapter . . . who knows you.

So let's position you to win.

NEXT COMES LIST-BUILDING (AND HERE'S WHY)

If you're serious about running, you have to get serious about lists. We often say (stole from our mentors) it comes down to money, people, lists. We're covering all of them extensively throughout the book, but here is the last one for your reading pleasure.

Now, despite what the sleazenuggets of internet marketing may advise, list-building is *not* where you slam, bam, thank-you spam your way into random internet strangers' inboxes, texts, or direct messages. There will be no buying of lists or scraping of numbers off the net. That's not how we do things around here.

List-building above-board means **building and maintaining organized lists of real people connected to your campaign**. And there are two types of lists you must care about from day one:

1. **Donors**
2. **Voters**

You will eventually get access to voter data through your state party, your local party, or a voter file vendor. We'll talk about that when we get into targeting and turnout. But for right now, we're going to focus on the part you can start today—**building a donor and supporter list from your own efforts.**

How You Build a List

There are two main ways to build your donor and supporter list before you ever file:

1. **Online petitions**
2. **In-person event sign-ups**

Both are simple, both are powerful, and both should be running constantly in the background of your life as a soon-to-be candidate.

Online Petitions

Instead of "Join my email list because I'm thinking about running for office and hope you'll give me money" as your call-to-action—which may be low-browedly honest—lead with value. Meaning, care about what other people care about. What are the "hot" fights relevant to your district? Specifically now, **we want you to put out an issue-based petition**. Like so:

- "Stop the property tax hike in [district]."
- "Protect girls' sports in [state]."
- "End unproven medical mandates for kids in [county]."

People are more motivated by issues than by how great you think you'll be. And it's not just national . . . maybe it won't attract the most signatures, but where can you also attract people who if they are concerned about a small issue, they are rabidly confirmed. For example, at the local level, the freedom to house backyard chickens is tyrannically banned on one's own private property . . . maybe you get twenty-five sign-ups, but when it comes time to vote, the backyard chicken freedom activists are ready to march into battle with you. We recommend you build petitions on the top three issues in your district. How? Simple . . . email platforms like Mailchimp and ConvertKit have email petition templates.

The "funnel" can go like this: You share your petitions on your social media, interested parties click through the link, they then sign your petition . . . and give you their email address in the process. If someone cares enough about this issue to hand out their email address, boy . . . that's at *least* a likely donor. If not a volunteer door-knocker and ballot-chaser for you (or all three).

In-Person Event Sign-Ups

Once you get in the habit of thinking in lists, you realize something: **Everywhere you go is an opportunity to harvest new contacts.** This is how you build them in person:

- **Meetings**: precinct meetings, central committee meetings, school board and city council meetings
- **Rallies**: "Stop the mandates," "Back the blue," "Save our kids," whatever fits your area
- **Events**: gun shows, county fairs, church conferences, business networking breakfasts, Rotary or Lions Club breakfasts

If you walk into these spaces without a way to capture names, you are burning opportunity. But if you walk in with a simple sign-up sheet or a QR code to your issue-based petition, you are building power.

Those interested can write their personal information and contact details—and **also** let you know also whether they're a "yes" to volunteering for you or accepting your yard sign (and if they're for either of these, chances are they'll also donate).

Notice now how list-building soft-transitions you into a campaign launch? It's a validation test, where, as you go out and about to meet in person the people you want to vote for you—and, of course, donate to your campaign as much as they are able—you'll get a feel for your personality's resonance among the people.

What You Ask For (and Why)

When you're building lists—online or in person—you want a baseline of information:

- First name
- Last name
- Email
- ZIP code

That's the core. With that, you can:

- Email them (obviously)
- Sort by geography
- Start organizing supporters by area

There are other fields we like, but they can impact response rates if you ask for too much too soon, but they include:

- Phone
- Address

If someone is already fired up (e.g., they're at a rally with you), you can ask for more. Online, you might keep it lighter at first, then ask for more info later once they've had a couple of positive experiences with you as a politically aspirational personal brand.

Here's a sample spreadsheet:

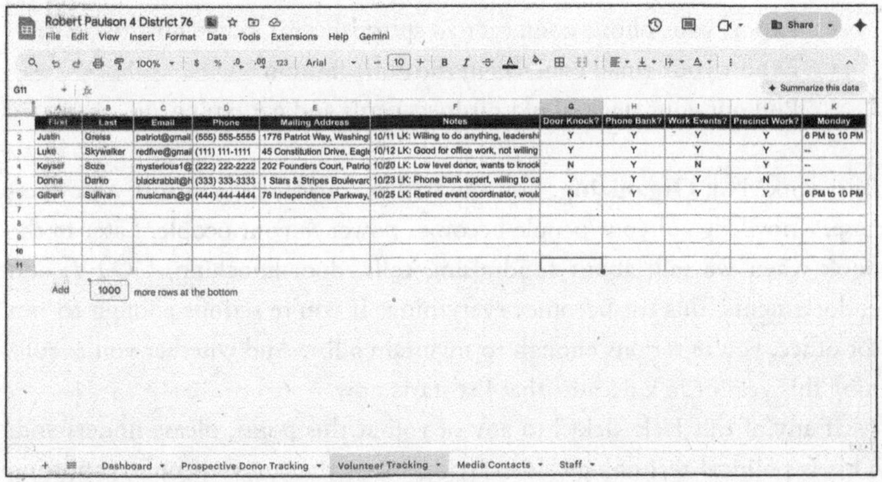

Robert Paulson 4 District 76

First	Last	Email	Phone	Mailing Address	Notes	Door Knock?	Phone Bank?	Work Events?	Precinct Work?	Monday
Justin	Greiss	patriot@gmail	(555) 555-5555	1776 Patriot Way, Washing	10/11 LK: Willing to do anything, leadershi	Y	Y	Y	Y	6 PM to 10 PM
Luke	Skywalker	redfive@gmai	(111) 111-1111	45 Constitution Drive, Eagl	10/12 LK: Good for office work, not willing	Y	Y	Y	Y	--
Keyser	Soze	mysterious1@	(222) 222-2222	202 Founders Court, Patrio	10/20 LK: Low level donor, wants to knock	N	Y	N	Y	--
Donna	Darko	blackrabbit@h	(333) 333-3333	1 Stars & Stripes Boulevarc	10/23 LK: Phone bank expert, willing to ca	Y	Y	Y	N	--
Gilbert	Sullivan	musicman@g	(444) 444-4444	76 Independence Parkway,	10/25 LK: Retired event coordinator, woul	N	Y	Y	Y	6 PM to 10 PM

We will say this again because it cannot be missed: Ask for enough to be useful, but not so much you scare people off from taking the first step.

All information you collect, either in person or online, must go into your central repository—your email management platform or also what's called a CRM, which stands for customer relationship management. Such apps can empower you to remotely, easily, and thoroughly track, connect with, and manage everyone who indicates interest in the same issues and causes you care about . . . up to and including the subject of your candidacy. A popular one in our circles is called **i360** (www.i-360.com). But keeping it simple works, too . . . a spreadsheet is the best way to get started right now.

We specifically recommend you add internal-only fields beyond contact information for each person that includes:

- How you met them
- Whether they're more likely to be a donor, volunteer, influencer, or voter contact
- What they care about (if you know)

And we'd be remiss not to remind you, your existing contact information matters too. One of the first tasks of your list-building mission is to assemble all your contact information into your database or spreadsheet.

- Export your phone contacts to a spreadsheet (Google how to do it)
- Export your email contacts in the same fashion
- Pull out your stack of old business cards and get typing

Busywork? No. **Organizing**. You can with a couple of clicks sort your database. Knowledge of your people becomes power *to* your people. Later in the book when we talk about fundraising calls, door-knocking, GOTV, and endorsements, this list becomes everything. If you're serious enough to run for office, you're serious enough to maintain a list. And whether you're running this year or in a decade, that list starts now.

If any of this feels "icky" to any of you at this point, please understand: This is political technology. Identifying issues that move people, capturing contact information, organizing people into lists, and following up strategically are all morally neutral tools and processes. The people who hate our values are already using them. The question is whether you're willing to use them to protect our people and our community. The goal is winning elections with a long-term vision. It is **not** to run, feel good about your process, and lose. Win so you can deliver real, durable change in the lives of the people you serve.

OK, now that you're building up your tribe one email address at a time, let's turn now to how these and others are going to feel about you. Yes, that's something you can control. And if you have ever been even barely careless on the internet . . . you've got some work to do.

THE PERSONAL BRAND DETOX: CLEAN UP YOUR CONTENT

Before you file, before you announce, before you boost your "I'm running" video with paid advertising, you need to detox. To do so, scrutinize all of your social media. And as you do, **delete any and all questionable posts, tweets, memes, and anything else you can.** If it makes you wonder, *Could this be used against me?* The answer is **yes**. If you don't find it, your opponent or a journalist will, and their interpretation of it with subsequent headlines next to your picture will be *worse* than the least charitable one you yourself could possibly imagine. Assume the worst person you've ever had the displeasure of meeting will go looking in an energized attempt to destroy you—and that they're very good at it—and pre-handle that situation accordingly.

Pro Tip: Use "On This Day" features in your self-censorship. Sorry but not sorry . . . that's what this is that you'll be doing. *But I want to be authentic! I want people to vote for the real, genuine me!* some of you are thinking. Cool. Have fun losing. Or did you want to win? Then do as we advise. Thank you. Platforms like Facebook will often surface old posts. Don't just smile at these old memories, like the one with you doing a keg stand (yep, that one). Clean up what doesn't match who you are now and the seriousness of the race you're entering. This is not to pretend you've never made a poor-taste, NSFW dad joke or had an extremist-adjacent opinion on anything. We refuse to let your decade-old meme distract from the issues that actually matter. Are you here to win or not?

Detox now, quietly. Don't wait until someone forces you into a scandal-cleanup mode later. Otherwise, you'll be talking about property taxes at an event, and some loon starts shouting about a spicy meme from 2014. You'll be advocating for parental rights, and the replies are lit up with screenshots of a dumb argument you had at 2:00 a.m. on Twitter six years ago. Your focus is on your vision for your district, but all would-be voters think about when your name comes up is your least-mature, caught-on-camera moment that your opponents' political-hack of an opposition researcher sleight-of-handedly made go viral. And you're done before you've run. Just say no, to all of this. Detox. Delete. Trust us.

And for those of you who think this is beyond obvious, even the big boys screw it up . . . just ask the number one Republican U.S. Senate challenger of the 2024 cycle, Tim Sheehy, who almost saw his campaign implode on day one due to not following the detox advice.[29]

LEARN THE LAY OF THE LAND

Alright, so you've got your online act together, and you're putting a team together, those potential donors and prospective volunteers. Next, we want you to learn the lay of the political landscape in your district.

First, the Network Nodes

Here there are the big-three questions about the very important **people** of your locale:

1. Who are the influential people?
2. Who are the influential groups on key issues?
3. How do you join or add value?

It's called we do a little reconnaissance. Map power and trust. Your findings might include, for example:

- A pastor whose church anchors hundreds of families
- A gun club board that can turn out volunteers on short notice
- A homeschool co-op leader who knows every parent fighting the school system
- A county GOP activist who's run every Lincoln Day Dinner for ten years
- A local business owner who is a walking chamber of commerce

What do they all have in common? They're nodes—people whom lots of others naturally follow.

What do you do with this information? Support what they're already trying to do. This does not look like parachuting in, taking over, and handing out your American flag–themed brochures. It means you show up, help out, and build trust over time.

Next, the Political Power Players

Now, those are the key people of community influence, but there are also **political players** you ought to become familiar with because these individuals can make your run significantly easier—or devastatingly harder. Groups to become familiar with that may be helpful for you to learn about include:

- Party activists
- Party socialites
- Party donors
- Elected people
- Social organizations of significance

Due to their potential direct impact on election results, each deserves details. Here they are.

Party (or Anti-Party) Activists

This is the grassroots. They sometimes identify with the GOP, but usually, they are more frustrated with "our" party than with the Democrats. These operators and activists are true believers and want to work to advance the pure mission of their affiliation. Many will identify as "constitutional conservatives" or perhaps "patriots" or by some other Right wing–coded moniker other than strictly "Republican." You'll find them showing up at obscure committee meetings, organizing protests and sign-waves, fighting with school boards and precinct committees, and getting angrier than anyone when our own side sells us out. You'll hear them speak ill of RINOs with great pain and disdain. And if you respect them, listen to them, and treat them like adults, they can become your most loyal volunteers and promoters. Dismiss them as "crazy" or "radical," and you have just lit your own base on fire. Good luck.

Party Socialites

These are your Country Club Republicans opposite the Left's Limousine Liberals. Sometimes they're donors, but mostly they control the social club and want to be loved by important people also seeking status. More often, they're senior in age and less knowledgeable about technology, social media, and the like. But they love young people and volunteers. You're most likely to find them organizing dinners, golf outings, VIP receptions, and various holiday parties. More often than not, their social media profile photos depict them standing next to a president, senator, or other high-profile elected elite. They love to command (and demand) respect. They may not be your door-knocking army, but they might introduce you to people with money. Maybe they have an email list that you can help them communicate with. Otherwise, you can add value by helping them modernize communication, run events, and look good. Still, we want you to treat them as peers. Don't grovel. Don't resent. Work with them where you can—only remember that they're a piece of the puzzle, not the whole picture.

Ideological Donors

These are donors that give to candidates because of their positions on issues. Do not confuse them with "access donors" (who are those who explicitly or implicitly fund you because they want to influence you for their benefit in the event of your electoral victory). Ideological donors give because they are as passionate as you. You can meet them at party fundraisers or other candidate fundraisers, cause-related banquets, and issue-focused events (e.g., pro-life dinners, gun-rights banquets, parental rights summits, etc.) They're usually in possession of "VIP" entry tickets at such outings. Your job—besides buying yourself a seat at their table to meet and greet—is to keep track of their names, phone numbers, what they care about . . . and then follow up afterwards.

We shouldn't have to say it, but we do: Please treat them like humans with convictions, not just checkbooks. They are often the ones who can get you from "idea" to "viable" if they believe in you. Receiving respect from a political hopeful is likely going to be a welcome change for them.

Elected People

Rather obviously, these are your current officeholders—legislators, council members, commissioners, school board members, sheriffs, and so on. Unfortunately, these people are often transactional and will perceive you as a threat, even if you're not running against them or have any plans to. Because you, in their minds, hypothetically could one day challenge them, now that you've entered the political combat arena. That doesn't mean they're all villainous combatants, but it does mean that their first instinct will be to protect their position and their relationships. They will try to figure out whether you are a potential ally, pawn, or danger. Never, **ever** rely on their private promises (many such cases). **BUT** . . . if you treat them as peers and work with them, it may limit their desire to politically destroy you. ☺

If you decide you don't want to be a bomb-thrower, then you may be able to use elected people to make the transition from citizen to politician easier.

That said, you're allowed to feel gross about how transactional some of this is. Just don't be naïve. Understand how they think, even if you refuse to become like them.

Social Organizations of Significance

There's a little overlap here with the network nodes from earlier, but the focus now is on the whole organization versus an individual community influencer. These are groups that are not explicitly political but have great sway with the people. Think:

- Faith-based groups (e.g., churches, ministries, etc.)
- Gun clubs
- Veterans groups
- Social institutions (e.g., Lions Club, Rotary, Chamber of Commerce, etc.)

The orgs are different in every community, but they all serve a common purpose: secular socializing and community volunteering. As we said earlier, don't join or support for nakedly political reasons, people can tell the difference between a climber and a leader. Participate to support the mission, make friends, and do some good in your community. After all, these organizations are respected for their good works. When you show up and do real work there, these positive images rub off on you and citizens begin to see you as, for example, "coach," "the guy who runs the pancake breakfast," "that lady who organized the food drive," "the person who always shows up to stack chairs and stay late," and such. Then when you finally run, that reputation is worth more than any mail piece. And no decades-old selfie with RINO Lindsay Graham will change their minds (because you already deleted it).

All of these relationships—activists, socialites, donors, electeds, churches, civic groups—are about one thing: **GAINING INFLUENCE**. We suggest you be visible and volunteer as much as possible within these groups, especially the local majority party. Start as early as two years out but no later than six months away from Election Day. **You are laying down the roots, not sneaking through the back door.** Your eventual supporters, donors, volunteers, and of course voters will already know you, like you, and trust you. You will seem like the *perfect* fit for the office you intend to pursue. Authentically. Naturally. Genuinely.

POSITION YOURSELF TO WIN: ACTION STEPS (12 MONTHS OR MORE BEFORE THE ELECTION)

To review, here's what you'll do having read this chapter and having become ready to make it all real.

1. Register with Your Party Now

If you have not done this yet, fix it today. Register with your chosen party. Confirm that your registration status matches the primary you intend to run in. Also check any timing rules (e.g., "must be registered X days before filing" or similar). This is freshman-level stuff, but campaigns implode over freshman-level stuff all the time.

2. Keep a Clean List of All Aspects of Your Campaign

That means:

- Donors
- Volunteers
- Influencers
- Endorsers

- Event attendees
- Petition signers

Remember list-building? This is how you get them. They've signed your petition, agreed to get your emails in some way or shape or form, and you've sorted them according to what you suspect their role could be (or they themselves told you as much directly upon sign-up).

3. Clean Up Your Social Media (Detox)

We already covered this, but it belongs firmly in your action steps. Scrutinize all your accounts, all your websites, all your everything. Delete what you can that doesn't serve your future as a serious candidate. Don't be like Democrat Susanna Gibson, the former candidate for Virginia's state legislature whose homemade adult entertainment featuring herself and her husband got leaked mid-campaign. Own goal.

4. Lay Down Roots in Your District

Learn what local groups will allow you to serve your community. Volunteer, be visible, and gain influence in these groups. Get to know your local party activists and donors. It's easy to say, hard to do, but so is political victory, and that's why we're all here. Don't just "attend" semi-occasionally; become a regular.

5. Find Groups That Provide a Network

Think potential donors, volunteers, and endorsers who all exist in the same place. Add **five** civic groups that you can join to help you in your run for your target office):

1.
2.
3.
4.
5.

These might include a church where you're actually involved, a gun club, Rotary, a homeschool group, or the local TEA Party (yes, those still exist).

Here is a quick test to vet your five: *Can I genuinely support their mission? If yes, I join and serve with real enthusiasm. If not, I pick something else.*

To bring this chapter to a close now . . . if you take us seriously, you won't be "some guy with a Facebook page" who files at the last minute, you'll be the person in your district who, when your name appears in the news, makes people think, *Of course he's running. It's about time.* This is what you want. And then, you'll touch their hearts with a fitting message. You already know why you're running; now the people just need a reason to put in the effort to vote for you. Let's do that next—refine your political purposes into a message that fits your district and confirm that your story, your public life, and your campaign all line up.

Become the one people feel good about voting for.

CHAPTER 6

A WINNING MESSAGE (AND HOW TO REFINE IT)

There's something you should know.
Voters form split-second judgments of a candidate's competence—and those first impressions predict the winner in up to 70 percent of races.[30]

One of the fastest ways to lose a winnable race is to pick the "right" fights in your head instead of the best fights for your district. Most first-time candidates make such an amateurish mistake. It's well-meaning, and also, well-losing. They'll build a big, beautiful platform covering bold, principled, comprehensive conservatism. They run on lower taxes, more guns, better schools, fewer mandates, sounder money, rolled-back censorship, stronger borders, weeded-out corruption, highlighted election integrity, and whatever else made them furious this morning on X.

Meanwhile, this dude is running for county clerk. Why the hell are you talking about abolishing the United Nations and the Federal Reserve when your county clerk role will never, ever directly or indirectly affect monetary policy?

Understand that politics doesn't reward the candidate who has the most "correct" opinions according to either the principled conservative or the die-hard liberal. **Politics rewards the candidate who can align what they believe with what actually moves real people**. Thus, your campaign messaging must be all about where your liberty philosophy aligns with what actual voters are concerned with *in your district.* Not at the border and not in Washington (unless your target office is directly associated with either). This alignment becomes your message, becomes your strategy, becomes your **fights.**

But if you pick these fights emotionally—because you're angry, online too much, or have a chip on your shoulder—you will unfortunately likely pick a fight that feels right to you but loses you the district.

So before we talk about how to speak, how to pitch, how to handle attacks, and how to win . . . we need a decision-making tool.

Enter Red Fox Four.

ENTER RED FOX FOUR: PICKING YOUR CAMPAIGN'S FOCUSED FIGHTS

Red Fox Four is a powerful confrontational politics tool used by candidates for office, conservative and libertarian group leaders, and anyone trying to move a district—or a community such as a college campus—more toward Right-wing sanity.

To that end, Red Fox Four is a decision-making tool, a comparative analyzer, and quite simply a way to go from hypothetical food fights to deciding the best fights (for you). For example, it causes you to stop asking yourself, *Should I run on anti-taxation or pro-gun rights?* in such a vague way so instead you can start scoring each issue-option so you can choose the set that actually wins.

One rule before the tool: Friends don't let friends do Red Fox Four alone. Meaning don't run this in your own head and all by yourself. Involve other people. Smart people, people who know your district, people who will tell you the truth. Score. Compare. Decide. Together.

How it works is you end up with a score for each issue, and you go with the issues that score highest. That becomes your campaign messaging topics list. It's not hard, but you have to do it. And that's what's hard.

How Red Fox Four Works (0–10): The Four Questions

Red Fox Four is painfully simple. You take each issue you might run on and score it 0-10 across four categories.

#1 — Will it bring in new money / new people? (0–10)

This is your growth and fuel score. Will this issue bring in:

- Donors?
- Volunteers?
- Yard sign requests and sign locations?
- Door-knockers and phone bankers?
- Issue ID (petition signatures)?
- Positive news coverage?

If the issue excites your own brain but doesn't bring new money or new people into your campaign, it's probably not one of your top three issues.

#2 — Will it help my friends and allies? (0–10)

This is your coalition score. Will this issue:

- Help your campaign in your district?
- Play well with your supporters?
- Make you and your people look good?
- Help candidates in neighboring districts or up- or down-ballot?
- Empower another outside organization to get involved in your race?
- If you take this issue on, does it create allies and momentum—or does it isolate you?

All essential to know.

#3 — Will it hurt my enemies and their allies? (0–10)

This is your pressure score. How much does the issue hurt your opponent? Does it:

- Put them in a tough spot?

- Force them to explain away an unpopular position?
- Force them to go against the people in the district?
- Put them on their heels playing defense?

A great issue energizes your side *and* traps the other side.

#4 — How much freedom is at stake? (0–10)

This is your stakes score. For example, is this fight against a major tax hike, or small potatoes? It's hard to get people to care about small potatoes. Not impossible. Just hard. Most of the time, you want to steer yourself toward fights that:

- Mean the most to people
- Have substantial consequence to your liberties

Example: Why One Score Means Nothing Until You Compare

Let's say you score: "Oppose a gas tax hike your opponent voted for." You might end up with something like:

#1 People/Money: +5
#2 Friends/Allies: +3
#3 Enemies/Pressure: +7
#4 Freedom Value: +4
Total: +19

What does "+19" mean? Well, nothing. Nothing until you compare it to other issue scores. That's the point of Red Fox Four—it's comparative. The tool helps you stop romanticizing one issue and start choosing the issue mix that wins. Ultimately, you might end up with a comparison list like:

Constitutional Carry: +25
Anti–Gas Tax Hike: +19
Fix Potholes: +17
Audit the Federal Reserve: +5
Pass Sound Money Protection Act: +3
Secede from the Union: +0

The tool is not telling you what's morally valid or theoretically correct; it's telling you what is strategically powerful in your district and for your candidacy. Notice the deeper lesson: ***Your campaign is not "about you"; your message is for your audience.*** You're aligning your philosophy to what real people will act on (without losing your principles) so you can win and govern right.

Thanks, Red Fox Four.

LIST-BUILDING MEETS MESSAGING (YES, THEY'RE CONNECTED)

Now the list-building tactic reenters the frame. This is a fantastic way to test your likely-top issues for your overall messages. After all, your people are going to be more motivated by issues than by how great you are (no offense). Petitions will also help create an issue-name association (who cares about what, and what matters to them). Then of course those contacts become donors, volunteers, sign requests, voters, and they feel good about supporting you because they know you're issue-aligned with them.

Message is more than what's said. It's what you collect, what you learn, and what you prove. Now, for how you talk about it.

KNOW YOUR WHY: A PUBLIC WHY VERSUS THE PERSONAL WHY

You will need two versions of an answer to the question, "Why are you running?" They go like this:

1. **Your public why — the story donors, activists, and voters hear**
2. **Your personal why — the reason you get up in the morning and fight**

Your public why is not your diary; it's more like a mission statement, and it must connect to your three main issues. Your personal why is for the days the campaign gets hard. It's not inherently different from your public why, and it certainly isn't at odds with it, but it's what keeps you going and to be shared with your inner circle. If you can't talk about three most-relevant-to-your-district issues in twenty to thirty seconds within an elevator pitch for your candidacy, you don't have a message yet. You have a pile of opinions.

MASTERING YOUR ELEVATOR PITCH (HOW TO SOUND LIKE A WINNER)

Your elevator pitch is (obviously) not, "Hi, I'm Bob, I've lived here forever, and I love freedom." Your elevator pitch instead includes:

- Your why (public)
- Your top issue set
- Your contrast with the opponent
- Why the listener should care
- Why they should believe you
- Ask for the voter to vote for you

Later in this chapter—in the Action Steps, specifically—we'll give you a step-by-step process to write your elevator pitch. But before we do, we owe you one more tool. Your pitch and message don't exist in a vacuum, they exist in combat.

That's where the Leesburg Grid comes in.

THE LEESBURG GRID: HOW TO CREATE YOUR POLITICAL IMAGE (AND ATTACK YOUR OPPONENT'S)

Red Fox Four helps you pick the best fights. And now the Leesburg Grid helps you understand the battlefield of perception—this means who *you* are to voters, who *your opponent* is to voters, and how *attacks* and *defenses* will land. Sometimes, the best defense is a counterattack. Other times, it's to respond as if no attack hit you at all. You'll soon learn why.

To use the grid properly, you have some boxes to fill out:

- Your positives (white box)
- Your negatives (black box)
- Opponent positives (black box)
- Opponent negatives (white box)

These will include categories personal and political points. See the image below.[31]

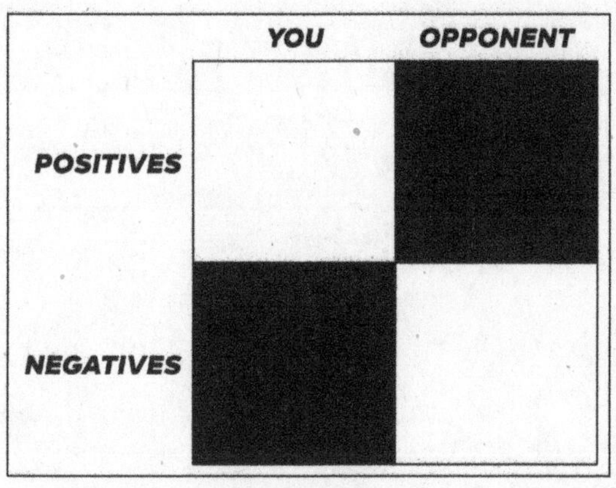

Like nearly everything in this book, this is not theoretical. For every campaign I (Cliff Maloney) manage with Justin Greiss, we run this exercise. And all serious people do the same.

To run the exercise, you must bring in the most trusted people from the campaign, and only those people. The candidate, the candidate's spouse, the core campaign team, and only those who can be trusted until the end.

Presidential campaigns will spend an entire day running this exercise with giant Post-it notes on all four walls to represent these boxes.

For your race, the exercise should be held over one to two hours in person or on a video call. Get time on the calendar and take it seriously. Use the Post-it note method or simply a spreadsheet with four distinct sections. You're not done until each section has at least fifty items listed.

This is the time to go deep and list out everything. There are no bad ideas here. We'll parse down the lists we build at the end of the exercise.

So let's sort it all out—honestly.

Leesburg Grid: Your Positives

This is where candidates get weirdly bashful. You have to force yourself to talk. You have to tell the truth. You have to list what's real. Do it. It's OK.

Personal positives might include:

- Married
- Kids
- Veteran
- Community service
- Non-political hobbies
- Family
- Faith

- Eagle Scout
- Business owner
- Farmer
- Gun owner

Political positives might include:

- Served on party committee
- Won political battles
- Endorsements
- A winning message based on Red Fox Four
- Led a group
- Served on boards or commissions

Taken together, these all help to build the story of the campaign. In fact, use all the construction materials. Tell the people everything and let them decide what's enough. Don't pre-edit your story because you're embarrassed or shy or unhelpfully humble. Better we know and shape the positives now for maximum impact.

Leesburg Grid: Opponent Positives

This is where immature candidates fail; they refuse to admit anything good about the other person. Don't be that candidate.

Your opponent may have **personal positives** such as:

- Military service
- Police background
- Popularity
- Charity work
- Education
- Speaking skill
- Work experience
- "Lived here since I was born."

Their **political positives** might include:

- Backed by unions
- Planned Parenthood endorsement
- Environmental groups support
- House leadership are on their side
- PACs are lining up
- Tapped into networks like the Fraternal Order of Police (FOP)

You have to admit . . . there may legitimately be some good things about your opponent. So, force yourself to think like they would, predict what their winning message would be. How would they frame themselves? What would they emphasize? And if you can't imagine your opponent's best argument, you aren't ready to defeat it. If you're running against an incumbent, your job may be pretty easy here. Go to their website. Go to Google. See what they said in past campaigns on mailers, texts, and traditional media.

Leesburg Grid: Your Negatives

Now we go to the dark place. It will be worth it.

Personal negatives might be:

- Affairs
- Divorce
- Tax liens
- Back taxes
- Criminal record
- DUIs
- Court records
- Quotes you forgot you posted
- Online forum comments
- Family members who bring drama
- Kids in trouble

Political negatives might be:

- You're divisive
- You gave your opponent opportunities to skewer you

- You were endorsed by a radical
- Past quotes that make the district furious
- A photo with someone your district despises
- You're on the Epstein flight log

If there's something you couldn't bear for people to know, don't run—because it will come out.

Knowing your weaknesses as a candidate so starkly doesn't always change your plan. But it always changes your preparedness. You'll stop being shocked when the hit mailer arrives. So you'll stop panicking. So you'll stop driving your team insane. So you trust the plan instead. We make the Leesburg grid BEFORE the campaign lets the candidate, and especially the spouse, get emotional. As Justin Greiss says, "The moment a candidate files for office, he loses 50 IQ points." Campaigning is stressful, that's why we prepare when we are of a clear mind.

Leesburg Grid: Opponent Negatives

This is where you identify what the enemy has as vulnerabilities. About time.

Personal negatives:

- Scandals
- Ethics questions
- Court records
- Criminal or public records
- Quotes, comments, old posts
- Anything that matters if the district would care

Political negatives:

- Bad votes
- Dumb statements
- Affiliations they can't defend in your district
- Prior contributions that look ugly
- Endorsements that make them pay a price

This is also where Red Fox Four shows up again. **Opponent negatives are often your RF4 #3, what hurts your enemy and their allies.**

Additionally, negatives do not necessarily mean being nasty. Not every race is as insidious as House of Cards. Maybe, perhaps even hopefully, your opponent is a fine person, they just are not as principled as you are. It's not all fraud, scams, and scandals. Your opponent's negatives can simply be issues that are not aligned with the district. And if they are an incumbent or have been elected to any office previously, they have a past voting record; use it.

Leesburg Grid: Putting the Tool into Action

Understand we directly control just two of the four boxes. . . . Our positives, and the opponent's negatives. They are represented as the "white boxes" in the graphic. When we message our campaign those white boxes are what we stick to. We get no choice as to what the opponent decides to campaign on, represented as the black boxes, and we certainly do not repeat the opponent's positives or our own negatives. Stay out of the black boxes!

You are not done quite yet. You now have your written list of nearly fifty, or maybe more, items in each section. Within the white boxes you control, you now pick the top personal and political issues that matter to develop your tagline, primary issue set for the website and palm cards, and build your narrative around.

For example, your tagline running for state legislature may be "Proven Conservative Fighter" and your top issues may look like:

1. Lower Cost of Living
2. Parental Rights
3. Deport All Illegals

Wherever the team determines you all go, know this . . . the Leesburg grid only fails if you fail to use it.

Politics Is Basketball (Not Soccer): Why You Don't Respond to Every Attack

Politics is like basketball, not soccer. In soccer (which is for English ladies) one goal will likely decide the difference in the game. Each goal is a monumental moment of the game. In basketball, players get to score frequently. Every time the opponent scores you don't pause the game and reset. You head right back down the court in the opposite direction. In campaigning you do the same. When your opponent scores, you don't change your message or react to what they're saying. In general, don't respond to attacks. Because if you do, you prolong the news cycle, give the opposition another reason to keep talking, waste time off-message, and give the issue legs when you could have cut it off at the onset. Instead of a two-point layup, you allowed a sixteen-point run.

But if you absolutely *must* respond, you do it like so, as a one-two punch:

- **Always pivot to your positive box. (white box)**
- **Pivot to their negative box. (white box)**

For example: "Kamala Harris is telling lies about Donald Trump because she doesn't want you to know she wants to use your tax dollars to pay for sex changes for illegals in prison . . . while Donald Trump will end the woke madness and put American citizens first." [insert opponent negatives, and you're back on offense].

The Secret Weapon for Political Persuasion Counterattack: Door-Knocking

How can I just ignore negatives about me out there, guys?

By door-knocking. Door-knocking is the ultimate way to overcome negatives because the voter often has direct experience with you (or a door-knocker supporting your campaign). You don't defeat smears primarily with press releases; you defeat them with contact, presence, and credibility on the ground.

If you've successfully knocked on a voter's door, you substantially increase the likelihood that a voter will be on your team. When your opponent starts slinging mud, the voter is much less likely to believe the lie. Voter Smith: "What do you mean he kicks puppies. I met him. Seemed like a stand-up guy to me." Now your campaign message is back in your white boxes.

Rejoice When They Attack (but Be Strategic)

Every competitive campaign is a race to the gutter. Rejoice and double down when the enemy attacks; it just means you are a serious threat and on your way to winning. We then go negative right back because it works (they haven't read this book, so they don't know).

That said, we want you to get mad on purpose. Don't just attack to attack (or react). Ask one question first: *Will people in my district actually care about this?* If they won't care, you're wasting ammo and self-inflicting drama. If they will care, put it to work—cleanly, deliberately, on-messagely. This is what *we* do. Candidates always believe a rumor or attack has more legs than it does . . . Why? Because good people in your circle who follow the race closely are telling you about the rumors and lies to help you. They mean well, but you as the candidate will now think every Mary Joe Beercan (our term for a blue-collar voter) in the district knows about it. Remember what we told you about those 50 IQ points. It's stressful.

Did We Warn You About Spouses?

If you have the fortune of being married, I am warning you in the clearest terms now. Your spouse will be a joyful blessing to your campaign or an unintentional saboteur. Here is the premise . . . your spouse loves you more than anyone else in the world. They chose you. They will believe you can win any race because you are the best person for the job. That could not be more false . . . remember how we got to this point in our Republic? As readers now know, the best man for the job rarely wins. But back to the well-meaning spouse. Your spouse will typically do two things:

1. Lead you to believe a negative has more legs than it does.
2. Want you to sell your positives and never talk negatively about your opponent.

But here is where we remind you once more, especially those running against an incumbent, you are asking voters to admit they made a mistake and voted for someone who sold them down the river. That's a tall order. But you need the voter to understand your opponent's negatives. After all, this is why you're running to replace them.

A WINNING MESSAGE: ACTION STEPS (MINIMUM 6 MONTHS BEFORE FILING)

Use the following worksheets and trackers months before filing so that by the time you announce, you're not "finding your message," you can already be executing it.

1. Complete the Red Fox Four Spreadsheet (Comparative Issue Scoring)

Open a spreadsheet and create a table with the following columns:

- Issue
- #1 New People/Money (0–10)
- #2 Helps Friends/Allies (0–10)
- #3 Hurts Enemies/Opponent (0–10)
- #4 Liberty at Stake (0–10)
- TOTAL (Sum of 4 scores)
- Notes (Why you gave each score; what evidence you're using)

Now list ten to twenty possible issues and score each one with other people involved (friends don't let friends do Red Fox Four alone). You're looking for your best fights among good fights.

Rule: A score means nothing until you compare it against other issue scores.

Your goal: Identify your Top 3 issues with the strongest combined score in your district.

2. Complete the Leesburg Grid Fill-In Worksheet (Your Image Versus Their Image)

Create a one-page worksheet with four boxes and fill it out honestly.

As you can see, you'll label the boxes, dividing personal and political. The four primary categories include:

- Your Positives (white box)
- Opponent Positives (black box)
- Your Negatives (black box)
- Opponent Negatives (white box)

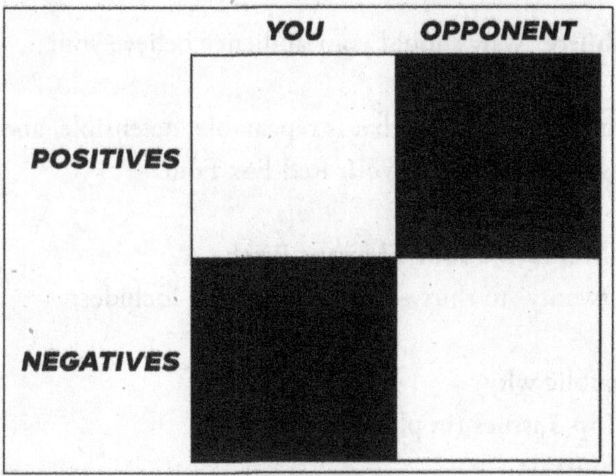

Under each box, write bulleted facts and examples. Don't "protect yourself" by leaving things out. If there's something you couldn't bear for people to know, assume it will come out and decide whether you should run.

Pro Tip: Do Google searches on yourself and your opponent. Check Facebook, Instagram, YouTube, and X. Check public records including criminal and domestic relations court. Dig deep. Everything must be brought into the light.

Your goal: Know instantly how to react to attacks—or ignore them—and know what "boxes" you will pivot to under pressure.

3. Draft Your Message Using $M = EC^3$

We teased you this earlier in the chapter, the process by which you'll actually craft your campaign message. You will write a one-paragraph message draft using this formula:

$$M = EC^3$$

In algebraic fashion, these letters correspond to:

Message: What will your overall campaign message be?
Emotion: How do you want your audience to feel?
Contrast: How are you different from your opponent?
Connection: Why should your audience care?

Credibility: Why should your audience believe you?

Your goal is to draft a message that is repeatable, defensible, and anchored to your Top 3 issues according to your Red Fox Four.

4. Write and Memorize Your Elevator Pitch

Next, write a twenty- to thirty-second pitch that includes:

- Your public **why**
- Your **Top 3** issues (in plain language)
- Your **contrast**
- A short **credibility** marker (service, community roots, track record, etc.)
- A simple **call-to-action** ("Will you help?")

Say it out loud until you sound like a person, not Robo-Candidate 3000.

5. Maintain Message Discipline (to Stay on Offense)

Write these rules at the top of your campaign notebook, be yours a real physical one or a word processing document on your computer:

* Always be on the offense. Always stay on message.
* Don't respond to attacks directly (and don't prolong their news cycle).
* Instead, counterattack; pivot to your positives and their negatives.
* Door-knocking is your ultimate way to overcome negatives; people who meet you will know claims about you don't really matter (or simply don't ring true based on how they know you).

Now that you've chosen your best fights, discerned your Top 3 issues (the public will actually care about), and sharpened your message into something that can survive cruel and unusual personal and political attacks, you're ready for the next step:

File.

It's about to get real—so you can become a real candidate and get yourself legally and operationally positioned to file and launch without botching, stumbling, or pitfalling.

CHAPTER 7

FILING TO RUN (KNOW THIS, OR GAME OVER)

> ***There's something you should know.***
> In some states, the window for candidates to file to run and get all necessary paperwork submitted is as short as four days.[32]

It sounds ridiculous until you see it happen in real time. Imagine the perfect candidate. She has the district. The donors. Volunteers. The pulse of the momentum, she's got it. But someone important on her team forgot something even more important: the deadline. A form. A paperwork mishap. Somebody misunderstood the signature rules.

And so suddenly she goes from being the shoo-in to a write-in. On Election Day at 10:00 p.m. local time with 99 percent of votes counted, the perfect candidate loses. By sixty points. Many such cases; we've seen them, even with congressional incumbents.

Before your campaign proceeds, we have to talk to you about preventing a self-inflicted disaster. The filing-to-run step is more than clerical; it's a visible, symbolic, newsworthy, public moment that ought to be treated as such.

But put it off like a chore, and you've wasted the otherwise incredible content of free media coverage. So don't do that. Do this chapter instead.

TWO TYPES OF "FILING": CAMPAIGN COMMITTEE AND FILING TO BE ON THE BALLOT

When the political class and activists talk about "filing" this refers to one of two things and is inaccurately used interchangeably: 1) filing your campaign committee and 2) filing to be on the ballot. We're going to clear it up for you in this section.

GETTING STARTED: FILE YOUR CAMPAIGN COMMITTEE

To begin officially running for office, the first task you will need to complete is filing your campaign committee. This can look slightly different in each state, however the theme is the same. You may not be that interested in the government . . . but boy are they interested in you.

Before you raise a dollar, get your campaign committee legally compliant. This typically involves registering the campaign with your Secretary of State and isn't an arduous process.

First, what you'll need is an EIN from the Feds. DO NOT PAY ANYONE TO DO THIS. This is free and your right as a heavily surveilled American. Just go to this website:

https://www.irs.gov/businesses/small-businesses-self-employed/get-an-employer-identification-number

Pro Tip: When you do this, you will receive a nearly instant PDF that serves as your official EIN letter. SAVE THAT IMMEDIATELY. You will need this in the future and a replacement takes twelve weeks. Easy to get, but hard to re-get. Trust us.

After you secure an EIN, find your Secretary of State website to register your committee. Usually this is just a one-page form with basic information you already have. This will be made public so just think carefully about what address you are going to use and the name of your committee. Simple is better. "Justin Greiss for Pennsylvania" is a go-to. If you ever switch races at the state level (e.g., state representative to state senate) you won't likely need to change your committee name.

Lastly, once you are registered with the state, you can now open a campaign bank account. Use the bank that works for you. What you are looking for is a bank that offers a debit card, allows you to deposit checks on mobile, and (this one is the difference maker) saves images of the checks you deposit. The last one will save you and/or your treasurer much heartache. Again . . . trust us. We've learned the lessons the hard way.

We do not typically recommend messing around with exploratory committees or any of the cute stuff. File when you are ready to raise money. Do not announce until you are legally able to raise money. Simple.

BALLOT FILING DAY MINDSET: DUCKS IN A ROW

The day you decide to file for the ballot (referred sometimes as "qualifying"), make sure you have all your ducks in a row. Start with the most underrated move in politics: **Call the governing body**. Yes, on the phone. Yes, you can do that. You can call them on the phone and ask them what you need to bring—and more. For some races/states you file with the political party. For others you file with a government office.

- What forms are required for my office?
- Do I need an ID? What kind?
- Is there a filing fee for petitions? What are the rules?
- Must I bring a personal check or money order?
- Do I need a financial disclosure form?
- What time window do you accept filings?
- Can I submit early?
- Are there appointment requirements?
- What would cause the filing to be rejected?

Then build a checklist and physically bring it with you along with all materials needed for filing. You are not above administrative tediousness. Administrative tediousness decides who gets on the ballot and who stays off. This process can be worse than the satanic DMV so be prepared.

Part and parcel with required documents, you also need to know timing.

KNOW YOUR IMPORTANT DATES (OR RISK EMBARRASSMENT)

You need a deadlines and events calendar that is obsessive. Not "somewhere in your email." We're talking about a living document you update. Include important dates for your chosen office such as:

- Campaign finance dates and deadlines
- Candidate petition circulation dates
- Filing dates
- Withdrawal dates

Don't just "know them." Put them in a calendar with reminders—and make at least one other person responsible for tracking them with you. One sloppy miss here can wipe out months of hard work.

KNOW THE PROCESS (DON'T GUESS)

Filing is not "one thing." Filing is a system. Besides the documents and the deadlines, understand what may be additional **requirements** for running (state and federal—especially if you're in a race that triggers federal rules). We mean laws for operating a campaign committee and laws regarding political expenditures, for starters. Always refer to the governing body and reference the packet the Department of State provides. Go to your state's Secretary of State website, specifically the Election Division page, as well as the Federal Election Commission (for federal rules or general guidance), which is at www.fec.gov.

There will be rules around signatures; we've mentioned this crucial aspect of running for office before. Let's devote a section to this plus filing fees, as we see otherwise well-prepared candidates botch both.

FEES AND SIGNATURES: TWO WAYS YOU'LL SEE CANDIDATES SCREW UP

"If you want it done right, do it yourself."

This is perfectionist cope; it's also wise self-advice for running your campaign. Petitions, fees, campaign finance . . . the buck stops with you because the buck *will* stop you if anyone on your team completes the wrong form, forgets a key signature, misses a field on a petition form, and so on. The buck stops with you. Read all rules. Strictly comply. Triple check. Document everything. It's not that hard, in our opinion; what's hard is announcing to your supporters that you have to withdraw because you technically never ran because someone did something wrong and you have no one to blame but yourself.

Here is an example of filing fees and petition requirements in Idaho:

Filing fees and petition signature requirements for partisan candidates		
Office sought	Filing fee	Petition signature requirements
United States Senator	$500	1,000
United States Representative	$300	500
Governor	$300	1,000
Lieutenant governor, secretary of state, state controller, attorney general, and superintendent of public infrastructure	$200	1,000
State legislator	$30	50

Pay the fee and/or get the signatures. This is what you must do.

STATE LEGISLATURE
PETITION FOR CANDIDACY

In lieu of the filing fee, this petition must be filed in the Office of the Secretary of State with the Declaration of Candidacy by candidates of all political parties for State Legislative office during the filing period below. The statutorily required number of signatures of qualified electors must be verified by the appropriate County Clerk prior to filing.

CANDIDATE FILING DATES *(I.C. 34-704, 34-708)*
February 28 - March 11, 2022*

CANDIDATE WITHDRAWAL DATES *(I.C. 34-717)*
Primary Election Deadline: March 25, 2022*
General Election Deadline: September 7, 2022*
*All deadlines are at 5:00 PM Local Time

OFFICE INFORMATION
Filing for the Office of: ☐ State Senator ☐ State Representative A ☐ State Representative B
Legislative District #
Party Affiliation: ☐ Constitution ☐ Democratic ☐ Libertarian ☐ Republican

CANDIDATE INFORMATION
Candidate Name *(As it will appear on the ballot.)*

SIGNERS STATEMENT
I, the undersigned, being a qualified elector in the State of Idaho, do hereby certify that I reside at the place set opposite my name, and that I join in the petition of the candidate for the party and office listed above to appear on the Primary Election ballot on May 17th, 2022, and that each for himself says: I have personally signed this petition; I am a qualified elector of the State of Idaho and my residence address is correctly written after my name.

	Signature of Petitioner	Printed Name	Residence Address	Date Signed
1.				
2.				
3.				
4.				
5.				
6.				
7.				
8.				
9.				
10.				

CERTIFICATION
State of Idaho
County of ______

I, ____________________, being first duly sworn say: That I am a resident of the State of Idaho and at least eighteen (18) years of age: that every person who signed this sheet of the foregoing petition signed his or her name thereto in my presence: I believe that each has stated his or her name address and residence correctly, that each signer is a qualified elector of the State of Idaho, and a resident of the county of ____________.

Circulator Signature: Address:

Subscribed and sworn to before me this _____ day of ______________, ______.

Notary Signature: ____________________

Notary Public in and for the State of Idaho, residing at

____

My Commission Expires: ____________________

SC-1P - Petition for Candidacy for State Legislative Office – Approved by the Idaho Secretary of State *Revised 09/02/2021*

If you had started this entire political adventure with "get signatures," you would probably be at a loss for what to do next. But you're not. If you'll have followed what we've advised so far, you've built community. You're going to events. You're connecting with likely voters and supporters. You know who these people are, where they go, and what's important to them. And now that you know the rules on petitions and you've downloaded and printed yours, you know what to do: **show up and ask people to sign**.

It's not sexy, it's systematic. You'll be done soon. Sooner than if you started this whole adventure with this step, ironically.

MAKE FILING A MOMENT (BECAUSE IT'S NEWSWORTHY)

This is one of the freebies in campaign coverage, and you'd be crazy not to accept it. The day you file is newsworthy, so make sure you have somebody to snap your photo while you are making it official. Make sure it's a clean, well-lit shot you can use everywhere. And then? Use it everywhere. Post across social media. Everywhere. This moment is a credibility-builder. It signals seriousness. Real.

PRESS RELEASES: TURN A CLERICAL ACT INTO FREE MEDIA

You should have your press release ready to go in advance; then attach that official-filing photo to it.

Read that again: ". . . *ready in advance.*"

With our fake news media, there are only two instances where a journalist with even a sliver of integrity left has to ethically cover your campaign as news: 1) filing day, 2) election night.

You do not write the press release after filing. By then, you're tired, the photo is sitting on someone's smartphone, and the news cycle has already moved on. So have this bad boy drafted, proofed, and formatted before you walk in the door. Your press release will include:

- Your public why (Chapter 6)
- Your top issues
- Your contrast
- Your credibility

- Your tone
- A quote from you that lazy journalists will copy and paste

This is where the reader learns what kind of candidate you are. How a candidate does anything is how a candidate does everything.

How to Write the Press Release (Without Embarrassing Yourself)

Press releases are neither English essays nor elegant poems. They are a specific format that seem clunky to the public relations–uninitiated. You will craft the narrative and message you want, but you will never, ever, lie. Grok AI can once again help you here. In fact, we encourage it. It's 2026 . . . let's act like it.

The Inverted Pyramid Template

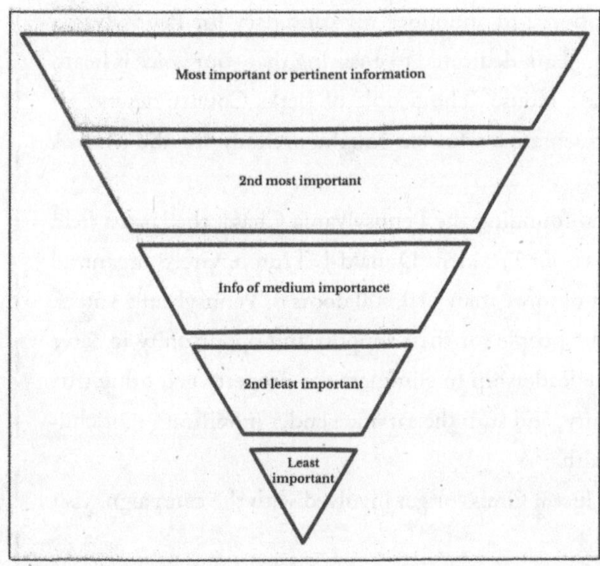

Follow the inverted pyramid as you write yours.

Meaning, lead with the most newsworthy facts first, then expand with supporting detail and add background, then finally . . . end with the least essential info. Use the standard close; write "###" at the end of the release.

Sample Press Release

Contact
Justin Greiss
justin@justingreiss.com
484.867.5309

FOR IMMEDIATE RELEASE **Justin Greiss Announces His Candidacy for the 2026 Pennsylvania State House**

Berks County, PA – Justin Greiss announced his candidacy for the 2026 Pennsylvania State House election in Berks County on the steps of the Pennsylvania Capitol Building.

"I am pleased and honored to announce my candidacy for Pennsylvania State House," said Greiss. "I am dedicated to ensuring that your voice is heard loud and clear at the State House. The people of Berks County deserve an honest and diligent representative who has fought tirelessly for the MAGA movement."

Greiss is known for co-founding the Pennsylvania Chase, the largest field effort in the state to reelect our President Donald J. Trump. Greiss organized the get out the vote effort of more than 510,000 doors of Pennsylvania voters.

Greiss humbly asks the people for their support and opportunity to serve them with bold and fierce leadership to eliminate the property tax, bring true school choice to our county, and stop the satanic gender modification of children in the Commonwealth.

To learn more about Justin Greiss or get involved with the campaign, visit www.justingreiss.com

###

You Need a Media List (Before You Need a Media List)

You cannot send press releases to "the media" if you do not have said list. We advise you to build and retain your list of media contacts, which can include:

- Local reporters
- Local editors
- Radio hosts
- Podcast hosts
- Community newsletter owners
- Bloggers (yes, some are influential locally)
- TV assignment desks (if applicable)

Keep this list clean, current, and backed up. It becomes an asset you'll use repeatedly, from first filing to announcing key endorsements to hyping up events to countering any controversies to getting attention for any debates to pushing out your closing arguments on election eve.

THE TIMELINE FOR EVERYTHING

This chapter should be executed from six to twelve months before the election, or the soonest it's legal for you to do so. That window is when you should already have:

- Your deadlines calendar locked
- Your packet and legal requirements confirmed
- Your petition/fee plan executed
- Your press release drafted
- Your media list built
- Your photo plan ready (who's taking it, where, what shot)

And then, filing becomes clean, official, and useful.

FILING TO RUN: ACTION STEPS (12 TO 6 MONTHS BEFORE FILING OR AS SOON AS LEGAL TO DO SO)

1. Call the Filing Office and Get the Checklist

Call the governing body. Ask what you need to bring and what causes rejections. Request or download the official filing packet. Make your own one-page checklist and print it.

2. Build Your Deadlines and Events Calendar

Add, at minimum:

- Campaign finance reporting deadlines (for your office)
- Candidate petition circulation window
- Filing date window
- Withdrawal deadline
- Election dates and early voting windows (if relevant)

Set multiple reminders. Share the calendar with at least one other responsible person.

3. Choose Your Path: Fee Versus Petitions (and Execute It)

Confirm you know (and will closely follow) rules for petitions versus filing fees.

If petitions are required: learn valid signature rules, circulator rules, formatting rules, and submission rules.

If a fee is required: confirm amount and acceptable payment methods.

4. Prepare Your "Filing Moment" Photo

Choose who will take the photo. Plan for a clean, well-lit shot of you signing/submitting. Decide in advance where the photo will be used—website, social media, email lists, press release, etc.

5. Draft Your Filing Press Release (Before Filing)

Our guidelines for you for this include:

- Use Grok AI (prompt it with something like, "I need you to write a press release for my campaign announcement.").
- Follow the inverted pyramid.
- Include your message and your "why" (from Chapter 6).
- End with ###.
- Do not lie. Ever.

6. Build and Maintain Your Media List

Create a spreadsheet that includes outlet, contact name, email, phone, beat, notes. Start local, move to regional, then add niche-specific. Keep it up to date. Retain it as a permanent campaign asset. Win.

7. Make the Post

Post that filing photo with a clean caption, and keep that text on-message, meaning it's short and sweet and says:

- Why you're running
- What your Top 3 issues are
- How grateful you are
- How supporters can get involved

You've positioned yourself to win, chosen your message, and made the candidacy real in the eyes of the district. Next, we move from *I filed* to *I can fund this*. In the next chapter, we're going to talk about budgets, burn rate, and the uncomfortable but unavoidable discipline of raising the money you need. Let's get it done.

CHAPTER 8

DETERMINE YOUR BUDGET (OR YOU'RE NGMI)

There's something you should know.
The higher-spending candidate wins nearly 94 percent of U.S. congressional races—and 87 percent of U.S. senate races.[33]

In our opinion, the most overlooked business profession is accounting. "Bean counters," they're called—as sales and marketing and operations all ignore the red flags of finance and the company wrecks *kaput*. Unideal.

Don't cook your books; study them. Rather, get someone you trust who will—and have visibility into all their doings at all times.

This is where we talk budget. We've personally witnessed up-close campaigns in which the candidate wanted to front-load investments and expenditures. They felt like they were doing great, as they always do . . . right up until the moment they can't afford the mail, can't afford the door program, can't afford the list, can't afford the tools, can't afford the staff, and can't afford the one thing a campaign exists to do—get votes. Money is how you get your message out. Simple as that.

If you don't determine your budget early, you're NGMI (internet slang for "not gonna make it"). A campaign is a cashflow operation, and the district doesn't care about your intentions—only whether you can execute. And so budgeting covers two things:

1. **How** much money you need to win, and
2. **What** you must spend money on to buy votes, not vibes

WHERE DO YOU START?

With evidence. Look at how much winning candidates in your district raised. Then look at what those candidates spent their money on—good or bad.

If you can't find this for your exact district, don't use that as an excuse to guess. Find information from a comparable district and use that to inform your decision-making. You're creating a working model, not writing a graduate dissertation.

While you're doing this, you need to answer this question: **Will there be a competitive general election, or is it primary only?**

Also ask: **Are you challenging an incumbent in a primary?** Is it an open seat? Are you headed for a bloody primary and then a sleepy general, or the reverse? The budget is more than a number, it's a ballot strategy.

THE RULE: EVERY DOLLAR MUST EQUAL MORE VOTES

Write this on the whiteboard and don't let anyone talk you out of it:

"Every dollar spent needs to equal more votes."

This is how you prevent the classic campaign failure where you spend thousands on things that feel like campaigning—banners, swag, vehicle wraps, constant logo refreshes—and then can't afford the one mailer that would have moved 1,500 persuadable households.

Your spending priorities must be focused on votes. Everything else is secondary.

What Are You Spending Money On?

At a high level, most campaigns spend money in a few categories:

- Voter contact (mail, door program, phone/text tools, digital ads that actually reach voters)

- Infrastructure (website, compliance tools, donation processor, basic software)
- Compliance and admin (filing requirements, accounting, reporting, treasurer support)
- People (staffers, contractors, consultants—sometimes necessary, sometimes a money pit)
- Volunteer enablement (food, supplies, cutting friction so volunteers keep showing up)

Next, you're going to decide what's worth it based on what historically worked in your district—and on what your opponent is already doing.

KNOW THE BENCHMARK: WHAT WINNERS RAISED HERE

Again, to use our Idaho example, in statehouse races, the average winning GOP primary candidate raised **$31,337**. Specifically, these winning candidates made it through the primary election in a *competitive* race, meaning a challenger garnered at least 20 percent. Depending on your district and your office, your number could be far higher—or lower.

This is why you must do the comparison homework for your race:

- How much have winning candidates raised in this district in the past?
- How much has your opponent raised in the past?
- How much has your opponent raised this cycle?

If you're facing an incumbent who routinely raises $120,000 while you're dreaming about winning with $15,000, you're not a maverick; you're mad. You likely do not need to raise more than your opponent, because you are going to outwork them by following this formula, but you need to be competitive. The point is, know the battlefield before you fight.

Have a look at this graphic put together for a Citizens Alliance candidate training seminar:

CASHFLOW *IS* THE CAMPAIGN

Your budget is both *how much* and *when*. Campaigns don't fail only from raising too little, they fail from raising too late. For example, you can't buy

District	Candidate	House	Senate
District 1A	Mark Sauter	$28,249	-
District 1B	Sage Dixon	$33,868	-
District 1	Scott Herndon	-	$54,401
District 2A	Heather Scott	NC	-
District 2B	Dale Hawkins	NC	-
District 2	Phil Hart	-	$19,460
District 3A	Vito Barbieri	NC	-
District 3B	Jordan Redman	NC	-
District 3	Doug Okuniewicz	NC	NC
District 4A	Joe Alfieri	$16,259	-
District 4B	Elaine Price	$25,834	-
District 4	Ben Toews	-	$49,449
District 5A	Ron Mendive	-	-
District 5B	Tony Wisniewski	NC	-
District 5	Carl Bjerke	-	$11,878
District 6A	Lori McCann	$45,090	-
District 6B	Brandon Mitchell	NC	-
District 6	Dan Foreman	-	$4,430
District 7A	Mike Kingsley	$23,675	-
District 7B	Charlie Shepherd	NC	-
District 7	Cindy Carlson	-	$45,090
District 8A	Matthew Bundy	$40,795	-
District 8B	Megan C. Blanksma	NC	-
District 8	Geoff Schroeder	-	$6,701
District 9A	Jacyn Gallagher	$16,367	-
District 9B	Judy Boyle	$15,200	-
District 9	Abby Lee	-	$19,471
District 10A	Mike Moyle	$38,000	-
District 10B	Bruce Skaug	$23,325	-
District 10	Tammy Nichols	-	$20,380
District 11A	Julie Yamamoto	NC	-
District 11B	Chris Allgood	$17,350	-
District 11	Chris Trakel	-	$22,411
District 12A	Jeff Cornilles	$15,026	-
District 12B	Jaron Crane	$14,851	-
District 12	Ben Adams	-	NC
District 13A	Brent Crane	NC	-
District 13B	Kenny Wroten	$9,650	-
District 13	Brian Lenney	-	$12,791
District 14A	Ted Hill	$38,257	-
District 14B	Josh Tanner	$45,863	-
District 14	C. Scott Grow	-	$33,262
District 15A	Steve Berch	NC	-
District 15B	Dori Healey	NC	-
District 15	Rick Just	-	$21,725
District 16A	Soñia Galaviz	NC	-
District 16B	Colin Nash	NC	-
District 16	Alison Rabe	-	NC
District 17A	John L. Gannon	NC	-
District 17B	Susan Chew	NC	-
District 17	Carrie Semmelroth	-	NC
District 18A	Ilana Rubel	NC	-
District 18B	Brooke Green	NC	-
District 18	Janie Ward-Engelking	-	NC
District 19A	Lauren Necochea	NC	-
District 19B	Chris Mathias	NC	-
District 19	Melissa Wintrow	-	NC
District 20A	Joe Palmer	$43,500	-
District 20B	James Holtzclaw	$24,052	-
District 20	Chuck Winder	-	$53,300
District 21A	James Petzke	$38,077	-
District 21B	Jeff Ehlers	$47,211	-
District 21	Treg Bernt	-	$69,448
District 22A	John Vander Woude	$34,000	-
District 22B	Jason Monks	NC	-
District 22	Lori Den Hartog	-	NC
District 23A	Melissa Durrant	$20,579	-
District 23B	Tina Lambert	$9,088	-
District 23	Todd Lakey	-	$24,750
District 24A	Chenele Dixon	$35,035	-
District 24B	Steve Miller	$14,580	-
District 24	Glenneda Zuiderveld	-	$25,285
District 25A	Lance Clow	NC	-
District 25B	Gregory Lanting	$17,833	-
District 25	Linda Wright Hartgen	-	NC
District 26A	Ned Burns	NC	-
District 26B	Jack Nelsen	$28,150	-
District 26	Ron Taylor	-	$10,740
District 27A	Douglas T. Pickett	$29,935	-
District 27B	Clay Handy	$7,940	-
District 27	Kelly Anthon	-	$86,606
District 28A	Richard Cheatum	$20,087	-
District 28B	Dan Garner	$31,079	-
District 28	Jim Guthrie	-	$39,400
District 29A	Dustin W. Manwaring	$23,656	-
District 29B	Nate Roberts	$13,107	-
District 29	James Ruchti	-	NC
District 30A	David Cannon	NC	-
District 30B	Julianne Young	NC	-
District 30	Julie VanOrden	-	$62,473
District 31A	Jerald Raymond	$48,759	-
District 31B	Rod Furniss	$24,163	-
District 31	Van Burtenshaw	-	$36,869
District 32A	Stephanie Mickelsen	NC	-
District 32B	Wendy Horman	NC	-
District 32	Kevin Cook	-	$18,500
District 33A	Barbara Ehardt	$33,566	-
District 33B	Marco Erickson	NC	-
District 33	David Lent	-	$18,722
District 34A	Jon Weber	$19,850	-
District 34B	Britt Raybould	$130,292	-
District 34	Doug Ricks	-	NC
District 35A	Kevin Andrus	$12,182	-
District 35B	Josh Wheeler	$90,997	-
District 35	Mark Harris	-	$39,950
	Average	$30,375	$32,300
	Min	$7,940	$4,430
	Max	$130,292	$86,606

effective voter contact three days before Election Day, you can't hire the tool after you needed the tool, and you can't decide you're doing a mailer after your opponent already defined you. This seems obvious. From the way campaigns blow too much too early, it's obviously not. We want you to think in cashflow terms:

- What must be paid early? (e.g., website, filing, compliance setup, list access, baseline printing)
- What ramps later? (e.g., paid voter contact, digital, persuasion operations)
- What must be held back? (e.g., final-week GOTV for turnout)

Here is a sample breakdown of a month-to-month cashflow:

ESTABLISH A CAMPAIGN BANK ACCOUNT (NO EXCEPTIONS)

You need a **separate bank account** for all campaign cashflow and right from the start. Never mix personal and campaign funds. They are not the same. Mixing funds creates compliance risk, reporting nightmares, audit vulnerabilities, opponent ammunition, and internal confusion that kills momentum. Just don't. Run it clean from day one.

FIND A TREASURER (AND A PLATFORM)

The campaign treasure is a key risk-management position. You'll want someone who is competent, honest, and experienced (with industries where bookkeeping compliance is a big deal). For some campaigns, this person already does this for a living, and it may absolutely make sense to do so in your situation. In others, it's a friend with real accounting understanding who is invested in your success and takes precision seriously. You could also involve someone apolitical you trust, someone who isn't emotionally caught up in the drama and will keep the books clean. Just don't be casual here. The treasurer is the person who keeps you out of preventable trouble resulting in bad press and fines. You're looking for a conscientious numbers nerd known to take everything literally, to be frank. Get as close to that with this paid or volunteer position as you can.

Budget Line Item / Action	Prior cost to campaign	Prior raise for campaign	March cost to campaign	March projected money raised	April cost to campaign	April projected money raised	May cost to campaign	May projected money raised	June cost to campaign	June projected money raised	July cost to campaign	July projected money raised	August cost to campaign	August projected money raised
Actual	$0	$0	$0	$0	$0	$0	$0	$0	$0	$0	$0	$0	$0	$0
Voter outreach - Voicemails	$0	$0	$0	$0	$0	$0	$0	$0	$200	$0	$200	$0	$200	$0
Voter outreach - Digital	$0	$0	$0	$0	$0	$0	$1,000	$0	$4,000	$0	$4,000	$0	$0	$0
Voter outreach - Radio	$0	$0	$0	$0	$0	$0	$0	$0	$1,500	$0	$1,500	$0	$0	$0
Voter outreach - Mail	$0	$0	$0	$0	$5,600	$0	$4,550	$0	$9,100	$0	$18,200	$0	$0	$0
Voter outreach - Paid Doors	$0	$0	$0	$0	$0	$0	$0	$0	$0	$0	$0	$0	$0	$0
Voter outreach - Texting	$0	$0	$0	$0	$0	$0	$0	$0	$500	$0	$500	$0	$500	$0
Donor outreach - Dialing for dollars	$0	$0	$0	$15,000	$0	$7,500	$0	$7,500	$0	$15,000	$0	$10,000	$0	$0
Donor outreach - Donor events	$0	$0	$0	$0	$0	$0	$0	$3,000	$0	$0	$0	$0	$0	$0
Donor outreach - Email	$0	$0	$0	$250	$0	$250	$0	$250	$0	$250	$0	$500	$0	$0
Donor outreach - Mailer	$0	$0	$0	$800	$0	$0	$0	$0	$0	$0	$0	$0	$0	$0
5411 Staff	$0	$0	$2,000	$0	$2,000	$0	$2,000	$0	$2,000	$0	$2,000	$0	$3,000	$0
Donation processing fees	$0	$0	$321	$0	$155	$0	$215	$0	$305	$0	$210	$0	$0	$0
Website	$0	$0	$1,200	$0	$0	$0	$0	$0	$0	$0	$0	$0	$0	$0
MailChimp	$0	$0	$35	$0	$35	$0	$55	$0	$55	$0	$55	$0	$55	$0
I-360	$0	$0	$0	$0	$350	$0	$350	$0	$350	$0	$350	$0	$350	$0
Office supplies	$0	$0	$50	$0	$50	$0	$50	$0	$50	$0	$50	$0	$50	$0
Campaign Swag	$0	$0	$600	$0	$0	$0	$0	$0	$0	$0	$0	$0	$0	$0
Volunteer Incentive	$0	$0	$0	$0	$100	$0	$100	$0	$200	$0	$200	$0	$100	$0
Travel	$0	$0	$0	$0	$0	$0	$0	$0	$0	$0	$0	$0	$0	$0
Event Tickets	$0	$0	$100	$0	$100	$0	$200	$0	$200	$0	$200	$0	$0	$0
Yard Signs	$0	$0	$1,471	$0	$0	$0	$0	$0	$1,471	$0	$0	$0	$0	$0
Big Signage	$0	$0	$1,000	$0	$0	$0	$1,000	$0	$0	$0	$0	$0	$0	$0
Printed Materials	$0	$0	$486	$0	$0	$0	$500	$0	$0	$0	$0	$0	$0	$0
Miscellaneous	$0	$0	$300	$0	$300	$0	$300	$0	$300	$0	$300	$0	$300	$0
TOTAL	$0	$18,273	$7,563	$16,050	$8,690	$7,750	$10,320	$10,750	$28,231	$15,250	$27,765	$10,500	$4,555	$0
Primary Date = August 8th														
	$0	$18,273		$26,760		$25,820		$26,250		$21,269		$4,004		-$551

Then when it comes to online donation platforms, consider using Anedot or WinRed. You can delegate this setup to your treasurer, but again—don't hand over the keys, so to speak. Create a second set. Anything anyone on your team has access to, you must be able to get into as well.

DETERMINE YOUR BUDGET: ACTION STEPS (12 MONTHS BEFORE THE ELECTION)

1. Determine What It Costs to Be Competitive

Estimate what it will cost to be competitive in your district:

$________________________

Is this for the primary? General? Both?

____

Now, answer honestly:

- Is your race primary-only competitive?
- Or will you need to survive both a primary and a general?
- Are you challenging an incumbent or running for an open seat?

Your budget changes based on that reality. That said, here is a **sample budget**:

Sample Campaign Budget:

Launch party	-$500	______
Website	-$200	______
Literature	-$2,500	______
Staffers	-$12,500	______
Mailer 1	-$7,000 ($1 per piece of mail)	______
Mailer 2	-$7,000 ($1 per piece of mail)	______
Mailer 3	-$7,000 ($1 per piece of mail)	______
Yard signs	-$5,000 ($2 per sign)	______
Volunteer food	-$500	______
Volunteer incentives	-$500	______
Digital ads	-$1,000	______
Door app	-$250	______

Donation processor fees	-$250	____
Filing requirements	-$500	____
Graphic design	-$500	____
Banners / Swag	-$500 (Go easy here)	____
Office supplies	-$500	____
Overhead	-$3,000	____
Total	**$49,200**	____

Can you raise this amount?

2. Research Past Raise-and-Spend

Look up how much recent candidates who won raised in your district. Look up what they spent money on (good or bad). Look up your opponent's current and historical fundraising (if applicable).

If district data is scarce, use a comparable district.

Write down your benchmark range:

Past winners raised: $________ to $________

My opponent raised (last cycle): $________

Comparable district winners raised: $________ to $________

3. Build Your Budget (Then Your Cashflow Plan)

Convert your topline budget into a cashflow plan.

What must be paid in months 12–9 counting down to the election?

What ramps in months 9–6 before voting?

What spikes in months 6–0?

If your spending is planned but your fundraising timeline doesn't match, you don't have a budget, you have a fantasy.

4. Open the Campaign Bank Account

Establish the campaign account for all cashflow.

Confirm who has signing authority.

Set up clear documentation for deposits, expenditures, and reimbursements.

Rule: never mix personal and campaign funds.

5. Secure a Treasurer

Decide whether you will:

Hire a professional treasurer/compliance service, or
Recruit a trusted person with accounting competence.
Write the name here once chosen:
Treasurer: ______________________________
Contact: ______________________________

6. Set Up Your Donation Processor

Select and configure your online donation platform:
Anedot / WinRed / Other: ______________________________
Donation link created: Yes / No
Thank-you note confirmation set: Yes / No
Recurring option enabled: Yes / No
Make it easy to give. Make it easy to give again. Make it easy to win.

So! Now you know what it will cost to be competitive, and you've set the basic financial infrastructure to handle money cleanly. The next problem is that you have to actually raise it.

In the next chapter, we'll get practical about fundraising, specifically how to make asking for money feel like leadership instead of begging.

CHAPTER 9

RAISE THAT MONEY (OR, AGAIN, NGMI)

> ***There's something you should know.***
> Overall, 30 percent of registered voters report having donated to a campaign in the past two years. Rates vary based on party affiliation, with Democrats most likely to donate (37 percent) compared to Republicans (26 percent) and independents (22 percent).[34]

If you won't ask for money—for **a lot** of money—you shouldn't run for office. We don't say this to be rude. We say it because it's the single-most common point of failure for first-time candidates who otherwise have everything going for them. Passion, message, the right issues, even momentum. But campaigning is not a vibes contest. It's getting your message out. That is why we raise money. Period.

Remember our example benchmark? The average winning Republican primary candidate raises $31,337. So now we ask you: **How are you going to raise $31,337?**

If you can't answer that in detail, you're NGMI.

FIRST: DON'T WING CAMPAIGN FINANCE

Before we talk tactics, let's talk law. We advised you to go legal earlier; that will also include understanding campaign finance laws in detail. Contribution limits exist, and they vary by office and jurisdiction. Here is an example from the state of Idaho.

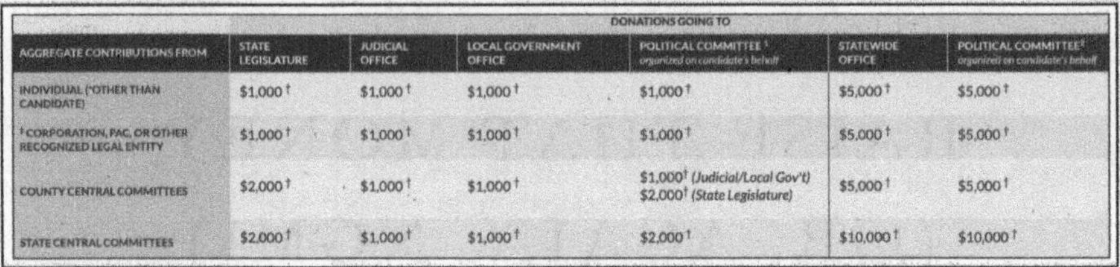

	DONATIONS GOING TO					
AGGREGATE CONTRIBUTIONS FROM	STATE LEGISLATURE	JUDICIAL OFFICE	LOCAL GOVERNMENT OFFICE	POLITICAL COMMITTEE ‡ *organized on candidate's behalf*	STATEWIDE OFFICE	POLITICAL COMMITTEE‡ *organized on candidate's behalf*
INDIVIDUAL (*OTHER THAN CANDIDATE)	\$1,000 †	\$1,000 †	\$1,000 †	\$1,000 †	\$5,000 †	\$5,000 †
† CORPORATION, PAC, OR OTHER RECOGNIZED LEGAL ENTITY	\$1,000 †	\$1,000 †	\$1,000 †	\$1,000 †	\$5,000 †	\$5,000 †
COUNTY CENTRAL COMMITTEES	\$2,000 †	\$1,000 †	\$1,000 †	\$1,000† *(Judicial/Local Gov't)* \$2,000† *(State Legislature)*	\$5,000 †	\$5,000 †
STATE CENTRAL COMMITTEES	\$2,000 †	\$1,000 †	\$1,000 †	\$2,000 †	\$10,000 †	\$10,000 †

Treat limits the same way you treat ballot filing—comply perfectly. Document everything. No improvising. Then with this last duck in your row, you can focus on the next fact: **You have to raise \$5,000 minimum in the first ten days.** Let's talk about it.

YOUR FIRST BENCHMARK: \$5,000 IN THE FIRST 10 DAYS (REAL MONEY)

Raise \$5,000 bare minimum in your first ten days—from other people. This first five grand cannot include you self-funding or self-loaning to the campaign. Yes, you may be able to loan your campaign legally, but that's beside our point. And our point is that it's mission-critical to prove you can persuade other human beings to invest in you. If you can't do that early, the rest of the race slips into slow-motion embarrassment.

THE FOUNDATION OF FUNDRAISING: YOU HAVE TO ASK

Fundraising is not sexy. It's uncomfortable, boring, and repetitive in every single way. As easy as this chapter was for us to write, it is that inversely difficult to execute. The challenge is both practical and psychological. Campaigns starve when they otherwise don't have to because candidates try to "be polite" and accidentally choose the one behavior that guarantees political death: they avoid the ask. Call it "building relationships," "educating the voter," "getting the word out," if any of those help you feel better about fundraising. Even so, you've still got to do it. You are the chief fundraiser for your campaign. You cannot outsource this to anyone. There is no magical fundraising staffer to hire that is going to solve this for you. Fortunately, to ease the pain a little, we have a little formula for you. It's pretty rad; we'll introduce it to you in Step 3 of Dialing for Dollars later in this chapter. For now, let's zoom out.

YOUR TRIPART ASK STRATEGY

Broadly speaking, how-do-I-ask-for-money is a concern that will bring you to a specific tactic or a technique. And we will do exactly that in short order. But prior and overall, you'll need a fundraising strategy for which to implement said tactic. Let's think big; big thinking includes **package**, **offer**, and **list**.

> **Package** — how you present the campaign and the why (your story, credibility, message discipline, seriousness)
> **Offer** — what the money does (what it funds, what it accomplishes, what it buys in voter contact)
> **List** — who you're asking (warm leads, cold leads, host committees, donor upgrades)

Most candidates obsess over package (i.e., "I need a better pitch") and spend all their time tweaking their fundraising script; winners zoom out beyond the ask to the entire package surrounding it and also include offer and list in their perspective. Even an emotionally compelling campaign pitch hits nothing if you're asking the wrong people for the wrong thing. Speaking of people, let's cover who you'll be calling—and how your ask of them will differ.

Warm Leads: The Phone Is the Weapon

Warm leads are your personal contacts. They're people who know you, know your character, and will pick up—at least some of them.

Warm Leads Fundraising

- Create a document with all of your personal contacts (we reviewed this earlier).
- Audit them and write down how much you believe they can give.

- Call and ask them for 4x the amount you wrote down.
  - If they say no, ask them for *twice* the original.
  - If they say no, ask them for the original amount.
  - If they say no, hang up the phone.

This will be very clarifying for you.

Note: people are rarely offended if you believe they have more disposable funds than they actually do, i.e., you ask for more funds.

Cold Leads: There Is No Perfect List (but You Still Call)

Cold leads are potential donors who simply don't know you yet. You'll obtain a list of donors to target and track (yes, in a Google Sheet if that's what you've got). Then you call.

Cold Ask Fundraising

- Ask for $1,000
  - If no, ask for $500
  - If no, ask for $250
  - If no, hang up

There is no perfect list, even if the cold leads you're dialing aren't frigid. These will likely be people who signed your petition a little while back, but they may not remember you by name. In that case, jog their memory as you dial for their dollars.

You will never find a list that makes this feel effortless. There are not donors sitting in a cocktail bar somewhere just waiting for your call in order to hand you money. You build a list and you work it.

4 STEPS TO DIALING FOR DOLLARS

Whether the lead is warm or cold, the workflow is the same.

Step 1: Response

If they do not answer, you have a 0 percent change of success. So you work the response:

- voicemail
- text
- email

You're not annoying them. You're doing your job. OK, maybe you're being a little annoying. That's OK. You have a country to save.

Step 2: Engage

The first five seconds matter most. We suggest you immediately engage your leads voice-to-voice via:

- a topical issue (something real happening in the district or nation), or
- a simple personal hook (brief, no rambling)

The engagement stage is complete when the lead joins in with you by asking a question, sharing an opinion, or showing emotion. That's when you know—you've got a live one.

Step 3: Ask

Now, transition the engagement topic to **YOU** and your campaign being the solution. Then make a firm ask. And once you make the ask . . . **shut up**.

But how, exactly, do you ask? We have that answer for you now, teased earlier. Let's get to it.

RAD: How to Ask for Money

The simplest fundraising formula you'll ever need is RAD:

RAD: Reason – Amount – Deadline

Let's break down the effective ask's three elements:

Reason — why this matters and why now
Amount — an actual number (not "anything helps")
Deadline — a real time constraint ("before Friday," "by the end of the month," "before our first mail drop")

In short, RAD will turn "support me sometime" into an action and force you to treat fundraising like an operation, not a mood.

Give Donors Choices (and Tie Gifts to Votes)

Your call-to-action can be more than a yes-no question. Ask them to fund something; give people choices. For example:

- "Will you fund a mailer?"
- "Will you sponsor a caller?"
- "Will you cover our door-hanger print run?"
- "Will you underwrite the donation processor fees so every dollar goes to voter contact?"

Donors appreciate impact and specificity.

Step 4: Lock

All amateur salespeople melt here. They'll ask for, say, $1,000, hear "no," and start negotiating against themselves. The whole conversation fizzles, and the can-still-be-negotiated-with would-be donor abruptly hangs up or makes up a (usually false) reason they have to hop off the phone right away.

Skip this crap; instead, lock in. In Warm Leads Fundraising and Cold Leads Fundraising earlier, we advised you to alter your ask at every negative. Don't simply ask the same question again. A simple workflow, to jog your memory, might go:

> **Ask $1,000** ⇨ if no, capture a nugget, step down
> **Ask $500** ⇨ if no, capture a nugget, step down
> **Ask $250** ⇨ yes/no

If YES: process the gift on the phone or give the address to send the check
If NO: say thank you and hang up immediately

Why People Don't Give (It's Always One of Three)

There are three reasons people don't give. There are only ever these three.

1. They don't believe in you.
2. The amount asked for is too much.
3. The timing is poor (for them, the donor).

That's it.

When you hear no, don't panic. Diagnose which of the three it is—then alter your game accordingly as needed. And know that there is more than one way to get your campaign paid.

FUNDRAISING EVENTS 101

More than a party in your honor, a fundraising event is a structured donation request in a controlled environment. There are a few straightforward steps to pulling this off without losing money your campaign can't afford to anyway (e.g., don't spend $5,000 to raise $3,000 and call it a success; that's vanity):

- Lock in on a host (local patriots group, homeschool parents network, an old friend, etc.; you will know these by now because you've built your network as instructed).
- Get the host to commit to:
  - a day and time
  - a personal gift to your campaign
  - and a total amount to raise.
- Legitimize it with a professionally designed invitation.
- Budget to keep costs low (e.g., drinks, not food).
- Host event; let your host make the ask on your behalf.
- Collect checks.

Events exist to raise money, build a donor and likely-donor list, and upgrade donors (i.e., someone pitched in fifty bucks but showed up to your event and wrote a check for a few hundred; more on that below). All else is unnecessary.

Here is some additional guidance to help ensure you pull yours off.

Event Sizes and Tiers

Consider running multiple tiered events, like so:

Small ("coffees"): The point is intimacy and conversion. Candidates often "show up" and hope people donate. Don't. You still pitch and you still ask.

Medium (almost always includes a meal): If it's a paid event, know your costs and your margin. At free events, include a pitch for money. At paid events, consider an extra fundraising push beyond tickets.

Large (meal and a celebrity): These events can attract press. They can also fail spectacularly. Don't waste money on stupid shows. If you go big, go big for strategic reasons, not ego.

Here's an example of a high-profile event's PDF invitation. Consider doing something similar.

At the event itself, attendees received the following handout:

DONOR UPGRADES: TURN ONE GIFT INTO MANY TOUCHPOINTS

Who is the most likely next donor to your campaign?

Someone who has already given to your campaign.

Fundraising doesn't have to end at the first yes. In sales, this is the art of the cross-sell (and upsell). Anyone who gave before, you may:

- Call them again.
- Mail them again.
- Email them again.
- Text them again.
- Invite them to an event (again).

Now, make sure you've marked every past donor as such. This way, you can update your RAD (Reason, Amount, Deadline) when you ask so you come across as offering a time-sensitive opportunity to show their support for the cause of your campaign, which they care about already. Phone this one in, so to speak, and you risk your donors left feeling treated like your campaign's ATM. Don't risk it. Keep donors in the loop, offer chances to deepen involvement, address them as insiders with special access, and provide (ideally photographic) evidence in your updates that your campaign spent their money on what your first RAD pitch promised them you would. Do all this, and your donors are likely to become the political equivalent of recurring revenue. In business, that's the holy-grail business model. In politics, it's the same.

RAISE THAT MONEY: ACTION STEPS (12 MONTHS BEFORE ELECTION OR AS SOON AS LEGAL)

1. Know When You Can Start Raising

When is the soonest you can begin raising money?

____

Confirm this with someone who knows campaign finance law in your jurisdiction if you're not 100 percent sure.

2. Build Your Donor List (Now)
Create a list of every person you know. Warm leads first. Do not wait until you "feel ready." You get ready by doing it.

3. Set Ask Amounts (Before You Call)
For each warm lead, write down what you think they can give—then plan to ask for:

- 4x the amount
- then 2x the original amount
- then the original

For cold leads, use the ladder:

- $1,000 ⇨ $500 ⇨ $250

4. Make Calls Daily (Response ⇨ Engage ⇨ Ask ⇨ Lock)
Set a daily call block and treat it like training. You're building a skill. Candidates who run for Congress are spending twelve hours per day on the phone. Skill beats motivation.

5. Schedule Your First Event (Low Cost)
Identify a likely host and lock:

- Date
- Host's personal commitment
- Total goal

Then create the PDF invite, keep costs low, and make the ask happen.

6. Hit Your First-Month Minimum
Raise $5,000 minimum in the first ten days (excluding self-funding and self-loans). If you can't do this, pause and confront reality. Everything downstream gets harder, not easier.

7. Complete the Worksheet: 15 Prospects to Ask Right Now

First	Last	Min. Amt	x2	x4	Contact Date
Justin	Greiss	$500	$1,000	$2,000	01-01-26

Alright, you now have a fundraising machine—list, asks, call discipline, events, and donor upgrades. Excellent. Moving right along, let's turn from the internal to the external, from what you tell your people . . . to what some very specific people say about you.

CHAPTER 10

SET YOUR MEDIA STRATEGY (OR THEY WILL SET IT FOR YOU)

There's something you should know.
An astonishing 96 percent of newspaper readers vote—compared to the average voter turnaround of roughly 40 percent to 60 percent depending on midterm or presidential elections.[35, 36]

Picture two Republicans running at the same time in two different districts. Loveable Baby Boomer John Doe with his incredible local name recognition is sitting pretty in an R+22 district. The seat is so certain, it comes with office furniture. Past the primary, he's virtually guaranteed to win. His campaign manager tells him no intraparty challengers have a shot; John starts acting like it.

Meanwhile, in the D+10 one district over, barely-out-of-her-MBA-program Jane Smith has "no shot." Not even a longshot. No shot. Family and friends smiled politely, awkwardly, when she announced. Jane doesn't get the luxury of believing her own press; she doesn't have any.

Then things get weird—for both candidates. John Doe—the one who can't lose—completely botches his media strategy and sputters his advantage away. He becomes addicted to attention. He chases every interview like it's oxygen. The local paper doesn't run his exact quote, misnames his wife (she gives him hell for weeks), and he spirals. There he is in the comments on Facebook waging World War III. He's winning the arguments. Except the one that matters. The ballot box. He's friendly-firing goodwill with the public. Worse still, his website looks like a scammy landing page from 2009, and his "issues" page reads like an anarcho-libertarian manifesto that scares normal people. He refuses direct mail because he thinks it's "old school" (the irony!), so the only people who hear from him are the people already obsessed with politics. And he's not exactly winning them over. *This guy has issues*, the collective online Republican base will think. He's trying to "clear the record" but only wipes out the previous positive one that gave him his whole advantage coming into this.

Meanwhile, Jane. The D+10 underdog. She retains her graduate-school discipline coming into politics. She accepts there is no silver bullet, no ace in the hole, so she rolls up her cardigan sleeves to do it herself. Her campaign is a mix of messaging *without* mixed messaging. She's got door-knockers, phone-bankers, direct mailers, and more. Plus, of course, media outreach. She treats digital like a tool for list-building and reinforcement, not her true identity. She also uses mail to define herself locally and to create contrast without sounding . . . you know . . . insane. She builds credibility with boring but effective moves, like a complete Ballotpedia profile, clean website, weekly emails, consistent social media posting, get-out-the-vote text messaging, and earned media exposure—including popular niche podcasts and livestreams with local influencers.

Favorite son John Doe blew the layup and gave himself a dogfight; Jane Smith is grinding her way into a competitive race. She's probably going to run opposed in the primary—and she now has an opportunity to win the general outright.

Now, transitioning from narrative to straight-up nonfiction, this little hypothetical is hyperbolic, we admit. But still, it's directionally accurate. We see upstart candidates like Jane **decide in advance** how her campaign's messaging is going to go; meanwhile we see local celebrities **become reactionary self-parodies** and let everyone and everything else set their media strategy, from journalists to opponents to social media rumors to their own addiction for attention. Take it from us; we'd rather work for a Jane campaign than a John debacle in any election season, whether Donald Trump is up-ballot or not.

That said, the top takeaway from our little story is as follows:

NO SILVER BULLETS!

Effective political communication requires a combination of tools, including:

- Doors
- Phone calls
- Text messages
- Direct mail
- Online advertisements
- Email blasts
- Social media (e.g., Facebook, X)
- Traditional media (e.g., newspaper opinion-editorials, meet-the-candidate interviews)
- New media (e.g., livestreamers, podcasts)

If you're hoping for the one magical tactic that replaces the rest or at the very least obsolesces them, you're not running a campaign . . . you're shopping a fantasy.

But notice what's **not** on the list: TV ads! For the overwhelming majority of races this book is used for, local-market ads on television are a complete and total waste. If your head is full of presidential-campaign instincts, you're going to waste time and money (NGMI).

Your campaign communication objective is, simply, as follows: **Reinforce the same message, across multiple channels, to the same voters, over time, till polls close**. There is, however, one little caveat: **Don't let communication replace campaigning.** The media supports door-knocking, fundraising, and getting the turnout; it does *not* substitute for them.

Another tool there is not a substitute for is a particular website you as a voter have probably used more than once. Let's set up your candidate profile there.

BALLOTPEDIA: FIX THE THING GOOGLE IS GOING TO SHOW PEOPLE ANYWAY

Organic searches for every election, every candidate, sends traffic to a website called Ballotpedia. You need a profile there. You need to check your profile there (in many elections, profiles for candidates are created automatically if not set up manually by the individual or their campaign already). Then update your profile. Finally, complete the Candidate Connection questionnaire that informs voters what matters to and motivates you personally and politically.

Ballotpedia is free credibility; it's one of the first "official-looking" pieces of content voters will see when they search your name. Do not let your opponent look legitimate while you look incomplete. Both of us have written off candidates we didn't know much about in local primary elections because they didn't take a few minutes to update and complete their Ballotpedia. How a candidate does anything is how a candidate does everything. We understand this.

BUILD A WEBSITE (ONLY IF IT'S NOT CRAPPY)

A simple but professional website is a sound idea for the vast majority of elections. It should include, at minimum:

- Sign-up for email updates and/or sign petitions (for list-building)
- Contact information and meaningful bio (a real family picture helps)
- Issues (remember your Top 3; less is more)
- Volunteer sign-up
- Online donation link
- A real campaign email, phone, and a P.O. box (not your home address)

In the current year, website design is one-click easy. Simple web-builder platforms like Squarespace, Wix, Kajabi, and WordPress will give you a beautiful website in minutes. Then have your people add the content and click-throughs above.

As for donation processing tools, we've mentioned WinRed before, but alternatives include RallyPay and Anedot (which we recommend above all).

Our one rule for all tools and features is that your website must be standard in appearance. No comic sans typeface, no weird colors, no Microsoft Paint–style designs like it's 1999. Better no site than a bad one.

On to the next.

DIRECT MAIL: THE ADULT CHANNEL (THAT STILL WORKS)

You will not win an election by having the dankest online presence. Most people who decide local races are not trolling your opponent and owning the libs on social media. They're Boomers and above. We both have living family members who remember World War II—*pre*-Boomers. Older generations read every piece of mail they get, front and back. We highly, highly, highly recommend you persuade them with direct mail.

Mailers empower you to define yourself, reinforce your Top 3 issues, create contrast with other candidates, deliver get-out-the-vote reminders, and reach consistent voters consistently.

The Direct Mail Program

Options here include "slicks" called **postcards** but also in-envelope **letters.** Postcards are cheaper and are good for micro-biography moments (e.g., "apple pie" moments to humanize you), broad-issue stance communication, contrast hits, and event reminders, including mail-in ballot deadlines and poll hours for Election Day.

Letters are likelier to be unread and thrown away and cost more. That said, they work and have a tremendous persuasion effect by those who do read them—if only they get opened. If it looks like junk mail, people assume it is, even our eightysomething and ninetysomething friends.

If you do letters, you can:

- Write a detailed four-pager (page one tells your story, pages two through four each cover your Top 3 with plenty of bullets).
- Enclose a donation envelope with a one-page fundraising ask (remember to keep it RAD).

- Help your spouse write what's called a "wife letter," where family is strategically yet non-cringily deployed on a candidate's behalf for a direct mailer. This is particularly effective to overcome negatives in a race.

Now let's talk about the next-level program: the chase.

The Chase Program

For future reference, **Appendix A contains the entire *PA CHASE* program run with unprecedented success to support Donald Trump's Pennsylvania win in 2024.** Ballot-chasing differs from mailer-chaser. In this context, "chase" means reinforcing your message through the mail and includes:

- Personal notes to undecideds
- "Sorry I missed you" to no-answer doors
- "Thank you" notes to sign locations (with a donation ask)
- Issue-based mail based off petition responses

Mail-chasers can be done alongside postcards and the different formats of letter. *But won't that cost a lot of money to do all that?* Yep. See Chapter 9.

EMAIL: USEFUL, CHEAP, AND EASY TO DO BADLY

Emails will not win an election by themselves, but a sloppy email program can absolutely weaken, worse, and wane everything else you're doing.

For starters, use a free or low-cost service like Mailchimp, Constant Contact, or ConvertKit. Your use for email will be to (no surprise here) reinforce your Top 3, drive donations and volunteer sign-ups, convert attention into action, and end any uncertainty or confusion the public has when searching your name or seeing a sign.

Email best practices and rules include:

- Send one email per week
- Keep paragraphs short (two to three lines)
- Provide useful content, more than just campaign updates, such as happenings at the state capitol

- Use indentation, bolding, underlining to control the reader's eyes
- Use images and video to communicate the message
- Recycle your best direct mail copy here (don't reinvent)
- Resend to non-opens within twenty-four hours
- Put time into crafting the subject line
- Always include an action item in every email
- Often include a P.S. line

Also, integrate your data. Import your email database into i360 or your spreadsheet so your communications and targeting don't live in separate worlds.

Let's continue the writing theme into the next stage of media strategy.

LETTERS TO THE EDITOR: CREDIBILITY (USE SPARINGLY)

Remember the Boomers and above. Do they subscribe en masse to a decent newspaper with real circulation in your district? Then that's where you need to be, too. Letters to the editor (LTEs) can be worthwhile because they (if actually read) build name recognition, establish credibility, and present your ideas to a high-turnout block: senior citizens.

LTEs and opinion-editorials, their sister format, serve other functions for you. You can "use spear-carriers"—other people—to promote your message, especially if the message is "the incumbent is failing" and you don't want to sound like you're whining. If you see a strong pro-liberty or otherwise aligned editorial, check the author against your list. That person could become a donor, volunteer, or validator for you, i.e., write an LTE or op-ed in support of you or in opposition to the other candidate(s). Just remember—deadlines don't move. Know the publishing turnaround time for your local papers.

ALL THINGS SOCIAL: NO COMMENT WARS, NO TROLLING, NO BS

Facebook, X, and the like should be for work, not play. And certainly not "play." No fighting, no rage-baiting, no doomscrolling. We're here to chase votes, not dopamine. That said, we *do* want you to get likes, comments, and shares, as these boost organic reach. But we don't want your profiles to become sentiment-synonymous with anything toxic or trollish.

Sample Letter to the Editor

Dear Editor:

I have been blessed to live in Berks County for the majority of my life, but in recent years I've seen a change that I am not proud of.

The folks at the Pennsylvania State House and in Washington don't always have our best interests at heart, but I'm here to change that. As a medical professional, I've been through the highs and lows with many members of this community, and I know the best way to uphold Pennsylvania values.

I want you to have more money in your paycheck every month. I will never vote for a tax increase. In fact, it's time to cut taxes . . . We all know that Berks County is a beautiful place to live, but it's time to make our home a more affordable place for our working families and seniors.

Hundreds of people are leaving the area due to the huge tax burden our state puts on us, but I'm ready to fight for the middle class. Along with cutting taxes and reducing spending, I understand the importance of having good schools and a safe community.

I have two children in grade school, and I am committed to ensuring that our schools succeed. I'm here to serve our students and teachers in the best way.

I will ensure that your voice is constantly heard at the State House. You are better equipped to make the best decisions for you and your family than the government is. I'm heading to the State House to stop the government from interfering with your life.

I humbly ask the people for their support and opportunity to serve them with bold and fierce leadership to restore freedom to the community.

Sincerely,

Ron Paul

Pennsylvania State House Candidate

Put Your Face on Facebook

We suggest you post here daily; post content normal people would like to see on their social media newsfeeds, such as:

- family pictures
- pets
- livestreams
- community events
- retiring teachers
- meaningful endorsements
- apple pie and kissing babies
- only broad-appeal issues for your district

Convert social reach into real information. If your presence isn't feeding your list-building and volunteer pipeline, it's probably waste-of-time entertainment. Sorry. Fix.

NOTE: Verify your account with that little blue checkmark before someone makes a fraudulent account with your name and face on it.

Online Ad Ideas (e.g., Facebook, Google)

Ads should do one of three things and in this order:

1. Build your list.
2. Deliver pain and show contrast.
3. Promote a message.

In social media marketing, there's a term called **cost discipline.** This is where you run the numbers to confirm you're getting at the bottom of the "funnel" what you're truly paying for at the time. Our rule is as follows: **If it costs more than $0.50 per new name (potential donor or volunteer), turn the ad off.** Cost discipline.

Upload voter files to Facebook or Google when appropriate. Exclude certain groups. Target key voters. Treat ads as a measuring tool that produces data—not a magic wand.

Lead generation is highly recommended:

- Use Facebook's native form (one-click, better conversion, cheaper).
- Downside: it doesn't auto-direct to a donate page.
- Use Google paid search to boost your website listing.

But don't just think list-building exclusively. Digital ads in 2026 and beyond are wildly powerful. These give you ability with relative certainty to target specific voters with digital media. Not until very recently in the history of campaigns has this been possible. It is a big deal. We're talking matching your ads on Facebook, Google, and across digital media with actual voters or at minimal households with targeted voters.

No longer are you simply limited to placing your ad on the 6:00 p.m. news and hoping your primary voters watch it. You can find them. Cookies.

Facebook and Google offer targeting and list matching. Services like i360 can plug right into your digital spend. Online platforms like RepublicanAds.com can get your ads on grandma's Candy Crush. And there are a number of services emerging making it easier to get on "Hulu" type services.

If you're running a big race, you may consider hiring someone to help with the matching. Smaller races give RepublicanAds.com, Facebook, and Google Banner ads a whirl.

You Are Not Donald Trump: Words for the Wise for X

Twitter, now called X after Elon Musk's purchase of the app, is generally less effective for campaigns in terms of moving voters. It is good for journalists, influencers, and in-office politicians, however. Odds are, you are none of these. You can get attention here, as it's become the *de facto* marketplace of ideas. That means it's easy to get in trouble.

You are not Donald Trump. If your tweet in drafts is potentially questionable—too spicy for undecideds—get another set of eyes on it. X rewards pithy one-liners, so don't get carried away trying to be clever. You'll most likely look ranty, not like a real candidate with poise and polish. A local campaign doesn't need virality, it needs seriousness.

MEDIA: THE CRACK COCAINE OF POLITICS

Don't get addicted. Earned media is valuable, but only when it meets **three criteria:**

1. The media is on-message (e.g., answer the question you wish they asked).
2. The media adds measurable value to your campaign (e.g., you recorded an uptick in volunteers following a given hit).
3. The media improves your name recognition and favorability (also measurable).

Your race probably won't make national or even regional news, and that's OK. Getting in the local paper is often easy and valuable—as long as it doesn't distract you from knocking doors and raising money.

The first media hits will come likely after you write and submit press releases; these should come right before and immediately following your announcement. Then onwards, issue additional press releases after (internal) milestones, like knocking on 1,000 doors; 5,000 doors; then 10,000 doors. Or hitting fundraising goals in a similar fashion.

When it comes time to give both traditional media interviews on radio or television—and the same goes for new media like podcasts—have your Top 3 issues memorized beyond memory. Meaning when you regurgitate them, you don't sound rehearsed. You sound like a person, not a politician. Genuine wins.

Gen-you-win.

TEXT AND PHONE: CHEAP, FAST, UNDERUSED

You can reach a lot of people quickly when it counts, especially for get-out-the-vote and Top 3 reinforcement. Let's run through a few now.

- **Robocalls**: Cheap and quick (about $0.02 per call, same-day deploy). Good for:
  - Negative messaging (used carefully and strategically)
  - GOTV / Election Day reminders
  - Polling in a pinch
  - Chasing your mail with robocalls

Note here: robo or prerecorded calls may not be legal in your state.

- **Text messaging**: Don't miss this. You can use software and/or volunteers to text a lot of people quickly. Text to:
  - Reinforce GOTV
  - Sign a petition
  - Donate (click to read / donate message)

Note here: we recommend a reputable texting platform such as RumbleUp which is American based and has real relationships with phone service providers. Don't fall for the "2 cent texting" services of Indian platforms that have no guarantee of delivery.

SET YOUR MEDIA STRATEGY: ACTION STEPS (6 MONTHS BEFORE ELECTION)

We freely admit—this chapter's action steps may take longer than most. Not just because we're giving you a long list of homework to complete. Also because many are recurring activities. You'll see what we mean below.

1. Build your channel mix (no silver bullet). Decide how doors, phones, direct mail, online, email, Facebook/Google, and selective media will reinforce one message instead of competing with each other.

2. Map your district's media terrain. What are the most influential news outlets overlaying my district? List the top five below, both old-school and new media (podcasts, etc.).

And of course, learn publishing turnaround times for each outlet you might use (especially local papers).

1)
2)
3)
4)
5)

3. Lock your "official public presence" early (so Google doesn't embarrass you).

Ballotpedia audit: complete Candidate Connection and fill out your profile fully/accurately.

Facebook page: create it as soon as you announce so you control the first impression and start building real reach.

Buy your website domain names early so your opponent doesn't scoop them up.

Create a professional email: Get an email at your domain name. (justin@justingreiss.com) Gsuite is the easiest. Protonmail purists go nuts.

4. Launch a simple, professional website (or skip it). Include email sign-up / petitions, Top 3 issues, volunteer form, donation link, and real contact info (email/phone/P.O. box). Better no website than a bad one.

5. Stand up your email system and cadence. Choose Mailchimp/Constant Contact, import your list, and commit to one email per week with disciplined subject lines and a clear action item.

6. Build your direct mail program and schedule (draft early, don't panic-write). Decide slicks versus letters, write/design the pieces, and map your mail calendar so it systematically reinforces biography ⇨ issues ⇨ contrast ⇨ GOTV.

7. Run Facebook like a campaign tool, not a personal brand. Post daily, avoid comment wars, prioritize broad-appeal content, and convert engagement into list growth, volunteers, and petition signers.

8. Test digital ads with hard thresholds (and kill losers fast). Run list-building ads first; if cost per new name is over $0.50, turn it off and revise. Use FB/Google to build a list, deliver pain/contrast, or promote a message (in that order).

9. Plan letters to the editor strategically (not obsessively). Create an LTE schedule based on publishing timelines, and recruit spear-carriers so credible third parties can echo your message when it helps.

10. Integrate text and phone into the overall plan (especially for GOTV and "chasing" mail). Decide how you'll use robocalls and volunteer texting for petitions, donation links, reminders, and Election Day turnout—without letting it distract from doors.

Now you have a communication strategy that serves the campaign. As you begin to implement it, you'll be greatly served by having high-value content to push—like endorsements from key allies. Let's get some of those for you now.

CHAPTER 11

ALLIES AND ENDORSEMENTS (AND HOW TO ATTRACT LOTS OF BOTH)

There's something you should know.

Endorsements from advocacy groups can strongly influence low-information elections where voters know little about candidates' records. That said, their impact depends on incumbency, helping challengers while often hurting incumbents.[37]

Endorsements are one of the fastest ways to feel like you're "doing politics." Yet they're also one of the easiest ways to accidentally weaken your candidacy. There's a rule that goes like this:

When you get an endorsement, you get 50 percent of their supporters—and 100 percent of their enemies.

In other words, proceed with caution. Endorsements are political leverage, but leverage has consequences. This chapter covers them. But first, a question from the idealists among us.

IS PARTY PARTICIPATION OPTIONAL?

Can you skip party politics and still win? Sometimes . . . technically . . . yes. Practically . . . no. Especially not in the game where doors, lists, volunteers, ballot access, and local credibility decide outcomes. Even when voters call themselves "independent" and are registered with neither major party, they still tend to behave in patterns. They still respond to identity, tribe signals, issues, and community validators. That's why party affiliation, ballot labels, and "who is this person aligned with"-type wonderings all (still) matter.

So, your question isn't, *Do I love the Republican party and everything about it?* No, you're asking, *Do I understand how the local political ecosystem works well enough to add more than my opponent?*

You might be curious what we mean by "add" here. Look, politics is a game of addition.

"In volunteer politics, a builder can build faster than a destroyer can destroy."
—Morton Blackwell, The Leadership Institute

Translation: The candidate who keeps building allies, validators, lists, and support structures outpaces the candidate who spends all day tearing others down. Addition, not subtraction.

HOW PARTIES ACTUALLY OPERATE

If you want endorsements, allies, and organizational support, you need to understand how political parties operate at the local level. Not the fantasy version advertised every four years in presidential elections. The real one. Parties (locally) do things like:

- hold meetings
- elect officers
- conduct business
- entertain nominations
- fill vacancies
- endorse candidates (if they do, it is handled at the local and county level)
- communicate with membership
- allocate resources

You don't have to worship the machinery, but if you ignore it, it will ignore *you* when you need help. Or worse, it will quietly help someone else.

ALLIES AND LEGITIMACY

Allies are more than "people who like you." In politics, allies are people (and organizations) with their political motivations, very important relationships, and protected assets. Your job is to map that terrain, all of that terrain. Categories of influencer you may want support from (and thus must build relationships with early and often) include:

- past elected officials (retired / termed-out / non-competitive; you do **not** want to try making friends but accidentally position yourself as a political threat)
- business leaders active with the party
- major donors and their network
- activists aligned with your Top 3

Your ability to build legitimacy with these individuals is what determines whether people take you seriously enough to invest. Now, just being known by these people is not enough. By **building legitimacy** with them, we mean an accumulation of signals. You have a reputation with these very important people whose word goes far even locally. You're considered consistent and are believed to have character. Yours is a results-first campaign.

In practical campaign terms, people assess you through political touchpoints like relationships with elected officials, contributors to similar campaigns and causes, previous volunteer and community involvement, career compatibility (does your life make sense for this office?), fundraising ability, volunteer recruitment, and likeability.

See? Legitimacy. You have it. Or can. Because the allies say you do. See how it works? Credibility is what gives you legitimacy; you prove yourself credible to your allies, and they dye-stamp you as legitimate, as it were. Make sense?

How Allies Help You Win

Allies can assist with real assets, assuming they like you. Starting with the obvious, think:

- formal endorsements
- financial support

- membership list(s)
- volunteers
- surrogate speakers
- participation in the campaign

This is the *total* endorsement. More than a few words of praise for you beside their name and photo, this is some serious help.

That said, before you publish any one endorsement, please confirm you want this person's reputation associated with yours.

FRIENDS IN LOW PLACES: TRUST BUT VERIFY

Competence counts. Public opinion matters. You must vet—before they do. Because they will. So get background information. Vet all social media. Seek a culture of follow-through. An unexpectedly disastrous ally can cost you weeks. A flaky one can waste your time. And a compromised ally can hand your opponent ammunition; instead of talking your talking points, you're apologizing on behalf of an integrity-free individual whose sins are now yours by proxy. Congratulations . . . should have read this chapter first.

PROCEED WITH CAUTION: SURVEYS, TIMING, AND *WHAT DOES THIS ENDORSEMENT MEAN?*

Most organizational endorsements require a survey. Before you send that survey back to anyone.

- research the organization
- know if or when they will share survey responses
- if they don't tell you . . . ask
- determine what the endorsement actually means

Now, a political "endorsement" is not one thing. An endorsement can mean a logo/graphic. Or it can mean outside uncoordinated voter contact. Those are worlds apart.

Also, know when surveys will be released. Timing matters. If you don't know the organization's schedule, you can't plan your own. This is nobody's first rodeo, so they have very likely endorsed candidates before. They just may have a process for doing it that you don't know about yet. That's OK. Find out. Play along. And know what you're getting yourself into.

TYPES OF ENDORSEMENTS (AND WHAT THEY REALLY GET YOU)

Behind Closed Doors

This is when someone won't publicly endorse you, but they can still help you. If an incumbent or local power player won't go public, press them to help you:

- fundraise
- find sign locations
- recruit volunteers

Don't be polite about the obvious. Press your supporter for their donor list. Ask them to personally introduce you to donors. Push them to meet donors with you.

One more thing. There's always a chance they're saying something similar to multiple candidates. So don't accept warm words; lock down actions.

In Name Only

This is the classic "endorsement graphic." But is the name worth the effort? If so, try to get these early so you can put them on your literature. There can be real value if it bolsters credibility with a specific voting bloc or enhances your credibility on an issue. Just don't confuse a logo with leverage.

Contributions

Some PACs or trade groups will give a contribution to your campaign. Research these groups. Use your personal background to your benefit when you pitch them, because memory and identity often drive giving.

Independent Expenditures (IEs)

These are the endorsements you really want because they're tangible. If endorsed, you may receive support in the form of uncoordinated door-knocking, mailers, phone calls, ads, and other paid voter contact. Lack of coordination can also give you plausible deniability when the opposition screams.

IE support typically comes in two varieties:

1. single-issue groups
2. vision groups

Single-Issue Groups

These endorsements are based on their issue. They might support a Democrat willing to move their issue, so don't assume loyalty is automatic. And if they support you, understand the deal: **You had better keep your word.** If you promise constitutional carry and don't deliver, you will face retaliation from the same group that helped elect you. Understand what they want, and don't promise what you won't do.

Vision Groups

Vision groups evaluate candidates holistically. Ideology across the board. Not one bill. For example, Citizens Alliance is a vision group.

Now, these endorsements are harder to get, often more valuable, and they can be ruthless about dishonesty. If you answer dishonestly, they are likely to release your survey answers and spend money against you in the future.

So don't lie. Ever. Not even a little. Not worth it.

BUILDING COALITIONS: THE MULTIPLICATION TRICK

Endorsements get stronger when you organize them into coalitions—or at least the appearance of them. You can stagger announcements of endorsements, make a social media post for every single one, and even connect your various endorsers through exclusive "inner circle"-only-type events. Remember the "celebrity" events that are a draw from some candidates? Think a budget like that . . . but for only your top endorsers who open doors.

That said, "big names" are great, but again . . . *coalitions.* Some of the most persuasive validators are local trust anchors such as:

- the high school principal
- teachers

- police officers
- little old ladies
- church elders
- respected business owners
- community volunteers

If multiple business owners support you, create a business owners' coalition for them. Same for other like-minded or professional groups. Politics is a game of addition; and coalitions are how you stack addition into momentum . . . and multiply it.

ALLIES AND ENDORSEMENTS: ACTION STEPS (MINIMUM 6 MONTHS BEFORE THE ELECTION)

1. Define What You Want from Endorsements

For each endorsement target, write down what it actually means:

- Name only?
- Contribution?
- IE support?
- List access?
- Volunteers?
- Surrogate speakers?

If you can't define the asset, you're collecting logos.

2. Build Your Endorsement Target List (Don't Be Lazy)

Study which groups endorse candidates in your area and track:

- Survey timing
- What they endorse based on
- What their endorsement typically includes
- Who to contact

3. Pre-Vet Every Endorser You Want

Research the organization. Ask when/if they release survey responses. Know the political tradeoffs, i.e., supporters gained, enemies gained.

4. Work the Relationship Like a Donor

Meet with them. Write letters. Send thank-you notes. Organize next steps. Follow through.

5. Stagger Announcements and Post Online

Don't dump ten endorsements in one day. Drip them with intention, always paired with the message you want reinforced.

6. Build Coalitions

Group supporters into visible coalitions like educators, business owners, veterans, faith leaders so endorsements feel like a whole movement.

Name	Who	Phone	Email	Notes	Contact Date
Justin Greiss	COO, The Constitution	(555) 555-5555	patriot@gmail.com	Promised to connect me with donor John Doe	01-01-26

With allies and endorsements in place, you're transforming your own personal candidacy into a movement with momentum. Incredible. Next, we turn that momentum into field power—volunteers, systems, and a ground game that converts supporters into doors knocked, lists built, and votes banked.

CHAPTER 12

RECRUIT VOLUNTEERS (WHO CARE AS MUCH AS YOU DO)

There's something you should know.
While volunteer labor for political campaigns is not assigned a monetary value for the purpose of Federal Election Commission (FEC) contribution limits or reporting, the value of a nonprofit volunteer hour across the United States is deemed to be $34.79.[38]

Forty years ago, an incredible business book was released that changed everything for small business entrepreneurs. Entitled *The E-Myth Revisited*, the work taught that most owners don't actually own an asset; they own a job. As only they know how to do everything in the business, what happens next is what you'd naturally expect—*they do everything!*

The owner wears all the hats, so to speak, and tries (and fails) to maintain quality of life while working minimum three different full-time jobs, that of business owner, general manager, and technician/specialist. Often, it's their skill in the labor trenches, being the technician or specialist, that motivated them to pursue freedom through self-employment in their craft. But the plumber who starts a plumbing business, for example, continues to do the plumbing. But now he has to be an accountant, a customer service representative, a CEO, and the intern who at his prior job was delegated every last administrative task that was too insignificant for salaried staff to do. And it really sucks.

We've seen the political version of this play out, where the very activities that win elections—doors, phones, follow-up, turnout operations—the candidate feels like they must do. If they don't feel overly busy to the point of exhaustion, frankly, they feel . . . lazy. *I'm supposed to be burned out. . . . I'm supposed to feel overwhelmed. . . . I'm supposed to sleep two hours a night, just like President Trump!*

Need we say it again?

We need.

You are not Trump.

What you are is someone who could use volunteers. Don't wear all the hats; pass the hat instead. Volunteers are not "supporters" or selfie-takers or even your personal fan club. They are your **workers**. They are here (or will be) because they want you to win—and they want to help. Many of them care so much, they would probably pay *you* to be able to work for you for free. In fact, we've witnessed a correlation between **people who donate to your campaign and then volunteer to provide unpaid labor**. Incredible. They'll multiply voter contact, build momentum, and create a campaign identity that voters can feel—all because of what you stand for. Incredible.

Volunteers matter. They replace money and they replace time—two things every grassroots campaign is short on. Volunteers are a force multiplier. They create more voter contact without adding payroll. They give staff (or you, the candidate) more time to do the highest-leverage work. They motivate other people to volunteer, because people follow people. They help define the campaign's identity, i.e., *Oh, that's the campaign that shows up.* Volunteers turn action into power—and action is power.

ACTION = POWER

A campaign with a thousand supporters who never really do anything but show up for free pizza and t-shirts is fragile. A campaign with fifty people who reliably knock doors, make calls, and recruit others is antifragile. Even, dare we say, dangerous—even in, but especially in, a district you "aren't supposed to win."

Plus, small chunks of volunteer time go a long way. A volunteer who gives you an hour and a half every Saturday is not "doing a little." They're part of a cumulative impact machine.

What we love about volunteer recruiting is it's building political muscle memory in your community. It's habit. Turnout identity. A network that can be reactivated again and again. Remember what all politicians want? That includes you, my dude or dudette. You want to get elected, get reelected, and get promoted. Your vision is the ladder, but your volunteers are the rungs. Treat them well. These people are not your task monkeys; they're your future frontline leaders.

THE SNOWFLAKE MODEL (NO, NOT THAT KIND OF SNOWFLAKE)

"Free labor" burns out. But future leaders? Well . . . they will self-organize into a self-improving machine of self-generated initiative. We've mixed a lot of metaphors in this chapter—in this whole book, admittedly—but we'll add another and call the volunteer experience a **snowflake model**. As the pattern of a snowflake repeats and repeats fractally outward from its center to its branches, so, too, will (or should) your campaign's volunteer experience. Leaders recruiting leaders recruiting leaders. And it's got levels, too. Instead of one campaign manager trying to personally manage sixty volunteers (impossible), you create layers, or branches, like so:

- A team lead who owns doors
- A team lead who owns phones
- A team lead who owns volunteer onboarding and scheduling
- A team lead who owns event staffing, sign crews, or ballot-chase support

WHAT MOTIVATES VOLUNTEERS (HUMANS ARE HUMANS)

A surprisingly effective tool is simple to push your people to give their all—give your best volunteers a title and a real lane of responsibility.

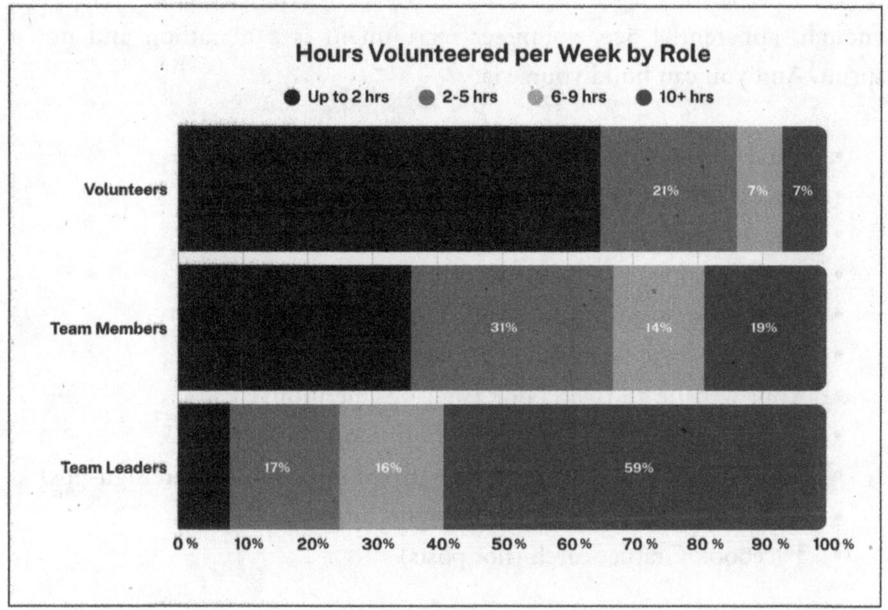

Source: 2012 Obama Campaign Legacy Report, pg. 22[39]

OK, maybe a little psychology of persuasion isn't that surprising after all. A title signals:

- trust
- responsibility
- belonging
- status (the good kind)
- and a reason to keep showing up even when it's inconvenient

That said, titles only work when they come with actual scalable responsibility. For example, don't give someone "Field Director" because you like them. Give them, say, "Neighborhood Team Lead" because their literal job is to recruit three canvassers, run two shifts per week, and report totals every Sunday. So it's not decorative; it's real.

PERPETUAL LIST-BUILDING

How many times have we talked about keeping and building lists? Not enough, apparently! See, volunteer recruitment is a marathon and not a sprint. And you can build yours via:

- Party town/city committees and county/state parties
- Access to i360 (where applicable)
- Special interest support groups and single-issue groups
- Former campaigns (yours or others)
- Low-dollar donors (often your most reliable volunteers)
- Your personal network
- Your website and Facebook (sign-ups, petitions)
- Google forms and a "Sign Up" button on Facebook
- Speaking at events (or sending staff/volunteers to capture sign-ups)
- Email blasts (quietly, in the background)
- Facebook Graph Search (not posts)

Campaigns are won by the people who keep the lists alive and growing. Not enough such cases!

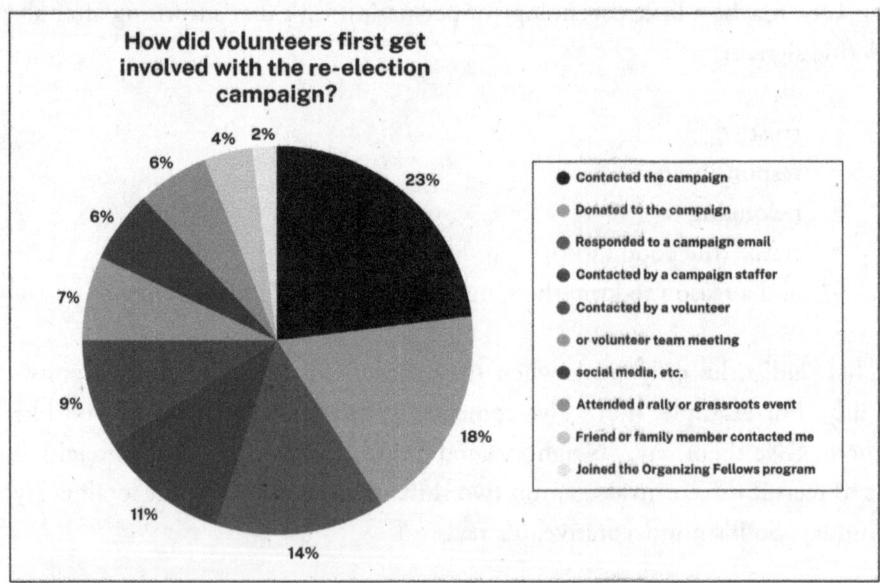

Source: 2012 Obama Campaign Legacy Report, pg. 27[40]

OK, so that's how to start and maintain contact. You know what they want once you've got them—a good title and a little bit of power to do something real on your behalf—but how do you get them involved for the first time, practically speaking? Let's talk about it.

FOLLOW-UP IS RECRUITING

Need volunteers? Call **everyone** on your lists, starting with the most recent submissions. Why most recent? Intent decays. Someone who filled out a form yesterday is warm. Someone who filled it out two months ago might not even remember why they did it. Even two weeks ago is too long.

If they don't pick up, you text them with an indirect ask—something that doesn't feel like you're immediately demanding four hours of labor. For example, you might text something like, "Hey, it's the campaign. Quick question: Are you open to helping with doors or phones this weekend?" Then you repeat until they answer yes or no. Most campaigns skip this; they treat non-response as rejection. It's usually not; it's usually life.

Your job is to follow a follow-up procedure that keeps contacting politely and persistently until they show up or show you up and unsubscribe.

Making the Ask (for What Actually Matters)

Notice the specificity of that sample text message above. It's a *what* and a *when*. Of course, the only volunteer activities that matter are the ones that produce votes. Everything else is support.

Method of Voter Contact	Contact Attempts to Earn a New Vote	Cost per New Vote
Paid Door-Knocking	36 Doors Knocked	$144
Direct Mail	273 Mailers	$205
Paid Phone Calls	700 Calls	$420
Literature Dropping	189 Drops	$756
Television	Not significant	$$$
Radio	Not significant	$$$

So, ask specific people to cover two specific things:

- doors
- phones

In other words, don't go from "can you volunteer?" to awkward silence. You go for the what-to-do ask and add the when-to-do scheduling. You'll have your team schedule in shifts so you're dialing and door-knocking for votes. Be sure to send a confirmation to each volunteer who agrees—and remind them twenty-four hours prior.

The above sequence is how you keep from losing volunteers who had the heart, but it just didn't work out. Make it work out. A tool called "Task | Owner | Deadline" packages this advice well; we'll cover that next.

MANAGING VOLUNTEERS: THIS ISN'T DAYCARE

Good volunteers become great leaders. First, you've got to empower them to be good. You do that by:

1. Training Volunteers. If you don't train them, they'll feel awkward, perform poorly, and disappear. Training should include:

- door-to-door basics
- phone bank essentials
- talking points and messaging (with scripts)
- directives on how to handle common responses without freezing or arguing

Event	Date	Start	AM/PM	Duration (Hr)	First	Last	Email	Phone	Recruited by	On date	Activity	Activity Location	Status
Super Saturday	01-01-26	9	AM	3	Justin	Greiss	patriot@gmail.com	(555) 555-5555	Fatal	12-05-25	Walk	Manchester	Confirmed

2. Assigning Clear Responsibilities. Every volunteer who matters should have a job that is definable and trackable. This is where **Task | Owner | Deadline** becomes your best procedural trainer. If you want volunteers to stay, you don't say "help whenever you can." You say:

"How about Tuesday 6:00–8:00, calling from home, and you'll report your numbers by 8:15?"

That's a real job.

3. Tracking and Following Up. Make a spreadsheet of volunteers with contact info, tasks, and outcomes. Assume the sale. In other words, treat "yes" like it means "yes," and build a system around confirmation and reminders. If you're using i360, pull lists and manage contacts there, too.

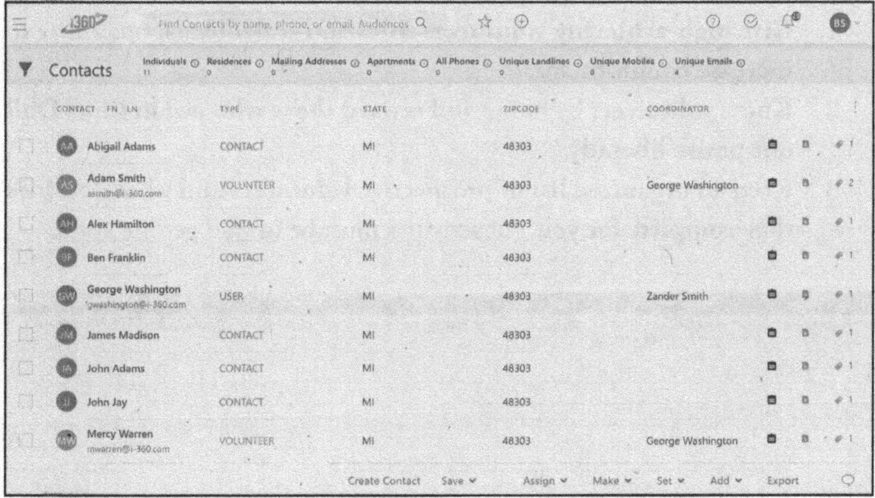

Retaining Volunteers, Forming an Inner Circle

Our procedure for this is pretty simple. To retain volunteers week to week, shift to shift, you'll:

- assign a staff member (or a volunteer lead) to volunteer care
- reward commitment and performance
- praise consistently and publicly (newsletter and social media)
- write thank-you notes
- provide face-to-face contact with the candidate (i.e., you)

Volunteers don't stick around because you're special; they stay because they feel useful, seen, and connected. Volunteers are people, too!

One last thing: Don't underestimate the power of physical space if you are running a large budget campaign. A "Victory Center" beats a depressing "office." This signals momentum. Everyone wants to be part of a winning team; nobody wants to go into an office space and work for free in drudgery.

RECRUIT VOLUNTEERS: ACTION STEPS (MINIMUM 6 MONTHS BEFORE THE ELECTION)

Volunteers are extremely important for multiplying outreach and building momentum. Here's how we can sum it all up so you'll be able to do just that.

1. **Give high-achieving volunteers titles and scalable responsibility to increase commitment.**
2. **Know volunteers by name and reward those who put in time. Doll out praise liberally.**
3. **Keep an organized list of prospective volunteers and what activities they complete for you.** All activities must be toward getting votes.

Title	First	Last	Email	Phone	Potential Contribution
Team Lead	Justin	Greiss	patriot@gmail.com	(555) 555-5555	Door-knocking / Phone banking

4. Make a list of ten prospective volunteers now. For each one, write down:

- what you will ask them to do (doors/phones first)
- what title or responsibility they can grow into
- when you will contact them and schedule their first shift

With your internal situation all buttoned up, we now turn to the outside world—to your message and how you'll be distributing it in print. Let's go.

CHAPTER 13

YOUR PERSONAL PROPAGANDA (AND HOW TO DESIGN AND BUY IT)

There's something you should know.

"[D]irect mail is the most effective and trusted channel to reach, engage, and motivate voters . . . 68% of voters feel less overwhelmed by direct mail than by other political advertising channels . . . [T]he majority (57%) . . . also agreed that direct mail is harder to ignore than online or TV ads. Perhaps surprisingly to some, the percentage with that view of direct mail is even higher (60%) among Gen Z voters than in older demographics."[41]

Imagine the try-hard candidate. We'll call him Mack as that happens to be his name. He's a political overthinker yet underachiever-in-the-making. He's got those big, wide eyes paired with eyebrows reaching escape velocity from his forehead during interviews. Pupil dilation. Wild hair, too. Mack's going to "go hard" and "blow people away" and "tell it like it is." He's running a campaign like a sideshow because he once read on X that "attention is influence" and so he's trying to steal as much as possible.

Mack's personal propaganda reads like it's inspired by a 1930s action-adventure pulp novel. It's all a saga. A manifesto of heroism. A quasi-religious quest against corruption, evil, and betrayal. The brochures and postcards and more have a smattering of typefaces and fonts, multiple exclamation points, photoshopped unflattering photos of his primary opponents, four USA flags, and a bald eagle. Mack alone stands against the forces of darkness, a George Washington patriot meets Ron Paul maverick.

It's amateurish fan fiction of a real campaign. And voters react exactly the way all normal people react when they see someone trying so hard, too hard, in public—with cringe. Some are repelled. Some are disgusted. Some laugh. Almost none of them vote for the Macks of the world.

All campaign literature has one job: earn votes. Ideological purity, personal appeal, political education, and ego demonstrations have no place in your printed material. We're about to show you, however, that some real-life candidates have taken Mack's route rather than recommendations like ours. Some of you, reading Mack's anecdote above, chuckled mentally but thought, *I get it, but there's no way anyone would pull stunts like this.*

Yes way. But first, we'll show you the way.

DESIGN AND BUY CAMPAIGN LITERATURE

All political persuasion featuring your name, image, and likeness is intended (or ought to be intended) to **drive name identification and feel-good correlation**, i.e., *Oh, right—I know that gal. I like her. She's normal, credible, and actually . . . kind of cute. I'll get up half an hour early and head out before the lines at the polls are too long.* All of that and more happens in milliseconds and subconsciously so. "Education" is not happening. **Reinforcement** is. Thus, all such literature—and all media, really—exist to remind the voting public why and how they know, like, and trust you.

Literature gets its own chapter as it's its own creature, separate from media including letters even. That said, the postcards we talked about *do* overlap here, provided there is more than a little text about your Top 3 issues. Literature we're talking about now also includes flyers for your campaign events that occur in person, brochures handed out, and anything else with pictures or illustrations that go out in the mail.

To these ends, understand the environment in which your likely propaganda-consumers will be in when they skim and scan your literature. Voters are not going to be reading your flyer the way your political friends read it. They'll be scanning it while they're walking through the door, wrangling children, thinking about dinner, tossing junk mail, packing things up, and more. If your piece requires effort to understand, you already lost, friend.

Effective literature is what a normal person can absorb in three-and-a-half seconds. Here's how to do it.

OPTICS: K.I.S.S. AND TELL (YOUR MESSAGE)

All media is narrative. All warfare is deception. All politics is optics. So keep it simple, stupid, i.e., K.I.S.S. Worthy literature almost always contains:

- A great photo of the candidate (non-negotiable)
- A campaign logo that looks like an actual campaign
- Three bullets that resonate in the district (likely your Top 3 issues written as three short phrases)
- A legal disclaimer (and correct placement)
- A third-party proofread (because you're not as careful as you think at 2:00 a.m.)
- A phone number and website

We love the three-bullet rule because it demands discipline. You have to pick what matters most to voters—what resonates in the district—without turning the piece into a drawn-out manifesto-novel. It prevents you from making the classic try-hard mistake—trying to persuade everyone with everything! We had you pick your Top 3 for a reason. Your literature should not attempt to prove you're right about the entire world.

Now, that last bullet, contact info, often goes without saying . . . and goes without appearing on campaign literature. Do you want everyone getting your material calling? No. Optics, remember? You want to signal legitimacy, accessibility, seriousness. People will be impressed you are handing out your personal cell. Few will call. It also gives your supporters an easy way to forward a real contact point when someone wonders, *How do I reach him?*

All in all, this little list-template will have your audience going, *I've seen this name before. . . . I recognize this face. . . . This seems normal and competent. . . . OK, that issue matters to me. . . . Hmm, yeah . . . maybe I really should vote for him.* But again, it all happens in a fingerful of seconds in time and below the conscious awareness of the voter. This is what we do.

Now let's talk design—how and where all that text gets laid out.

YOU DON'T HAVE TO DESIGN IT (AND YOU PROBABLY SHOULDN'T)

Remember *The E-Myth Revisited* from the last chapter? Let's continue that theme, perhaps calling it *The P-Myth*. As you might imagine, this is the self-fallacy that *because I can do everything on my campaign myself, I should! I wear all the hats. If you want something done right, do it yourself.*

Yeah, no. Candidates designing their own literature is one of the most reliable ways to end up with something that looks homemade, cluttered, and unserious. You are about to spend a lot of money on these . . . don't screw it up. Two better options:

- Let the printer design it (often free if you're printing enough).
- Bring in someone who has done political layouts before and can keep you from committing visual crimes.

Either way, the goal is not some weird art statement; it's clarity and credibility at a glance.

As promised, we'll now show you the Mack way—and the various misadventures in campaign literature we've noticed out there. Then finally, we contrast with how to do it right. In a world of try-hard Macks, just be you. Be your issues. Be normal.

Yes, Virginia, attention is influence. But the wrong attention is anti-persuasive—and convinces your otherwise likely voters to either stay home or show up for your opponent. Take it away, Mack.

POLITICAL ANTI-PERSUASION: CAMPAIGN LITERATURE EDITION

Some of these are going to surprise you, starting with . . .

The Ronnest Paul

When quantity of quality is not, in fact, more quality.

To be clear, we love Ron Paul. Cliff worked for him on Capitol Hill. We are not making fun of Ron Paul. He got us here and deserves credit for inspiring the current America First movement. But here is the story…

This literature was designed and distributed by well-meaning activists as part of a grassroots effort to support Ron Paul's 2012 presidential campaign. Dubbed "the Super Brochure" these patriots created this all-encompassing lit spectacle. It's accurate. It's factually correct. But it misses the point.

We can't even cover all the ways this is wrong but here are a few.

- Fourteen issue points… a voter finds one they disagree with and it's game over. NEXT.
- Issues that no one is talking about. Yes, phase out the IRS. 100%. Excellent today. This is why we love him. But you can't just drop that bomb and leave, in 2012. The people weren't ready. There is no explanation.
- Meaningless directions to YouTube videos by name…
- And perhaps our favorite point . . . there is so much stuff on here they just started writing things in the white space of the debt chart.

So again. Well-meaning. Factual. But messaged entirely amateurishly.

The Deer-in-the-Headlights

Don't look like you're the subject of an undercover predator-catcher show.

The Floater

How did they even take this photo?

The Microsoft Paint

When an attack ad becomes self-inflicted friendly fire.

The Way-Too-Far

Please don't ask us to explain this to you (please).

The Reading Glasses

Speaking of reading, this brochure somehow reads like a stock picking tips information product subscription from 2006.

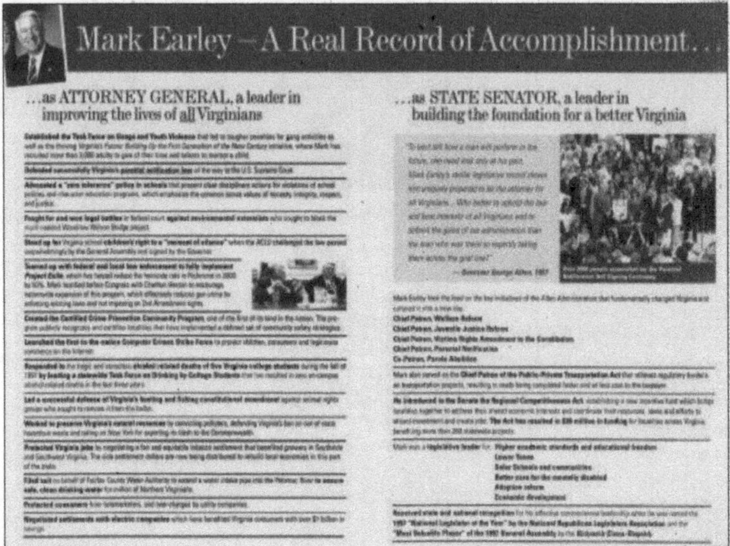

The Law Firm

Everybody knows most elected politicians are lawyers; everybody knows how we feel about lawyers. Don't offer any unnecessary reminders, even by visual association.

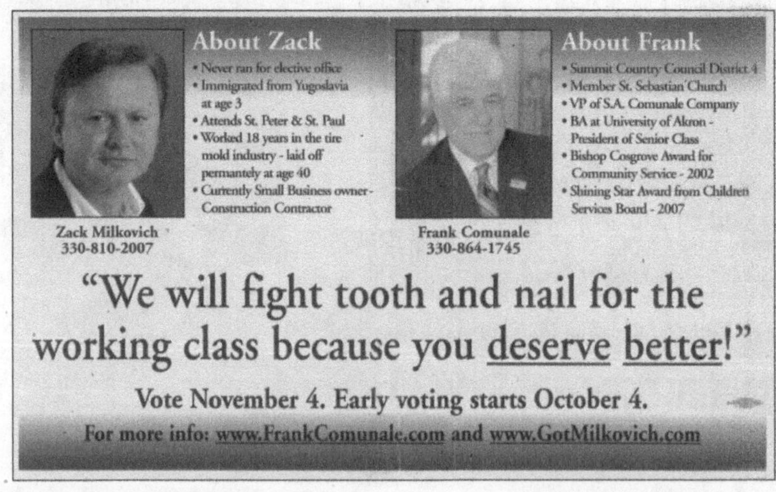

The Colorblind

This brochure appears in a weird shade of blue. Why? We don't know. Neither do voters. But we do all know one thing: How a candidate does anything is how a candidate does everything.

The Hard Crop

Why does this remind us of a true crime documentary? Hard pass.

The Might-Be-Racist

Just completely unforced errors at this point.

The Failed Movie Star

Spend a split-second looking at this. You won't know what it is. You might believe it's something it isn't.

The Photobomb

Do we really need to see this woman with her curlers in? We do not.

The Name Change I

Yeah, about that . . .

The Name Change II

We rest our case.

Wait a moment, Cliff and Joshua . . . did those candidates actually lose their elections?

To this mental objection some of you are thinking right now, we ask back: Does it matter? You and we both know how you felt upon glimpsing the above Mack-samples. Why risk it all by attempting to out-do Mack in his amateursmanship? Your campaign—your Top 3—are too important to try to prove us wrong and get away with it. Be normal. Be like this . . . **K.I.S.S. and tell!**

CAMPAIGN LITERATURE DONE RIGHT: THE PERFECT EXAMPLE

Notice the professional photo, campaign logo, limited bullets, legal disclaimer, contact information, and demonstration of proofreading (no embarrassing typos). Mack could never.

So good.

Let's zoom in. Notice the headshot, name, and title all present.

Simple, simple, simple bullets featuring his Top 4 issues.

The theme continues.

Also in the literature are endorsement(s) and personal bio; both are optional and innocuous. Notice both are each limited to a couple of bullet points apiece and simple.

YOUR PERSONAL PROPAGANDA: ACTION STEPS (MINIMUM 5 MONTHS BEFORE THE ELECTION)

Let's get to work.

1. Decide the outcome for each piece. Is it name ID? Bio and apple pie? Issue ID? Contrast? GOTV? Pick one purpose per piece.

2. Choose your assets. Include:

1. best candidate photo (and get a professional one if you haven't)
2. campaign logo
3. three bullets that resonate in the district
4. phone number and other contact
5. legal disclaimer text

3. Pick the simplest production path. If your printer will design it for free at your print volume, use that. If not, get a competent political designer. Don't DIY unless you want it to look DIY.

4. Proofread like a grown-up. Make a third-party proofread mandatory before anything goes to print.

5. Lock in printing and delivery timelines. Printers have lead times. So do mail houses. Don't discover that five days before you need it.

And that's it.

What we tell you to do works.

You just have to do it.

Mack still won't.

Not gonna make it.

CHAPTER 14

ANNOUNCEMENTS AND DOOR-KNOCKING (STARTING WITH A PARTY)

There's something you should know.

"We do not find evidence that our political message persuades voters to support the candidate. We do find, however, that a brief visit by the candidate dramatically increases the support for the candidate regardless of the nature of the message delivered. The actions of candidates seem to speak louder than words."[42]

We're fourteen chapters into campaign preparation, and we're only now covering the campaign launch itself. Why? It's called we do a little front-loading.

front-load

/ˈfrən(t)ˌlōd,ˌfrən(t)ˈlōd/

verb

gerund or present participle: front-loading

distribute or allocate (costs, effort, etc.) unevenly, with the greater proportion at the beginning of the enterprise or process.

"the candidate front-loads preparation in order to run a time-optimized campaign"

OK, so what's time optimization? Here you go.

time optimization: The strategic process of efficiently allocating resources and tasks to maximize output while minimizing wasted effort.

That's what all previous chapters have been about—allocating your attention, energy, and yes, money, on the highest-value tasks *first* so that you're not running from behind when you're running for election. This is what most (failed) candidates do, unfortunately. They make this chapter their real-life opening salvo, announcing their run, holding an event, and pushing press releases out. Often two weeks (or less!) goes into the planning. They're already scrambling, trying to pull together the first few donors and filing the right paperwork (oops, missed the deadline—guess I'll have to do the write-in) and publishing a website and hiring volunteers—no, wait . . . you don't hire volunteers, you recruit them. Shoot, you hire a campaign staff. Starting with a CEO. No, right . . . it's called a campaign manager. Right?

You see the frenzy. Sharp candidates do everything unlike all of that. We've discussed at length how you'll be planning, preparing, budgeting, recruiting, and so on *months* in advance. By the time you "launch," you've got volunteers, donors, even media lined up. You're ready to go (because you read the book).

Yes, we have touched on some aspects of your campaign launch already, specific to media and press. However, we want you fully prepared for media strategy and press relations—and know what to expect—long before you will be doing either. Front-loading. Time optimization. This is what we do. We want you running a winning campaign, not running like a headless chicken.

All that to say, first things first—and your campaign announcement is not it. Even if, technically, it's the "Chapter 1" of your campaign according to local normies who aren't sociopolitically active. Of course, every person you've been list-building with and getting a petition signature back from and expressing their interest in volunteering for the cause for liberty, upon seeing your "special announcement, save the date" email, goes, *Wow. Really? Wow. I didn't know that. You're telling me now for the first time.*

Now, what is your announcement, exactly, and what is it for? Obvious questions have obvious candidates.

THE PURPOSE OF AN ANNOUNCEMENT IS WHAT IT DOES

So, what does it do? Well, your announcement is one of the few moments in a campaign where you get a built-in burst of attention. Friends get curious, supporters have hope and want to help, local activists start watching, and even skeptical citizens pause and wonder, *Wait—is this really happening?*

Indeed it is. Which means your announcement event has a job. In fact, it has three jobs; you should treat them like non-negotiable outcomes, not nice-to-haves. And they are:

1. Get (more) volunteers.
2. Raise (more) money.
3. Gain (more) legitimacy and (free) media.

Anything that doesn't drive one of those outcomes is noise. Don't waste time. And don't waste money either; this event should run you $500 or less, absolute maximum. It should *never* be out of your pocket. If you can't get a donor to fund it, scale it down until you can.

ANNOUNCEMENT EVENTS 101

Your announcement event has three jobs, yes. That said, it's generally impossible to focus on all three and nail all three well. This is why we suggest you make one of the event's jobs your *primary*, another your *secondary*, and finally the last your *tertiary*. They are all must-dos, and yet you "must do" them in a certain order. And the reason has to do with calls-to-action. In sales strategy, it's long been known that the more options you offer a prospect, the less likely they are to buy, e.g., *click here and then add this to your cart and then you have to scroll down to hit accept but first there's a consent form and after that there's our privacy policy which yes you do have to in fact read in full and then enter your payment information but first we need you to—*

Yeah, no. We exaggerate only slightly. In politics, you can tell when a campaign didn't pick an outcome because the night is vague—no clear primary ask (followed by secondary then tertiary), no discipline, no follow-through. So decide, based on what you do and don't have as much of yet:

- Is this announcement *primarily* a volunteer event where you recruit and assign people to doors?
- Or is it *primarily* a fundraising event where you leave with commitments and checks?
- Or is it *primarily* a media event where traditional, new, and social media are buzzing about you for the next seventy-two-hour news cycle?

Pick your primary, set *one* call-to-action for it, then have the other two as your immediate go-tos next. For example, with that third announcement job being media and legitimacy, you schedule your event where and when journalists, influencers, and the like are likeliest to be available and actually show up. *Then* you, for example, invite the list you've built up, arrange volunteer sign-up tables at the entrance, and *then* print your little fundraising brochure with a QR code and your Top 3 issues and put that on every seat in the house, requesting fifty bucks.

See how it works? The options aren't exactly limitless, but you do have a certain creative freedom. That said, every announcement event has the basics:

- Press releases (one for before the event, one for after, as discussed in Chapter 7)
- A place for all attendees to sign in (this is not optional)
- Fifty-plus people expected (or at least a plan to make it *feel* like more than fifty showed up)

Now let's talk about perception.

How to Look Legit: The Experience of Your Event Is the Experience of *You*

Your announcement event is a signal that how you do anything is how you'll do everything (where have you read that before). If everything is neat and organized, you'll get great photos for donors and social media and you project competence. But if the event is sloppy, people will rightfully infer that *you* are sloppy—and in politics, "sloppy" quickly becomes "not serious" and "not electable" and worst of all "where can we find somebody with decency and volunteer and donate there instead."

So, create an experience for attendees, like so:

- Make it easy to arrive and know what to do.
- Make it social without being chaotic.
- Make it feel like a movement beginning, not a random meet-and-greet.

Remember the sign-up table. Volunteer sign-up. The brochures for fundraising. They can be one page only, that's fine. The purpose of an announcement is what it does.

Optics: Why the Room Should "Fit Twenty"

Earlier, we advised you to generate fifty or more attendees as best you can—or to make it look like there's that many. We can't let that slide past without additional comment, so we'll give you that now. Here is our little rule for that: **The capacity of the room should be 60 percent of the expected crowd size.**

In other words, if you expect fifty people, you want a space that "comfortably" fits about thirty. And go down from there if you'll have fewer. Optics are everything on politics. "Standing room only" is a media angle; a half-empty room is a morale killer. Understand?

Expandable rooms are ideal. Curtains can tighten the room. Plan ahead to have more chairs available. And if the crowd is bigger than expected, you can truthfully say it: "More people attended than expected." See? Optics. Momentum. Victory.

Venue Selection: Choose the Tone Before You Choose the Building

Don't pick a venue because it's available the day you had in mind and it's pretty cheap; pick a venue because it fits the campaign you're trying to run. More on that:

- What tone are you trying to set? Friendly? Serious? Grassroots? Professional?
- Who do you want in the room? And will they actually come to this location?
- Do you want media there, or do you want media coverage without the risk of a circus?
- What timing helps turnout and avoids community conflicts?
- What is the call-to-action and where does it happen physically in the room?

But again, keep it cheap. Ideally, in-kind donations such as a nice local house (friend of the campaign), a donated community space, or public options like parks, schools, community centers (when appropriate).

But **never** on a holiday. In our experience, the best timing tends to be a weekday evening, Saturday morning, or Sunday afternoon. That said, always check for conflicts in the community.

OK, so we've covered some dos and don'ts and decisions to make. We've suggested fifty attendees as your target. Regardless of how many ultimately show, you want a sense of how many *will* likely show so you can pick the place that feels *almost* too crowded. Regardless, how do you get people to commit to come in the first place so you can pick your venue? Here's how.

Who to Invite (and How to Actually Get Them There)

We suggest you invite a specific target audience, including:

- friends, volunteers, supporters
- donors (and donors-in-waiting)
- local activists
- civic groups
- the local party apparatus
- aligned organizations

We recommend you invite by phone, text, **and** email, not just via social media posts. Such posts are permission slips, but direct invitations are attendance drivers. Which do you suppose gets more people coming out? Get a confirmed "yes" I will attend in writing or on the phone.

Also—especially early, long before the event, as in a full **month** out—invite in a way that makes people feel needed, not simply marketed to. People will show up because you gave them a reason. Such a reason can be as straightforward as a **"because"** or a **"so that"** or an **"in order to"** or all three, e.g., **"I'm asking you to come because you joined my email list so that anything coming up about this critical issue in our community, you can show up in order to make your voice heard."** OK, that's overly stilted and overstocked, but you get the idea. Give a reason to get people there—that's important to *them* according to what you know about their level of sociopolitical interest and/or activism—and they will.

The Announcement Speech

This is the main course. Or is it? No, your words are merely appetizers. How people *feel* about what you said . . . that's the main course. That comes from preparation in areas like:

- mastery of the issues (enough to sound grounded, not rehearsed)
- developing relationships (so the room isn't strangers)
- public speaking (clear and calm beats fiery and chaotic)
- confidence and humility (both matter)

Some things can't be taught, only trained. If you are not 100 percent certain you will get up there and give flawless remarks, we advise you to join Toastmasters International (www.toastmasters.org) at least **one year prior** to your campaign launch date. Yes, twelve months. Yes, this is that important. There are few ways to win in politics; there are many ways to lose. Blabbing and blubbering when the eyes of your local world are upon you is one such way to lose bigly. Don't. Train. Then run.

Ultimately, your speech at any political event should be LESS THAN five minutes, ideally three minutes. Get on with it. People don't want to sit through a lecture series.

During the Event: Capture, Connect, Convert

We're ready to get even more tactical now. For the event itself (besides your prepared and memorized remarks), you'll need:

- name tags
- sign-in (contact info captured cleanly)
- time for you or staff to meet attendees
- a planned moment for the ask (volunteer and/or money)
- obvious "next steps" so people don't drift out

A simple way to do this is to build the event around **conversion moments:**

- Arrive ⇨ sign in ⇨ name tag
- Mingle plus photos (you meet people)
- Short remarks (you set tone, state why, make the ask)
- Immediate next steps (doors/phones assignment or donation commitments)
- Close with gratitude plus follow-up promise

If your event is fundraising-focused (or you're doing a money moment inside a volunteer-heavy night), pick one method and run it confidently.

Option 1: Ask Each Attendee at Sign-In. This works when your audience is already warm. It's direct, simple, and fast—especially if you have forms ready and someone designated to handle it.

Option 2: Reverse Auction (Start High, Go Low). This works when you want energy and public momentum.

The key is to pre-ask likely donors so you're not gambling in the moment. Then you can run it like, for example, *Who can I count on for $500? Great—thank you. Here are the contribution forms. Who else can match that? Wonderful. Now who can we count on for $250?*

It's a little theatrical, but so is everything else about politics. It works. Trust us. And you are allowed, and encouraged, to line up some commitments beforehand so your reverse auction doesn't flop.

Now, if you're instead primarily volunteer-focused for your event, then staff can run a short training right there—door-to-door basics, get-out-the-vote projects—so the night produces actual field capacity and not just vibes.

FROM ANNOUNCING TO DOOR-KNOCKING

This is our favorite play. Whatever your primary, secondary, and tertiary event jobs are, make this your immediate follow-up. *Let's go door-knocking!* Just be prepared, obviously. You need logistics ready before the first attendee arrives, including:

- Walkbooks built and assigned in your app
- Cell phones charged
- Campaign literature neatly stacked
- Volunteer forms for anyone who can't go that day (so they still become a volunteer)
- Brief training and consistent coaching

Supporter morale and motivation immediately after the event will be high. Don't let it go untapped. Chapter 18 covers door-knocking in full. Get ready.

ONCE IT'S ALL OVER

If you don't follow up, the event was entertainment—basically a Right-wing podcast live and in person and that's it. So after the event, you will:

- Thank attendees.
- Invite them to another event you already have scheduled.
- Put them to work immediately.
- Give high performers a title and responsibility.
- Keep them involved.

As a result, one night becomes a durable volunteer base and donor pipeline.

ANNOUNCEMENT AND DOOR-KNOCKING: ACTION STEPS (6 MONTHS BEFORE THE ELECTION)

1. Decide whether your announcement is primarily volunteer or fundraising focused.

2. Keep the budget $500 max and make it donor-funded.

3. Select a venue where room capacity is 60 percent of expected crowd size (or is expandable).

4. Build your invite list and invite directly (phone/email), including civic groups, party infrastructure, and aligned orgs.

5. Set up sign-in, name tags, and a clean photo moment.

6. Prepare your press release before the event and send a follow-up release after.

7. If **knocking** afterward, prep walkbooks, scripts, literature, and coaching logistics in advance. If **fundraising**, choose either sign-in asks or a reverse auction—and pre-ask key donors.

Complete the short activities below, and we're on to Chapter 15.

★ ★ ★

I will do a party focused on (circle one): **volunteers** **fundraising**

Potential venues:

CHAPTER 15

BUILDING (AND MANAGING) YOUR TEAM

> ***There's something you should know.***
>
> Field staff, including campaign managers for state and local campaigns, tend to be younger, often recent college graduates but certainly under age thirty. The political campaign world is often described as being "run by people who are under 30."[43]

The good news about all the volunteers you'll be amassing is that you don't have to pay them. The bad news about all the volunteers you'll be amassing is that at some point they will act like it. At some point, very much sooner than later, you will want the reliability, competence, and security of paid help. And this help, to be helpful, must not blow up your budget, your compliance, or your calendar. This chapter is here to help you do it right.

THE STANDARD

This shall be the rule that keeps you from hiring your way into failure: **Everything your team does must help you get votes.** All else flows from here, including to the role that for many is their very first real hire, even before campaign manager (if not very shortly after).

THE FIRST QUESTION: DO YOU NEED A CONSULTANT?

Candidates assume a consultant is the next step because that's how campaigns look on TV. But for a smaller race—think the $50,000 or less campaign reality—most "general consultants" are not a good use of your dollars unless you're in a larger district state race where the scale is genuinely different. So let us ask a better question: Do you have someone available who can answer the campaign questions that will arise, someone who has gone through the ringer?

If you do, that person might be your informal advisor, a mentor, or a trusted operator you can call when something weird happens. If you don't, you might be tempted to hire "the local consultant everyone uses."

Please don't. Do not be tempted to hire the local consultant everyone uses. They are not your friend. They are a vendor. They have their own incentives, their own history, and their own political philosophy. Their job is not to "love your movement." Their job is to invoice you. That doesn't mean they're evil. It means you must be clear-eyed.

At this level, the most common consultant mistake is hiring someone who provides meetings, memos, and jargon . . . while your vote-getting operations stay weak. There may be value in hiring a vendor to run your digital advertising, mail, etc. . . . but this is based on a per-service charge, not a general consultant's monthly retainer.

WHAT YOU ACTUALLY NEED: AN ACTIVE CAMPAIGN MANAGER

If you're going to spend real money on staff in a smaller to mid-size campaign, your best "hire" is usually not a general consultant, it's going to be an active campaign manager.

And "active" has a definition: **An active campaign manager devotes 90 percent of their working hours to your campaign.** This person is not dabbling. They are not "available when they can." They are not running three other races and calling themselves your manager. Nothing else. And if they are working multiple campaigns, they are a consultant, no matter what they tell you.

Also, campaign manager is **not** a remote position. This person must be in your area—or relocate—to execute on the ground. Campaigns are physical.

They are door lists, event setups, volunteer training, sign logistics, donor meetings, press moments, and constant small fires. A remote "manager" is often a fancy name for "someone who emails you advice."

A real campaign manager on a race this size plays an active role in:

- fundraising execution (call time systems, follow-up discipline, event structure)
- volunteer coordination (recruiting, training, retention, snowflake leadership)
- media execution (posting rhythm, email cadence, earned media moments)
- translating your campaign plan into reality week after week

In plain terms, they make sure the work happens.

WHAT TO LOOK FOR IN A CAMPAIGN MANAGER (THE NON-NEGOTIABLES)

A campaign manager is not your hype man. They are not your therapist. And they are not your best friend from high school. No, they are a co-runner of the campaign with you—often the person who sees your weaknesses more clearly than you do.

So you want someone . . .

Close enough that you can trust them—

. . . but not someone you couldn't fire.

If you can't fire them, you're not hiring a manager; you're adopting a liability.

Who could envision running for office themselves one day. That doesn't mean they have to want it now. It means they understand the job from the inside: the discipline, the pressure, the reputation risk, the need to win. If they can't imagine being in the arena, they may not have the instincts you need.

Who can stand up to you when you're wrong. This matters more than candidates want to admit. A yes-man is not going to win you the election. You need someone who can say, "No. That's a bad idea. That's off-message. That's not worth the time. That's not what wins." The candidate is emotional by nature; your manager is the counterweight.

Who dedicates full attention to your campaign. If they're splitting time across multiple races, you're buying fractional priority. And in a campaign, fractional priority becomes fractional execution.

Who is local and present. Again, not remote.

Whose age and experience fit the work and not your ego. Age and experience matter, but they are not the end-all. A hungry, organized twenty-year-old who lives in field operations might outperform an older "political professional" who's mostly a talker.

HOW MUCH SHOULD YOU PAY? (FOR A $50,000 CAMPAIGN)

A common range for a manager in a smaller race is $2,000 to $4,000 per month plus housing (if relocation is required). As for housing, do you have a relative with a spare bedroom? Can you create a stable living arrangement? Preferably not with the candidate for an extended period of time. If you can't, you need a local hire or a different staffing plan.

Another constraint that protects your budget is that paid staff should account for no more than 15 percent of the money raised. So hire carefully. If you are running a race of less than $100,000, you are probably relying on volunteers. Discipline. Anything to get votes comes first. Blow your donations on payroll operations, and you can't fund what counts when it counts most.

THE FOUNDATION OF EVERY CAMPAIGN TEAM

Campaign team structure depends on the type of race you're running, but the foundation is consistent across all races at all levels, from county commissioner to the House of Representatives. Regardless, you will need:

1) Campaign Manager

Think CEO energy but lower profile than a CNBC hound. Organized and leaderly. Has the confidence of the candidate. Drives execution. Got it?

2) Campaign Treasurer

This position is legally required anyway; you want someone responsible, trustworthy, and detail-minded. Sometimes a former elected official works well in this role because they respect the seriousness of compliance.

3) Campaign Counsel

This is someone who knows election law and state law well enough to advise you and keep you from stepping on landmines. Even if this counsel is "as needed," you want a relationship established before you're in trouble.

Sample Campaign Structure

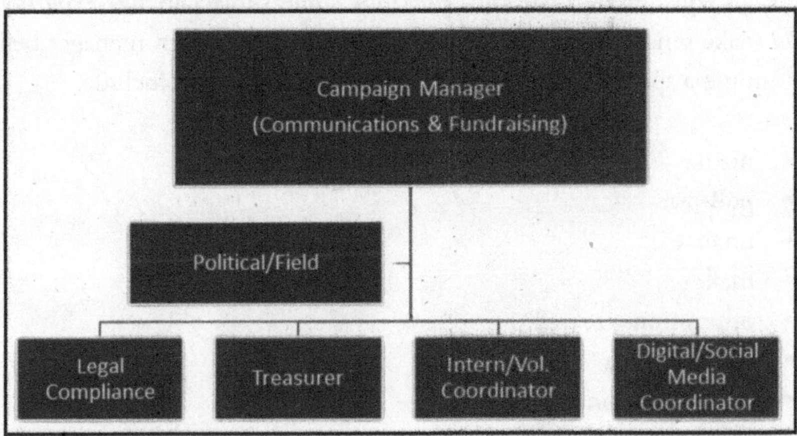

Diagram via the Leadership Institute.

Accounting and Compliance: Don't Be Cute with the Money

Small campaigns get sloppy here because it "feels" administrative. But compliance failures can end candidacies . . . or quietly drain you.

You need checks and balances, so hire an accountant/controller if feasible, get invoice payments handled cleanly, and ensure you, the candidate, do not personally sign checks. This last one is a protection for you, by the way; it reduces chaos, prevents mistakes, and creates separation between "candidate life" and "campaign finance reality."

Management Principles (Where Campaigns Either Scale or Collapse)

Once you have staff and layered volunteers, you're officially managing people, and management requires explicit structure, as you see above. Furthermore, we suggest you provide, besides a visual organizational chart of your team(s), a detailed job description that each person signs, along with their supervisor. Set daily, weekly, and monthly goals (the work must be measurable) and do **not** manage operations budgets with hope and prayer. Allocate resources based on outcomes. And outcomes are votes. We're a broken record on this. We will keep breaking.

Consultants: Use Specialists, Not a Generic "Wizard"

We warned you not to hire a pseudomanager for a small campaign, i.e., a campaign consultant. That said, there *are* some subject matter experts that *might* make sense on any issue you or your (real) campaign manager believe you can use a specialist for. Typical niche consultant areas include:

- media
- pollster
- finance
- mail
- opposition research
- PAC director
- legal/compliance
- voter contact

Specialists are special; managers manage. Never forget this distinction. Consultants have a political philosophy too. They have habits. They have methods. They have relationships. Be smart. Vet them. Make sure their incentives align with your outcomes.

Where your campaign manager and a specialist disagree, make it your default to side with your manager unless the consultant provides an overwhelmingly data-driven reason to go with their instincts and veto your manager. You will probably get only one such veto, however, maybe two, before your manager is one more away from quitting on you. Speaking of quitting . . .

Brace Yourself: When Team Members Quit

With paid staff on any campaign, some will quit, go nuts, waste resources, or all three all at once all together. Pessimistic? Yes. Preparative? Also, yes.

The best way to minimize and otherwise mitigate the damage of a quitter (we know of no single campaign in U.S. political history where literally *nobody* quit at any point), we suggest **the three-makes**. They go like so:

- Make expectations incredibly clear.
- Make expectations completely realistic.
- Make the reason for hire or fire abundantly obvious.

A campaign is not a family no matter what the corporate motivational posters of old all say. This is a mission with a timeline. Anyone falling off must be relieved of duty. No exceptions. Not even for your spouse (yes, there are some stories there; yes, they're as bad as you imagine; yes, the candidate failed to follow the three-make rules; yes, they lost the race; no, you don't have to duplicate their mistake).

Volunteers Can Fill Many "Paid" Roles (If You Structure Them)

Once you have a hierarchy and multiple levels of structure, you can begin grouping and subgrouping all the volunteers you've been accruing. There are now enough people to not simply build a team but *manage* them.

For a smaller campaign, volunteers can cover a surprising amount of what "paid staff" would otherwise do. Possible volunteer roles, grouped, can look like this:

Group 1

- Chief Advisor
- Personal Aid
- Event Coordinator
- Media Manager
- Precinct Director

Group 2

- Digital/Social Media Coordinator
- Research Coordinator
- Sign Coordinator
- Special Projects and Titles
- Director of Poll Watchers

One person can fill many roles in a smaller campaign. The idea is to assign ownership and outcomes instead of vague "help."

BUILDING YOUR TEAM: ACTION STEPS (6 MONTHS BEFORE THE ELECTION)

1. Prioritize an active campaign manager (90 percent hours, local, execution-focused).

Who may be a good fit? Write three names below. Interview them all. Vet like victory depends on it. Because it does.

____

____

____

2. Set compensation parameters early ($2,000–$4,000/mo. + housing if needed), and keep paid staff at 15 percent or less of money raised.

3. Define your core structure such as manager, treasurer, counsel, plus any party committee support you can leverage.

4. Create written job descriptions and measurable goals (daily/weekly/monthly).

5. Set up accounting and compliance checks and balances.

6. Build a volunteer role map to fill "paid" functions where possible.

7. Prepare mentally and structurally for turnover; hire and fire with clear expectations.

The next chapter is going to be a bit shorter than most previous; don't let that fool you. In politics, quantity is quality. In Chapter 16, density is quality. Data density. You'll see what we mean.

CHAPTER 16

DATA, SOFTWARE, AND ALL THE INTEL YOU'LL NEED (OR ELSE)

> ***There's something you should know.***
>
> "[P]eople aged 46 or older were significantly more persuaded by the microtargeted messaging than those in younger age brackets."[44]

You can just do things. You can just target voters and persuade, motivate, influence, and otherwise move them to vote. You just need to know who they are. How do you do that? Data. Here are a few choice screenshots so you can see what we mean.

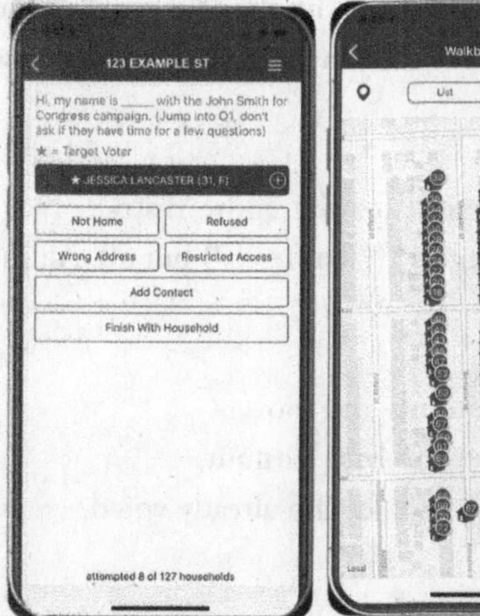

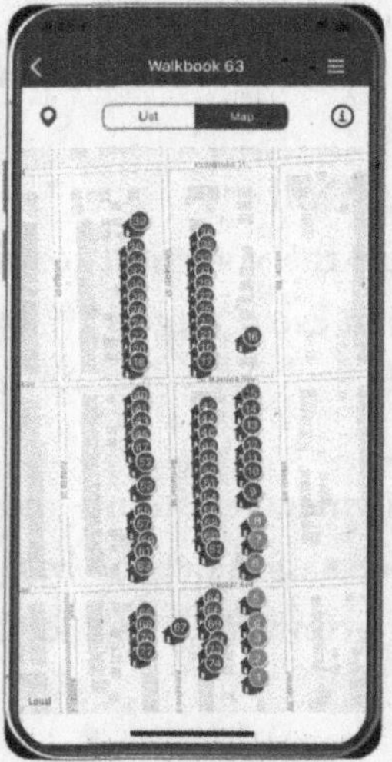

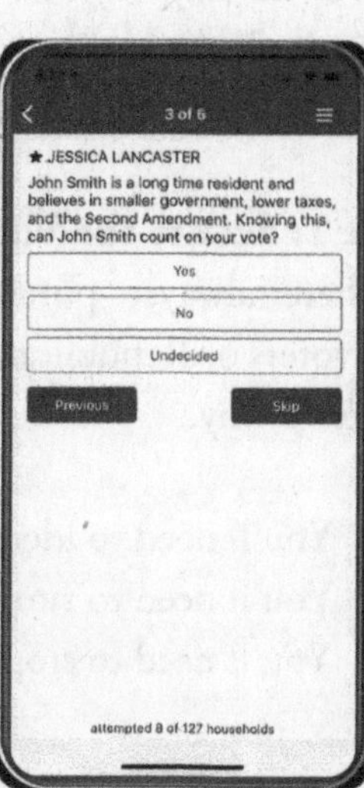

Mo' data, mo' voters. Here's how to get them.

FIGHTING FIRE WITH SOFTWARE

Let's explain voter data software with an intuitive analogy. Think of this like outfitting a firehouse. The voter roll is the map of every building in your district. Modeling data is the heat signature (i.e., who's likely Republican/leaning/right-of-center, who's persuadable, who's a donor type, who's turnout-prone). The front-end tools are the hoses, trucks, radios—all things that let humans do work fast and record it correctly. And you're ready to fight fires. In our case, that's find and win votes.

Got it? Got it. With the gist in your grasp, here's what you're buying, in plain English now:

1. **Voter roll = Who exists**
   - A list of every registered voter in the district, with IDs and basic attributes.
2. **Modeling data = Who they probably are**
   - Scores that estimate party/lean, turnout probability, persuasion likelihood, issue affinity, etc. This is what stops you from guessing.
3. **Front-end app = How your humans work**
   - The walk/call/text tool that volunteers actually use. This is where activity gets recorded and turned into actionable follow-up.

If you're missing any one of these, the campaign becomes a mess of spreadsheets, duplicate touches, and wasted volunteer hours. We recommend all three, and here's how to set them up—in three naturally sequential phases.

Phase 1: Secure the Voter Roll

Start here, always—purchase the voter roll for the entire district. Not just likely voters or Republicans or even "targets" (Chapter 17) but **all**. All means all! Here's why.

- You'll need to identify new registrants and movers.
- You'll need to run persuasion beyond base turnout.
- You'll need to stop re-contacting people who already voted.

- You'll need clean lists for mail, door-knocking, phones, and follow-up on all three.

You can get your Phase 1 data source from the following:

- Secretary of State / county elections (sometimes cheaper, sometimes clunky)
- County or state party (sometimes included, sometimes limited)
- Commercial vendors (often easier, often pricier, often comes with appends/models)
    - . . . specifically, i360, which we've mentioned before and will do so again because i360 also has what you need for Phase 2 and 3.

Whichever way you go, it will strike you that data can be pricey. If you can get it cheaper through official channels or party infrastructure, great. Just remember—cheap data that isn't refreshed is expensive later.

You will be asking these two non-negotiable questions of any vendors or data sources you ultimately consider for Phase 1:

1. **"When was your last voter file refreshed?"**
2. **"Will I receive daily AB/EV updates? How are they delivered?"** (AB/EV refers to absentee ballot and early vote.)

These make all the difference. We don't want you burning time chasing voters who already cast ballots but instead shifting resources to precisely who remains untapped as voter potential for you.

Phase 2: Add Modeling, Stop Guessing

Once you have the voter roll from Phase 1, you need modeling data layered on top of it. In any race other than a closed primary, you will have to distinguish between the voter party and conservative lean somehow. And if you don't buy modeling software, here's what happens:

- Volunteers "judge" voters based on yard signs and in-driveway vehicle bumper stickers.

- Thus, the campaign wastes persuasion time on hard opposition.
- And as a result, you will miss soft supporters who needed just one more touch to turn out.
- All while your get-out-the-vote plan is a generic blast.
- And then you lose.

Modeling will prevent the above fate as best you can avoid it. Specifically, modeling provides scores so you can build "universes" like:

- High-support / low-turnout ⇨ turnout operation
- Soft support / persuadable ⇨ persuasion scripts + follow-up
- Hard opposition ⇨ deprioritize
- High-turnout supporters not yet voted ⇨ late-stage chase list

This is how campaigns scale intelligently instead of the spray-and-pray approach common to amateurs and upstarts.

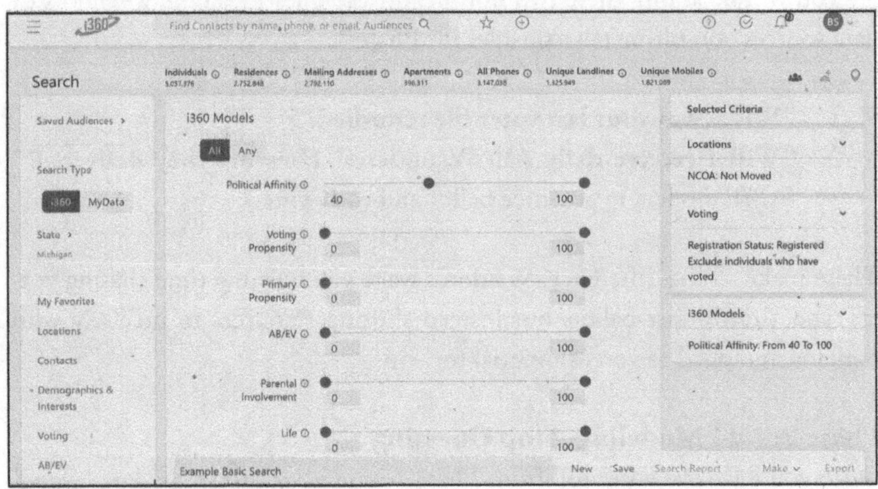

Phase 3: Select Your Front-End App

Now you need the software layer your campaign uses to execute canvassing (walk lists, turf cutting, mapping, routing), calling (dialing, scripts, dispositions), texting/email (depending on platform and compliance), survey scripts and data capture, and real-time synchronization so your campaign can see what's happening. This is the interface that joins up human effort to your database. Both previous phases build on this one. We highly recommend you *not* go cheap with this software. Ease of use is essential; if the volunteer experience is poor, your data will be poor, and then the campaign becomes unmanageable in the final stretch.

Which brings us to basically two buying paths: worst-case and best-case.

Worst-case scenario Phase 3 goes like this:

- You buy voter records from a vendor.
- You may pay something like $0.02/record for the list, sometimes including modeling.
- Then you separately buy a front-end canvassing/calling tool.
- This can work, but it creates friction:
    - multiple systems,
    - import/export issues,
    - mismatched universes,
    - "which file is truth?" arguments

You can survive this path, but you must be disciplined.

Now let's look at the best-case scenario for Phase 3 in which:

- You sign up for a subscription platform.
- Configure the integrated tools such as:
    - an original voter list
    - modeling
    - the ability to cut walk books and create universes (more on that last one in Chapter 17)
    - canvassing + calls + texts + email + analytics in one place

That sounds way easier, doesn't it? It is, and it means fewer sync problems, cleaner reporting, easier training, and faster volunteer deployment. Way easier.

Phase 3 Vendor Options

Let's cover which software are available to you, starting with our favorite platform that we've already mentioned before—and we half-hope you've already signed up with them.

Integrated platforms (data + tech in one system): i360

This is the top option for right-of-center operations, with subscription or per-record pricing, integrated data + modeling, built-in tools (walk, call, text, email), and analytics.

If you're going to win with discipline and speed, integrated is right for you because it reduces "duct-tape," i.e., throwing different data and software tools together to ramshackle something of a self-integrated, self-managed tech platform for your campaign.

Here is our quick checklist for vetting potential integrated platforms (i360 is not the only one):

- Do I get the full district universe?
- How often is the file refreshed?
- Do I get daily AB/EV updates?
- Can I cut turfs and build universes easily?
- Is the volunteer interface simple?
- Can I export my data any time, cleanly?

Data vendors (strong data, tech varies): Data Trust, Aristotle, L2

Data Trust, Aristotle, and L2 are alternatives to i360. You should know they:

- May sell to both Republican and Democrat candidates and campaigns
- Sell per-record pricing similar to if not higher than i360
- Sometimes have niche/nuanced data in certain places, which can be a plus
- Often offer no daily model updates
- May require a separate grassroots organizing app, resulting in a complexity-headache situation, in our opinion

On that last point, if your data provider isn't also your field tool for actually contacting people, you must plan the integration yourself. And you may not have the budget for a part-time information technology guy, much less a full-time one.

Front-end "grassroots apps" that require external data: Campaign Sidekick, Advantage, Numinar, Ecanvasser, Field Edge

These can work, but the core issue is they usually require external data—often from another provider. The result is that volunteer experience can be uneven as they have to figure out and remember how to use multiple tools. Both cost and complexity increase because you're running a multi-vendor situation. Plus, any vendor history of "access drama" during election season is a real operational risk. You do not want to be negotiating platform access in October.

Budget tools for the most modest budget: Ecanvasser

Ecanvasser can be cheaper, but you need to provide the voter data. This category is viable if:

- You already have a solid voter roll and modeling process.
- You want a simple volunteer canvassing interface.
- You have someone on the team who can manage imports/exports and hygiene.

Cheap software is fine. Cheap data discipline is rare. Make sure you have the latter if you get the former. As you can probably tell, we advise you to subscribe to a fully integrated tool. Consider i360 (www.i-360.com).

DATA, SOFTWARE, INTEL: ACTION STEPS (5 MONTHS BEFORE THE ELECTION)

1. Purchase your integrated software solution that covers all three phases.

2. Once you pick your stack, you don't hope it works. **Test it.** Import voter file (entire district). Then confirm refresh cadence + AB/EV updates schedule.

3. Build universes (covering this in Chapter 17 in full). Include base supporters, persuadables, and unknowns.

4. Create walk lists and outreach scripts (doors, texts, calls, emails).

5. Run the following:

- 1 canvass shift
- 1 phone bank shift
- 1 follow-up workflow

6. Confirm your voter data workflow is working. You should be able to answer:

- Are volunteer notes and tags syncing correctly?
- Are voter responses usable for follow-up?
- Can you generate "who to hit next" lists with confidence?
- Can you stop contacting voters who already voted (as AB/EV updates arrive)?

If you can't do those things, you don't have a system . . . you have a subscription. We want you to have both.

Now, we've teased this concept of voter **universes** throughout this chapter. You probably get the idea, but it's worth its own chapter. Now that you know the *how* of voter data and software, we're ready to dial into the *who*. Let's do.

CHAPTER 17

CREATE YOUR TARGET UNIVERSE (OF DEMOGRAPHICS)

There's something you should know.

Eight in ten eligible voters don't show up to primaries.[45] The shrewd candidate's job is to change that.

Your district has an observable universe—everyone registered to vote. Your **target universe** is much smaller, perhaps more like a galaxy dare we say of a few solar systems. Your target universe is the group of voters (or group of groups) that you will spend real resources on because they're the only people with a plausible path to voting for you—and the only people you can and need to realistically reach enough times to matter.

This is your commitment. To the doors you will knock, the calls you will place, the mail you will send, the texts you will deploy, the ads you will run, and the follow-up you will execute. Your target universe. Your commitment. The difference between activity and results. Target.

STANDARD TARGET UNIVERSE TERMINOLOGY

Campaign professionals shorthand voter behavior and likelihood with simple labels. You need to speak this language because your targeting decisions will be built out of it.

Turnout History (The "#/4" Language)

These terms describe how often a voter has participated in key election types, based on their voting record:

0/4 — Zero of the last 4 elections of consequence
1/4 — One of the last 4 elections of consequence
2/4 — Two of the last 4 elections of consequence
3/4 — Three of the last 4 elections of consequence
4/4 — Four of the last 4 elections of consequence

What is an election of consequence? Simple. If you're building a primary election universe, it is the last four primaries. If you're building a general election universe, it is the last four general elections.

However your data vendor defines those categories in your state, the practical meaning is the same—it's how consistently this person engages in either primary or general elections.

Why do these frequency signifiers matter? Because the most likely person to vote in the next election is someone who voted in the last election . . . and more likely than that someone who voted in the last two elections . . . three elections . . . four elections. You get it. Voting is habitual. In primary elections, it is not uncommon for 60 to 70 percent or more of the vote to be cast from 4/4 past primary voters. That's a big deal and understanding this is a massive cost saver. Mail, knock, call, advertise to the right people, many times.

KEY CONSIDERATIONS (BECAUSE YOU CAN'T REACH EVERYONE)

Creating a target universe is not just who you like; it's an operational decision that forces your campaign to sort voters into three buckets:

1. Who you absolutely must hit
2. Who you absolutely can't hit
3. Who you can hit if you overperform

If you don't force yourself to make these buckets, you'll default to the lazy and unnecessary fantasy of "we'll hit everyone." Fantasy dies the moment you ask the questions that matter related to your and your team's and volunteers' realistic capacity:

- How many doors can you knock?
- How many doors will you knock?
- How many mail pieces can you afford?
- How many calls can you make?
- How many calls will you make?
- How big is your texting budget?
- How big is your digital ad budget?

Notice the difference between *can* and **will**. Clueless candidates live in *can*; winning campaigns plan in **will**.

Remember your voter data from Chapter 16? It's time to filter it all down to must-contact territory by discerning the RULES of the election. This is most relevant in primary elections where many times not every registered voter can vote:

Closed, semi-closed, or open primary?

Closed Primary: A closed primary is one in which only registered members of a political party may vote in a political party's primary election. In many states, the political parties set the rules of their primary elections. This means you may have a closed Republican primary and an open Democrat primary in your state. Or vice versa. In a closed primary, voters must be registered with the political party BEFORE Election Day. If you show up to vote in the Republican primary and you are an Unaffiliated voter, you will be asked politely yet firmly to leave.

Semi-Closed Primary: A semi-closed primary is much like a closed primary, but with a key loophole, an individual may either change their party registration at the time of voting (Election Day or early voting) or participate if they are an unaffiliated/independent voter.

Open Primary: An open primary is one where any registered voter may vote in a party primary. In states without partisan registration all together, you'll find yourself in an open primary.

A guide to state primaries can be found here; you'll need to type in the website exactly. It's a long site address but worth your while:

https://news.ballotpedia.org/2025/09/12/understanding-primaries-state-primary-laws-and-types-explained-2/

The importance of these rules cannot be understated. If you don't understand this, you will waste significant resources sending your communications to voters who cannot even vote for you.

Let's give a concrete example . . . Kentucky holds a closed primary in the May 2026 elections. To participate in the Republican primary, a voter must be registered as a Republican before the end of the year in 2025. If you are running in a state house primary for the May 2026 election and are sending mail to a non-registered Republican, you are throwing money into a black hole. That non-Republican voter CANNOT VOTE FOR YOU. Do not speak to them.

So what if you are in a state without party registration?

Well in almost all cases you are still in luck. Nearly every state records which primary a voter participated in past elections. This is called a Primary Ballot Indicator.

For example, in Texas, voters do not register to vote with a party affiliation. However, the Secretary of State records which primary election(s) a voter participated in for past elections. This is why getting a good data source is key. If a voter has only participated in Republican primary elections in the past, there is a good chance that the voter will participate in the Republican primary next election. It's not complicated, but you have to get this right.

The Two Scores That Matter: Affinity and Propensity

Previously we discussed modeling as a consideration when purchasing your voter data. If you live in a state that does not have partisan registration you may run into a problem for certain types of voters . . . Let's give an example using Texas once more.

Texas is a high growth state. New voters are moving to the state frequently. If you live in a district with many new movers, you will find yourself needing to target these folks. But they have not had the chance to participate in a primary yet . . . how do we know if they are a Republican? Enter modeling data.

Modeling data takes their known consumer behavior (remember agreeing to the terms of service when you sign up for never-ending websites, email lists, subscriptions? Yeah, someone is buying that data). Serious data companies take consumer behavior indicators across tens of thousands of data points to create a score on how likely an individual is to be a Conservative or Liberal. This is often illustrated as a sliding scale of 0–100. Zero being likelihood of a Liberal, and 100 being likelihood to be a Conservative. How do they make those calls? Because Conservatives and Liberals consume differently.

For example, if a voter drives a Ford F150 they have a 90 percent likelihood of being a Republican. Inversely, if that voter drives a Toyota Prius, they have a 90 percent likelihood of being a beta male.

This understanding will prove immensely valuable when competing in a general election as a significant number of voters register as Independents/ Unaffiliated or never participate in a party primary.

A target universe for these types of scenarios is built from two fundamental measurements. **Affinity** (Partisanship / Political Lean) answers, *How likely is this voter to be ideologically aligned with you?* Typical scoring looks like:

0–30: Liberal
31–69: Swing / Unclear / Mixed
70–100: Conservative

Voting Propensity (Turnout Likelihood) answers, *How likely is this voter to actually vote?* Typical scoring for propensity goes:

0–30: Low
31–69: Mid
70–100: High

When you combine these two scores, targeting stops being a guessing game, meaning affinity tells you who might support you, but propensity tells you who will actually show up. Your job is to find the overlap you can afford to reach.

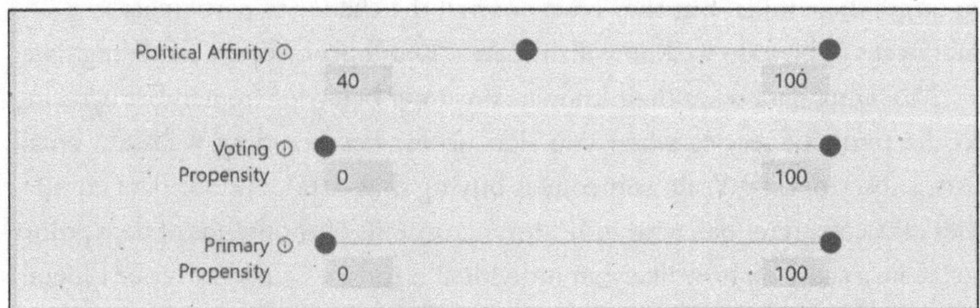

That last point is one of the most important lessons in this entire book.

Real District Examples: Why "0/4+" Doesn't Mean Anything by Itself

Let's run a scenario from a real-style legislative district breakdown, MS HD-40. If you pull 0/4+ voters with no limiters, you're staring at, in this example, 7,224 doors. Now, that's not a target universe, that's "everyone registered." Now apply one simple limiter: 4/4+ with MAJORITY Republican ballot indicators. Suddenly, your universe becomes merely 1,829 doors. Oh. Same district. Same voter file. Wildly different operational reality. Why? Behavior beats assumptions. Registration alone is not enough to tell you who is gettable. Duh.

Why All Voters Are Not Uniform Unicorns

In another example universe of voters, we have 6,048 doors of 0/4+ total (all registered voters). Breaking it down further, we've got 3,319 doors with 35+ affinity, 704 doors that have voted in at least one Republican primary ever, 623 doors with majority Republican ballot indicators, 906 new voter doors, and 156 doors that are 4/4 general voters.

Notice the ramifications within the data. Some 0/4 voters are actually Right-leaning but inconsistent at putting their conservative principles into voting practice. Some are new voters who might be highly persuadable. Some have Republican primary history (high-"signal" behavior). Some are statistical noise, e.g., records that may be outdated, inflated, or irrelevant to your ground operation.

What to do with this information? We're glad you asked.

The Real Question: Are 0/4s Worth Your Time and Money?

Now comes the point of the exercise—**operational feasibility**. If your district can be fully covered multiple times by your available door-knockers, that changes everything.

In the MS HD-40 example, ten door-knockers can easily do three passes, plus a GOTV pass of the entire district. If you have even a modest field team, you may be able to run a high-frequency contact plan that other campaigns will never match. That's why some professional targeting operations shrink the universe dramatically. For example, a professional target universe for that example district could be, say, 1,395 doors, not the 7,224 total 0/4s. Now it gets interesting.

THE THREE STAGES OF A CAMPAIGN (AND HOW UNIVERSE-TARGETING CHANGES IN EACH)

Like the universe itself, your voter universe changes throughout space and time. There are three distinct campaign phases that affect the who, what, where, when, and how of your voter universe–targeting plays. And they go like so.

Stage 1: Identification (6–3 Months Out)

Goal: Find your people and categorize the rest. This is when you use doors/calls/texts to label voters as:

- supporter
- leaner
- persuadable
- opponent
- unknown

Identification is where you build the map that makes persuasion and GOTV possible.

Stage 2: Persuasion (3–1 Month Out)

Goal: Move the persuadables and lock in soft support. This phase is where affinity matters most because you are trying to convert "I might" into "I will."

Stage 3: Get Out the Vote (the Home Stretch)

Goal: Turn identified supporters into ballots cast. GOTV is where campaigns collapse if they failed to build a disciplined target list earlier. At the end, you won't really need clever messaging. It's all clean lists and relentless follow-up from here on out, baby.

During All Three Stages, Capture All (New) Data

All targeting is theory until you capture data. Every door-knock without data capture is a missed compounding opportunity. Every call without disposition is a future duplicate touch. Every text without tagging is a wasted follow-up. Every voter who told you they already voted by mail is a wasted follow-up.

Campaigns with the same budget can perform radically differently based on one habit—capturing the data and using it. This ongoing, inter-stage effort allows you to tighten universes, increase contact frequency on the right people, stop chasing the already-voted, and move from simply working hard (or just feeling like it) to actually scoring votes.

AN IMPORTANT NOTE ON MAIL BALLOTS

Whine. Complain. Piss. Moan. Mail ballots exist. They are the entire margin of the election many times. Until you and thousands of America First patriots take power, they are going to stay. And if you are in a state with significant voting by mail ("universal vote-by-mail" states including California, Colorado, Hawaii, Nevada, Oregon, Utah, Vermont, and Washington) you definitely can't ignore this. There are additional states with majority or plurality vote-by-mail on top of these.

Sorry to break it to you but your "Election Day" may be thirty to ninety days before the final Election Day. If vote-by-mail is significant in your race, hear me out… your GOTV doesn't start in the final weeks of November or final weeks of the primary. It starts in the final weeks before ballots hit doorsteps. This is why we ran the PA CHASE. To solve the mail ballot problem. Not because we like mail voting… quite the opposite. Because we were tired of losing.

THE LAST RULE: CREATE THE LIST AND FOLLOW IT

If you remember nothing else from this chapter, remember this: **A target universe is only useful if it becomes a list your campaign actually follows.** That means:

- Don't constantly "expand the map" midstream.
- Don't chase shiny objects.
- Don't let a volunteer knock random doors because they "felt like it."
- Don't waste candidate time on low-yield voters while high-yield universes sit untouched.

Build the list, commit to it, execute.

CREATE YOUR TARGET UNIVERSE: ACTION STEPS (5 MONTHS BEFORE THE ELECTION)

1. Pull the full voter universe and create an initial "working universe" by excluding obvious non-targets (out-of-district, bad addresses, deceased where flagged, extreme age outliers, etc.).

2. Set your targeting ceilings (the hard math):

- doors you will knock (not "can")
- calls you will make
- texts you will send
- mail pieces you can afford

3. Build your first target universe using Affinity and Propensity. Start with high-affinity / mid-to-high-propensity voters, then add persuadables (mid-affinity) you can actually reach repeatedly.

4. Segment the universe into three buckets and lock it:

- Must hit (core)
- Can't hit (waste)
- Overperform (only if you have surplus capacity)

5. Assign each bucket to a phase and a timeline. Create lists you can hand to staff or volunteers. Remember, the three stages of a campaign are:

- Identification (unknowns)
- Persuasion (movables)
- GOTV chase (supporters not yet voted)

Phases Timeline

Identification	Start: ______	Wrap Up: ______	Doors: ______
Persuasion	Start: ______	Wrap Up: ______	Doors: ______
GOTV	Start: ______	Wrap Up: ______	Doors: ______

6. Capture results and rebuild weekly. Update IDs, refine universes, and tighten the list as you approach persuasion and then GOTV.

It's getting real. Let's keep going.

CHAPTER 18

WORKING YOUR TARGETED LIST (WITH DOOR-KNOCKING AND MORE)

> ***There's something you should know.***
> Since (at least) as far back as the 1950s, door-knocking has been the most effective tactic ever measured in political science.[46] Ground campaigns have increased voter turnout by as much as 7–8 percentage points.[47]
> Doors win wars.

This is the chapter that many of you have been waiting for. One of those people is John Brunner.

In 2017, I (Cliff Maloney) finally got a meeting I'd been chasing for a while—with John. John is the kind of guy you don't "network with." You earn (maybe) twenty minutes with him, and you don't waste them. He was a manufacturer, owned a family company, built up the whole thing, then sold it for hundreds of millions. It's public knowledge. Today, he sits on the board of Citizens Alliance. Also public knowledge. But back in 2017, I didn't have the benefit of hindsight. I just knew I needed to get in front of this man.

We met at a Starbucks in St. Louis. I sat down with my "fundraise the fundraiser" pitch ready. I thought I knew exactly what mattered most, copying a page from the Turning Point USA handbook—campus outreach. Getting younger people engaged, right? Bringing them into the fold, you know? Long-term culture shift . . . get it? That was my Turning Point–style pitch, but it was a bad parody of their actual work. All my ideas probably sounded noble and strategic when thinking high level in decades . . . not in the details of election cycles just months away.

I barely got rolling before John cut me off. No patience for fluff. I've come to love that about him.

"What are you doing to win elections?" he asked. "Because that's where the power is."

I doubled down; I kept talking about campus. I tried to explain why it mattered. I tried to justify the strategy. We were going to be Turning Point Two-Point-O!

But he pushed back again. Same question, same idea underneath it. *You can't influence the culture if you don't hold power.* It clicked; I broke from my script.

"Look . . . we do have this case study," I said. "When we take committed people and we knock on a lot of doors, we can flip state-level races."

"Go on," he said.

So I said I wanted 250 Ron Paul types around the country. Think dedicated America First yet liberty-loving state legislators. That many might sound crazed to you until you do the math—it would've been roughly 5 percent of all the statehouse seats in the country. If you can take 5 percent of the seats in the minor leagues, so to speak, you can start building an actual bench for the big game. These recruits become people who move up through the system and can eventually become congressmen, senators, governors . . . and more. A farm team. A pipeline. A real future. That's the future.

I ended my tangent, and John then said the line I knew I needed to remember.

"This I'm interested in."

From there, he taught some strategy.

"I've learned something in business. People tell you, 'Don't put all your eggs in the same basket.' They're wrong. Put all of your eggs in the *right* basket."

He then mentioned the classic business book *Good to Great.* Its key takeaway is focus, which comes from deciding you're going to be the best in the world at one thing and then ignoring anything and everything else that distracts you from that one thing.

John leaned in and then said something that felt less like encouragement and more like a challenge.

"Cliff, if you can be the best in the world at knocking doors to advance liberty, then be the best in the world at that."

I accepted. I walked out of that Starbucks with my thinking narrowed in the best possible way. John had pulled me out of long-term culture change work and brought to the imminent, to the urgent. From the potential to the real. The only scoreboard that matters if you actually want to change the country is election results. Charlie Kirk would figure this out as well, starting up Turning Point Action to become the politically active sister organization to college campus–organizer Turning Point USA.

Yes, politics is downstream of culture, to paraphrase Lawrence Myers (often attributed also to Andrew Breitbart). But this is a canal we're talking about, not a river. Politicians are the lockkeepers at the gates, who can raise or lower the water, redirect it, and decide which boats move forward and which get halted in place.

Once you accept this reframe, as I did that day, the next question becomes unavoidable: *If door-knocking is the highest-leverage, most repeatable way to produce wins . . . why wouldn't you build your whole machine around it?*

The culture war is waged at the front door. So that's where I went.

DOORS WIN WARS

Much campaign wisdom out there is simply inherited superstition. It's the sort of fluff I heard wannabes, students, and consultants repeat when I was getting started. They probably just heard it from someone who once worked on a winning race, then telephone-gamed it to the next person and then the next and then the next and so on until it reached someone like me. It takes voices like John Brunner's to replace noise with signal. The facts back him up.

In a well-known randomized field experiment in New Haven, scholars found that personal canvassing increased voter turnout by about 6 percentage points while direct mail had only a small effect and phone calls had no effect in that study.[48] The broader synthesis work behind *Get Out the Vote* (now in its fifth edition) exists for one purpose—to measure what it costs, per vote, to mobilize people using different methods. According to the book, a door-to-door canvasser must knock on an average of **nine doors** to make one successful contact.[49] Guess what . . . contrasted with other forms of campaigning, this door-to-door canvassing is the most effective way to increase participation, with other tactics trailing behind it. Door-knocking can cost as low as **$19** per vote with volunteers and minimal paid staff, or $144 per vote with a paid canvassing team.[50] Ergo, door-knocking is the main effort we are covering in this chapter. Everything else is a force multiplier. But we'll cover that too—and multiply your forces.

WORKING YOUR TARGETED LIST: DOOR-KNOCKING AND MORE

If you did Chapter 17 correctly, you now have a target universe—a list that is ruthlessly realistic.

Now you're going to work that list in three passes, aligned to the three stages of your campaign you've already read about, namely:

1. Identification (first pass)
2. Persuasion (second pass)
3. GOTV (third pass)

No surprise, we start with door-knocking.

The Gold Standard: Door-Knocking Timeline

Start knocking **five** months before Election Day. And you will keep score. Not "we've been working hard." Real numbers such as:

- 2,000 doors by 120 days out
- 5,000 doors by 90 days out (cumulative)
- 10,000 doors by 60 days out (cumulative)
- 15,000 doors by 30 days out (cumulative)
- 20,000 doors by Election Day (cumulative—per election)

Important: Doors knocked are not the same thing as conversations. Track both. Conversations are what move votes; doors are the input.

Door-Knocking Phases Explained

Three passes, one list. All map to the campaign's overall stages.

First Pass: Identification

Goal: Learn who's who and introduce the candidate.

This pass is an issue survey plus candidate ID. You are collecting usable data; what you want out of every contact includes:

- Supporter / Lean Supporter / Undecided / Opposed
- Top issue (from your own list, not whatever cable news is pushing)
- Voting method preference if you can capture it (absentee / early / Election Day)
- Permission to follow up, and ideally an email or phone if they volunteer it

This is where you build your "supporter file," which becomes your GOTV weapon later.

Second Pass: Persuasion

Goal: Move the persuadables and lock the soft supporters.

Now you return to the same turf with intent. Two rules make this pass work:

1. Use the issues you collected.
2. Remove negative interactions from your persuasion pool.

You are not trying to "win arguments." In fact, we advise no debates while going from door to door. You are here to secure votes. That means you spend time where time pays you back.

Third Pass: GOTV

Goal: Convert supporters into ballots.

This is where your data becomes your advantage; chase your identified supporters with precision.

KNOCKIN' DOORS: THE MECHANICS (HOW IT ACTUALLY WORKS)

The basic flow—simple, repeatable, trainable—goes like so:

- Approach the door with your literature already in hand.
- Knock; don't only ring the doorbell.
- Smile and introduce yourself immediately.
- Hand the literature as you begin speaking.
- Jump into the conversation.
- Ask for the vote—twice.
    - If they aren't home: write "Sorry I missed you! – [YOUR NAME]" on the literature or a sticky note and place it conspicuously. (That double ask matters because people dodge commitment. The first ask surfaces resistance. The second ask closes the gap.)
- "Can I count on your vote?"
- (If they hedge) "I hear you—so can I count on your vote?"

Is this a little pushy? Yes. Is being a little pushy your job? Also, yes. The psychological commitment of a **YES** is what you are chasing.

Dos Versus Don'ts of Door-Knocking

DO:

- Carry literature, a fine-tip marker, and a charged phone (plus battery pack).
- Dress appropriate to the district; comfortable shoes always.
- Knock doors with "No Soliciting" signs (you're not selling; you're campaigning).
- Keep literature in your hand as you approach.
- Knock and ring—don't rely on the doorbell alone.
- If you have the opportunity, leave a recorded message at the doorbell camera.

DO NOT:

- Cut through yards or grass.
- Leave gates open.
- Look in windows.
- Forget the doorbell cameras are *always* recording.
- Touch mailboxes. Ever.
- Go inside a home. (This is not just a safety issue but also a time suck.)
- Get sucked into national political drama or internal faction fights.
- Dive deep into policy explanations at the door.
- This is not a debate club. This is a persuasion + turnout operation.

Caveat: Still knock those "No Trespassing" doors but only where lawful and safe. Obey clear posted restrictions and your local campaign's legal guidance. Your safety outranks a single door. But of course hit every "No Soliciting" door you confront.

Pro Tips That Save Time (and Keep Your People Safe)

- Assume dogs exist. Don't reach through fences. Don't crowd doors. Take a big step back.
- Be aware of surroundings. Trust your instincts. Leave quietly if anything feels wrong.
- Apartments are not impossible. They're a systems problem: entry access + routing + persistence.
- Walk your turf in an order that makes sense. Don't burn an hour zigzagging.
- Implement the "Greiss Wave" and show motion at the door without peeking in windows. It opens doors. Humans respond to humans, but many people assume you're just Amazon dropping a package and heading out.
- Data accuracy is sacred. Track restricted access carefully. Bad data ruins second pass and GOTV.

A Note on Volunteers

Volunteers are imperfect. People are weird. Voters can be weirder. When "weird things" happen at the door, give your people the benefit of the doubt while still protecting data quality and safety. Remember, a voter contacting the campaign to complain about a door-knocker may just be ideological opposition messing with you. Your job is to make volunteer work easy to do correctly—and hard to do randomly.

YOUR SURVEY SCRIPT: WHY IT EXISTS (AND WHY MOST CAMPAIGNS WASTE IT)

This is a key tool to bring with you—or have your team bring with them—during door-knocking effort. A survey exists to:

- Keep you and your volunteers on message
- Collect data you can actually use for mail and calls
- Identify supporters for GOTV

A good survey is short, calm, specific, and repeatable. A volunteer should be able to run it after five minutes of training.

Your survey should never invite a ten-minute policy rabbit hole. It should create clear tags after the fact for you to record, such as:

- SUPPORT / LEAN / UNDECIDED / OPPOSED
- Issue A / Issue B / Issue C
- "Wants info" / "Wants yard sign" / "Wants candidate call"
- "Do not contact" when appropriate

Wait . . . isn't this survey thing just like the online petition thing and the list-building stuff from Chapter 5 . . . only for door-knocking?

Yes, that's correct. How a candidate does anything is how a candidate does everything.

Before we move on, here is a glimpse at a sample survey.

Sample Survey

1: Hello {VOTER NAME}! My name is {YOUR NAME} and I am a

volunteer concerned about our community. We're out talking with folks in the community ahead of the upcoming primary election on March 3rd. Are you planning to vote in the upcoming primary election? . . . Will you most likely vote early, by mail, or on Election Day?

- Early Voting
- Mail-In Voting
- Election Day Voting
- Maybe/Unlikely Voting
- Not Voting
- Already Voted
- Refused Voting

2. Great, Representative Justin Greiss is the conservative fighter in the State House who stands with President Trump and pushes back against the far left and RINOs. Justin is a husband, a father, a Christian, and a warrior who stands for Texas values. As State Representative, Justin has worked on issues like eliminating property taxes, securing the border, and protecting Texans from the globalist agenda. We're working to get him reelected to continue representing District 64. Can Justin count on your support?

- Would Support
- Unsure Support
- Would NOT Support
- Refused Support

3: Can we count on your vote for Justin Greiss for State House District 64?

- Hard ID Justin Greiss
- Lean ID Justin Greiss
- Hard ID {OPPONENT NAME}
- Lean ID {OPPONENT NAME}
- Undecided
- Other Candidate
- Refused ID

4: Great . . . Would you like a yard sign? [Multi-select]

- Wants Yard Sign
- Gave Yard Sign
- Possible Big Sign Location
- JG Call to Win Over
- JG Call to Thank
- Likely to Donate
- No Action

5: Note: Have a conversation and win the vote. How would you rate this interaction?

- Positive Interaction
- Neutral Interaction
- Negative Interaction

CHASE CALLS: HOW YOU MULTIPLY DOORS WITH PHONES

Door-knocking is the punch. Chase calls and text messages are how you throw combinations. We suggest you start these calls three months before the election. The to-do for this is simple: **Call every household whose door you have knocked to persuade them to vote for your candidate.**

But again, do this *after* the front door visit. A door touch makes your number less "random." Voters remember the knock more than the flyer, and this follow-up feels like continuity and not spam.

Yes, there can be costs here (e.g., tools, dialer, phone lines), but follow-up is everything. It's a theme we've repeated throughout this book so far. Phones are getting tricky in the modern era. Spam blockers, low answer rates, etc. Perhaps they'll fade out in the near future, however while the option still exists and visual voicemail adds a useful layer of opportunity, speaking to a human is still king in campaigning. The personal touch of a real, live phone call is becoming more and more rare, so use it as resource. Layer in meaning to text messaging for those you can't reach live. A candidate who is not persistently in front of the voting public is not a candidate they'll remember—or remember to vote for.

Lastly, if you're sour on the phone calls and not getting your desired outcome, there are other personal touches you can substitute. Handwritten follow-up post cards to the doors you've knocked is a premiere touch you can implement. But everything has tradeoffs and at the time of writing, a postcard stamp alone is 61 cents. This adds up quick, but may be a piece of your winning strategy.

MAIL PLAN: THE "TANGIBLE PROOF" LAYER

Mail is expensive, relatively, yes. But the right mail does something digital can't—it creates physical reality for a low-information voter. It shows your name, your face, and seriousness. This is no news to you, of course. We have written at length about the use of mail for your campaign. But now, it comes up again, when the time is now to follow up with those whose doors you've paid a visit and whose phones you've dialed.

To briefly review Chapter 13 takeaways, you'll write, design, and oftentimes pack your own mail. Use templates. Get a second opinion. Keep the language simple. Every piece asks for the vote. Nothing new here.

If your budget is tight by this point in the campaign, follow this **minimum plan**—send three mailers:

1. Intro / biography (about 6 weeks out)
2. Issue mailer (about 3 weeks out)
3. Personal appeal letter (about 1 week out)

Include in all three:

- a clear "Please vote" ask
- the voting method / dates info appropriate to your district
- donation envelope only if you're actively fundraising by mail (not always worth it late)

If you have a bit more budget, go with this **extended plan** for your mailers:

- 6 weeks out: Introduction bio + "apple pie" values letter
- 4 weeks out: Issue letter + donation envelope

- 3 weeks out: Issue/endorsements slick
- 2 weeks out: Positive issue slick
- 1 week out: Contrast/choice slick (careful, factual, clean)
- Closer: Spouse letter + final argument

And we're not done yet. We now follow up again—via email.

EMAIL LISTS: SUPPLEMENTAL, NOT SUBSTITUTION

List-building matters, especially at the beginning, but not just for emails. You want—and will have collected—phone numbers and mailing addresses, too. Door-knocking is the ideal opportunity for adding those emails to voters for whom you don't have that data field yet. You and your people can simply ask, "We're sending one simple reminder with voting info, so want me to add you?" You can now even purchase voter emails, but this takes some critical thinking skills . . . you can't just drop in 5,000 cold emails without hitting spam boxes.

So, now that you're getting all these emails, it's time to use them in sequence with your other follow-up efforts. Use email at this phase for:

- donations
- volunteer recruitment
- event attendance
- communicating relevant information on state politics and news
- reminding supporters to vote

But, guys, that's what we've already been using email for.

Yes, exactly. We repeat ourselves throughout this book because you will be doing the same things over and over again throughout your campaign.

And over and over and over again.

And over and over.

Again.

DOOR-KNOCKING AND MORE: ACTION STEPS (5 MONTHS BEFORE THE ELECTION)

1. Launch door-knocking immediately and commit to the cumulative

door-count timeline (2,000/5,000/10,000/15,000/20,000) with weekly targets and accountability.

2. Build a one-page survey script that tags every voter (support level + top issue + follow-up permission), then train volunteers until they can run it without freelancing.

3. Run your passes. Start with Pass 1 (Identification) across your full target universe. Each week produce:

- "Supporters to Chase" list
- "Persuadables for Pass 2" list
- "Do Not Contact / Negative" list

4. At three months out, start chase calls to every door-knocked household. Use door data to personalize the opener.

5. Lock your mail plan (minimum three pieces; ideal expanded cadence if budget allows). Write every piece to mirror the top issues you're hearing at the doors.

6. Build and continuously grow your email list from personal networks + donors + opt-ins at the door. Use it weekly for volunteer recruitment and voting reminders.

7. Every week, "shrink the universe" using your data. Remove negatives, prioritize high-yield turfs, and reassign resources to what's producing conversations and commitments.

This chapter covered much, in terms of ground game and more. But leading up to Election Day, urgency spikes. We'd like you to be prepared for what you'll be feeling and for what you should be doing as you reach the final home stretch leading up to the day of the election—primary, runoff, general—up to the very minute polls close. Let's go.

CHAPTER 19

GET OUT THE VOTE (BECAUSE MOST VOTERS REALLY DON'T CARE—SORRY!)

> ***There's something you should know.***
> After door-knocking and face-to-face conversations with eligible voters, working the polls is the most effective political persuasion tactic available.

People don't stay home on Election Day because they forgot; they stay home because they just don't care. Your job is to make them care. The final get-out-the-vote effort must not be a polite reminder. It's time to pull out all the stops on this high-urgency operation. The argument is over. It's all action now. Specifically, with, for, and on your supporters. The undecideds, hostels, and political hobbyists, their time is over. Supporters only.

But don't supporters naturally come out to vote for the candidates they support?

As we say on X with a biting sarcasm, "lol, lmao even." In 2024, Donald Trump won approximately 15 percent of the African American vote.[51] Contrast this with the 18 percent who said they "would" vote for Trump.[52] Not every aspect of this particular demographic maps onto the entire electorate, much less yours. That said, a three-point difference is **not** insignificant when there are 34.4 million eligible black voters.[53] Local and state elections are often decided by a few thousand, even hundreds. We've both supported and worked for candidates who won by a few *dozen* votes.

The closer you get to Election Day, ironically, the more electorally fatigued the voter gets—even your most ardent supporter who donated and possibly even volunteered. They're tired, probably distracted, and likely busy with other things now because they gave so much time and energy to your campaign. It's a bit like a hangover and unfortunately, the post-buzz crash often occurs *days* before the actual Election Day as opposed to after. This is just a campaign reality, unfortunately, which we must all contend with. The likely reason for the interest drop among, again, even your supporters is called the New Year's Resolution Effect. From *Psychology Today*:

> When we publicize our goal intentions, and others acknowledge the awesomeness of such "potential" changes, we get our dopamine reward all at once . . . The more others admire our goals, the more dopamine rush we get, and the less likely we are to execute the future necessary actions to implement them.
>
> Therefore we deplete our "feel good" gas, keeping us from reaching our final destination: our goal. Furthermore, publicizing our intention to succeed gives us a "premature sense of completeness."[54] It signals the brain to move on. If the brain believes that you have reached your goal, it might inhibit the specific brain circuits related to further pursuing this goal.[55]

Supporting a candidate in public, even and especially volunteering for them (you), fits the "publicize . . . goal intentions" bill. Your job becomes to drag your people across the finish line. Make them care; get out the vote.

YOUR TRIFOLD GOTV MESSAGE

Loud and clear, this is what you want your people to hear in the days and, yes, hours leading up to the opening of the polls.

1. **Purposeful**: "Vote for Stewart to protect our gun rights." (A reason, not a reminder.)

2. **Social**: "Everybody's doing it." (Peer pressure without sounding like a weirdo.)
3. **Simple**: "Here's when, where, and how." (Vote planning reduces friction.)

One last reality check before we get into the fundamentals of crunch-time GOTV: **You aren't normal.** You're reading a campaign playbook. Your supporters are not. So you must lead them like you're the adult in the room.

BEFORE YOU GOTV: KNOW WHAT CAN BE KNOWN

Before you knock another door or place another call, lock down what can be known:

- Who can vote (eligibility basics, party rules if it's a primary)
- Rules for voting (ID requirements, absentee rules, early-vote rules, mail ballot rules)
- Dates and deadlines (when voting starts, when it ends, ballot return deadlines)
- Polling-place restrictions (how close you can be, what you can hand out, what you can say)

On that last point: Every state has some restriction on electioneering near polling places, typically in a campaign-free zone measured in feet (often roughly 50 to 200 feet, but it varies).[56] Check www.ncsl.org for your state's rules. If you don't train your people on this, you're volunteering for conflict on the most important day of your campaign.

DEFINE THE ONLY UNIVERSE THAT MATTERS NOW

Practically speaking, all GOTV must be focused on your supporter universe—the people you've already identified through doors, calls, commitments, and prior contact. You need it cleanly separated into three lists:

- Already voted (do not waste touches here, they are dead to you, figuratively)
- Likely voted / needs confirmation
- Not yet voted / must chase

You know what you need to do now.

THE THREE TIME WINDOWS OF GOTV

Leading up to Election Day, your three universe-lists likely map onto the three time windows of voting.

The Early-Vote Window

Early voting and vote-by-mail represent a larger share of turnout each cycle, and it varies wildly by state. Some places are essentially built around mail voting (for example, Oregon and Colorado are widely recognized as universal mail ballot states).

If early vote or mail vote is a meaningful chunk of turnout in your race (say, approximately 20 percent or more), your campaign has to start turnout operation earlier because your supporters will be casting ballots earlier. Any grand "Election Day push" thus comes too late to influence these votes.

In the early-vote window, the most valuable asset is your universe sub-list—who requested a ballot, who was sent a ballot, who returned it, who still has not.

A Simple, Repeatable Early-Vote Program

Here's a basic workflow to GOTV for these people.

- Design a mail piece specifically for early vote and set the "drop date."
- Text or call the recipients within a day or two of expected delivery.
- The voter fills out a mail ballot request paper or online form and sends it back.
- Ballot is mailed to the voter.
- Voter completes the ballot and returns it.
- Campaign tracks ballot returns daily.
- Campaign calls and texts everyone on the early-vote list who has not yet returned a ballot.

In summary, early-vote GOTV goes **mail ⇨ call/text ⇨ list ⇨ chase ⇨ confirm ⇨ repeat.**

The Final Week Window

Similarly in this window, pull the latest data, map what you can accomplish, and run the last clean contact pass on your supporter universe. Here's your checklist of specifics.

Minimum Viable GOTV During Final Week

- Make one last door sweep on identified supporters (especially "not home" and "lean support").
- And make one last live call to lock commitments and clarify voting plans.

Note that all of this should already be in motion. It's not a new plan; it's the plan, narrowed.

The Election Day Window

Every minute on this day is an opportunity-cost decision, meaning if you have a volunteer or staff member do one thing, that leaves that individual unable to do another. For example:

- If someone is working a polling place, they aren't knocking doors.
- If someone is knocking doors, they aren't calling.
- If someone is calling, they aren't texting.

So, choose the mix based on staffing, geography, and the rules. Just know that 100 percent of the people going into the polls on Election Day are voting that day. Those sitting at home may or may not vote. Poll-working can be the single best use of time this day—when and where it's legal and logistically smart given everything else you'll know. Working the polls, which you may have seen before, is when a candidate and/or their team stands at an appropriate (according to the law) distance from the actual polling location, often with campaign business cards or small literature to hand out to imminent voters.

It works. We've seen it. And we have had dozens of election bureaucrats yell at us . . . why? Because voters are leaving the candidate business cards on the voting machines. That's the greatest problem to have. The voter took the card out of their pocket while voting . . . what else could you ask for.

Now, those are the three sub-universes; let's next talk about how best to reach them.

GOTV METHODS (AND HOW TO DO THEM)

Doors

Prior to Election Day, doors are still the most effective way to move turnout because they are human, immediate, and hard to ignore. As we said earlier, there is a measurable turnout increase. Door-knocking is all about instructions and commitment. For example:

- "Here's where you vote."
- "Here's when."
- "Here's how easy it is."
- "What time are you going?"

If nobody answers, leave specific voting instructions (and make it readable in just a couple of bullet points or less).

Calls

Calls work best when they are live and repeated. Attempt to reach each identified supporter three times with live callers if you have the capacity. And on Election Day, prioritize cell phone numbers, if available. Higher-propensity senior citizen voters are likely to also have a home landline phone number they've shared; scan your voter information data for those individuals who have two different numbers.

Example Live Call Script

"Hi, is this [Name]? This is [Caller] with [Candidate]. Today is Election Day, and we're turning out our supporters. Polls are open [hours] at [location]. Can I count on your vote for [Candidate]?

Great—what time are you planning to go? Perfect. If anything comes up, can I text you the address so it's easy?"

Example Voicemail Script

"Hello, this is [Candidate Name]. I just wanted to call and personally thank you for your support. Without wonderful supporters like you, we stand no chance of defeating [opponent / threat]. Polls will be open [day] from [hours] at [location]. I look forward to seeing you there!"

At this point, we should address a common GOTV concern we hear from candidates and their teams.

What if people get offended?

Who cares. Are you bothering them? Sort of. Who cares. The goal is turnout. Some feelings will be hurt. Some people will snap. Who cares. Keep moving.

Texting

Text is great for "vote planning" because it carries crucial details with zero friction. Text all supporters the day before Election Day and again on Election Day. All means all. Even your already-voted universe sub-list. Anecdotally, we're familiar with early voters who later decided to drive a family member (or more) to the polls to vote for their preferred candidate even though they themselves, the early voter-supporter, had already mailed in their ballot.

If budget allows, expand your text game beyond supporters (but again, your best ROI is still your supporter universe).

***Pro Tip*:** Add a little peer pressure without sounding insane, e.g., "Turnout overall is up, so supporters are making all the difference today. Half the victory is just showing up." People do not want to participate if no one else is . . . your logical brain may be telling you their vote matters more in a low turnout election. Resist the urge. People want to be a part of something.

Mail

Mail is the least effective mobilization tool at the very end and a much better persuasion tool earlier. If you're doing mail as a GOTV add-on, keep it short, instructive, and paired with other contact. Consider including a small box that signals accountability like, for example, "Voters may be contacted about their voting record after the election."

That said, does it work on everyone? No. But does it nudge enough people who don't want to be "the person who didn't vote"? Yes. Yes, it does.

Working the Polls

If the law allows it, and the logistics make sense, this can be the best thing you do on Election Day. Again, people already walking in are going to be voting. We've even seen success from working the polls during early in-person voting.

Key variables here include:

- number of polling locations
- distance between them
- staffing
- opportunity cost
- the electioneering boundary (feet)

If your volunteers have done little else for you at this point, asking them to commit just one day of active poll working may be just the ask they are looking for.

How to Communicate at the Polls

This is pretty simple. You or your team will:

- smile
- say one line (e.g., "Vote [Candidate Name] for [Office] for [1 of 3 Top Issues].")
- hand the campaign business card or pocket-sized literature
- *not* hover, block, or argue
- *not* "make a scene"
- actively work the polling location and parking lot

As for the campaign literature to hand out at the polls, cards are perfect here because they're fast, clean, and non-dramatic. The only thing beyond breaking the law we do not want you to do, is stand still and lazily thank people for voting . . . they already voted. You are playing it safe and dumb. Whether for or against you, they have voted and their job is done. Talk to the people who are going to vote. Way more people have no idea who they are voting for than you would ever imagine. Trust us and remember we told you.

STICK TO THE GOTV PLAN (BECAUSE THE INTERNET WILL TRY TO RUIN YOU)

The closer you get to Election Day, the more temptations appear. As examples, perhaps your opponent says something dumb, an old rumor about some personal exploits of yours reemerges suspiciously, a news story that "will change everything" trends, and whatever the issues, everyone wants a response and right away. Chase the fire, and it will burn your volunteers and scatter your efforts into ash. Plans can change, but wildly chasing headlines in the last forty-eight hours is how campaigns self-sabotage.

Down to the end, your campaign is a turnout operation. That is all.

GOTV: ACTION STEPS (48 HOURS BEFORE THE ELECTION)

1. Niche down your supporter universe. Pull the latest list and split into already-voted / not-yet-voted / unknown.

2. Create vote plans. For every high-priority supporter, record when they'll vote, where, and how.

3. Run the final door sweep. Hit supporter-heavy turfs first; leave explicit voting instructions at every not-home.

4. Call every identified supporter three times. Live callers, short script, log dispositions every time.

5. Text supporters twice—day-before and on Election Day. Include polling location, hours, and a "reply YES when you've voted."

6. Assign poll-working posts if legal and logistical. Train on the electioneering boundary and the one-sentence message.

7. Narrow the already-voted list continuously. Update throughout early voting and Election Day so you stop wasting touches and reallocate energy.

8. Do nothing else. No new persuasion projects, no last-minute issue crusades, no social-media rabbit holes. Turnout only.

Doors win wars, yes. But GOTV guarantees the terms of your opponent's surrender—or turns the tide in their favor.

Pro Tip**:** Write the following down now so you don't forget during the intensity of crunch time.

Why is ACTIVELY working the polls effective?

How should you communicate with voters at the polls?

How far must I stay away from the polls in my state?

CHAPTER 20

YOUR POST-CAMPAIGN PLAN (EITHER WAY)

There's something you should know.
"For state legislative elections, men who lose are 38 percentage points less likely to run again, while women are 39 percentage points less likely . . . In nationwide mayoral races, losing causes men to be 20 percentage points less likely to run again, while women are 32 percentage points less likely to run again."[57]

A campaign—run and done correctly—creates something valuable, a functioning political asset. The yard signs may or may not be reusable, and the meet-the-candidate selfies may be timed out. But you still have a donor list that proved it will give; a volunteer list that proved it will work; an email list that proved it will respond; data that shows which doors opened, which scripts worked, which issues landed; and a network of relationships that didn't exist before you ran. All of this has value **whether you win or lose**. That said, in the event of a loss, it will be harder to resurrect all of it, especially if you're running later for the same office you missed out on previously.

We warned you before that you effectively have one shot as a beginner in politics. The one caveat that we will give you now is that **the more local your**

loss, the more mulligans you get. A mulligan being a do-over, borrowing the term from golf. If your first run is for, say, state senate or State Supreme Court, much less a national office and you flop . . . yeah . . . NGMI.

But if you lose your first primary for State Treasurer, then run for your local Township Trustee three years later, OK. You get a mulligan. The data will be less useful with it being statewide now that you're dialing into your local area, but data it is nonetheless. And all of it retains value whether you win or lose.

Even in the event of a loss and you don't run again, your campaign assets can help someone else pick up the flag and run with it. We both know candidates who've lost not once, not twice, but three times . . . only to transition their failed system into a successful PAC. Now these men are effective kingmakers, supporting the candidates most aligned with their previous Top 3 issues and granting them the highest odds to win it all.

Movements collapse when they refuse to build on prior wins and losses. They keep starting at zero. So your first post-campaign job, no matter the result, is to retain and organize:

- Donor lists (including amounts, frequency, and notes)
- Volunteer lists (including who actually showed up, repeatedly)
- Your email list (the whole thing—segmented if possible)
- Supporter universe (identified supporters, leaners, persuadables)
- Door/call outcomes (where you performed, where you didn't)
- Vendor logins and assets (graphics, templates, mail pieces, scripts, website)
- Press and endorsement contacts
- Polling place notes (what was effective, what wasn't)

You have something valuable. Retain it. Utilize it. For yourself. For an ally. For America.

TWO PLANS AT ONCE: PREPARE FOR WINNING AND PREPARE FOR LOSING

Back to the campaign itself now, and prior to Election Day on the timeline. A mature candidate plans for both outcomes simultaneously. Pessimistic? No.

Professional? Yes. Election night is chaotic. You do not want to invent your post-campaign behavior in the middle of emotion, adrenaline, and a room full of people watching you. So, you'll have two checklists:

1. What you do if you lose
2. What you do if you win

Let's dig in.

If You Lose: Be Gracious, Don't Complain

The first thing to remember is simple: **It's not all about you.** If you ran a credible campaign, dozens if not hundreds of people helped you along the way with it. They took a risk and bet on you. As you went, so did they. Losing is public. It stings. But how you carry yourself in defeat determines whether people will ever trust you again with leadership, influence, or a future run. Blaming the voters, your opponent, your supporters, or any combination is a surefire way to abandon any future prospects of support.

So be gracious in defeat. Use grace and your best judgment. Do not draw attention to yourself. Keep your head high and also your integrity. People remember sore losers. Don't be that guy.

Do not create drama, hint at conspiracies, pick fights online, or turn your loss into a personal brand.

Even if you think you were wronged, this is not the moment for theatrics. The moment for building power comes next; theatrics destroy your ability to build it. Once again, you are not Trump. Nobody is going to believe that the Deep State in Washington, DC, stole your village council election, population 2,477. Don't go there.

Should I call my opponent on election night? That is solely up to you. There is no law requiring it. This isn't a TV show. If your opponent ran a respectable race, maybe give them a quick congrats. If your opponent was a horrific mudslinging RINO, maybe hold off on that call so you don't get recorded saying something you shouldn't. But either way, don't endorse them tonight. Sleep on it and decide a road map for what you will do next. You get one chance to do this right, after all, everyone who voted for Hillary Clinton remembers when she sent out John Podesta on Election Night 2016 instead of addressing supporters herself.

Thank people anyway. Send thank-you notes. Make calls. Express gratitude. And, of course, consider running again. Some candidates lose once and vanish (some even flee the state). They treat the loss like a verdict on their worth. That's a mistake. You can run again. And if you ran a real campaign, you will not be starting over—you will be restarting from a higher step with a better list, better name ID, and better instincts. Some people will stay with you. Some won't. So what? Move on.

If You Win: Celebrate but Don't Lose the Plot

Winning creates its own dangers. You'll be tired, relieved, euphoric. People will want your time. Your phone will light up. Money you wish you had previously will miraculously start coming in. New organizations will call. Influencers will want selfies. Consultants will smell the money. And if you're not careful, you'll drift into a victory haze and neglect to prepare for the next fight—the one for your political soul, which begins the moment you win.

Now let's talk about victory details.

The Victory Party

A victory party is worth doing, but only in a way that supports, not undermines, the operation. It cannot be a distraction from GOTV prior to Election Day. So keep the planning simple, like a reserved back room at a restaurant or a backyard. This is a great task for a family member to handle. The best way to do this is to host a "watch party" at such a place, shortly after polls close. Then as results come in, you're in a position to celebrate with some champagne . . . or console yourself with a merlot.

Overall, a well-timed victory party will prove to be a memorable re-motivator for volunteers and staff under pressure in the home stretch. It gives them a finish line. It tells them their sacrifice mattered. In the event of a win, thank your people—personally. Do not become a stranger to the people who got you there. Remember Hillary Clinton 2016? Don't be her. Ever. Thank your volunteers, donors, supporters, family, and staff. No mass gestures and "everyone" gratitude. Each person, personally. A candidate who wins and immediately forgets the specific people who carried the candidacy will be alone the next time.

The "Thank-You" Statement

You should have three versions of this ready:

- A short press statement
- A longer thank-you email
- A crisp social post

And all three should do the same thing:

- express gratitude
- honor the voters
- unify rather than spike the football
- communicate seriousness about the job

Here's what to prepare for next.

Expect the Calls

If you win, the calls begin and will include:

- leadership
- interest groups
- outside orgs
- future endorsements
- "we'd love to meet" invitations

Some are legitimate. Many are attempts to shape you before you've even taken office. That's why you must decide now what you are and are not going to be. Remember the pledges you took. Don't be a sellout. Not yet. You just got here. Give it some time. Kidding.

REELECTIONS, PROMOTIONS, AND THE NEXT RACE

Every politician wants three things:

1. get elected
2. get reelected
3. get elected to higher office

If you're honest, that trajectory will likely tug on you, too, either by ambition, by opportunity, or by necessity when term limits hit. Remember, this is not inherently bad, it possesses all politicians.

Whether you win or lose, you are not "done." You are going to be restarting the system at some point. **If you lose**, you might restart with improved targeting, refined messaging, and a stronger base (if and only if you believe your Top 3 are worth fighting for at the ballot box and with your name on it). **If you win**, you'll restart because governing doesn't eliminate campaigning; it simply changes the incentives and the calendar.

Either way, you return to the beginning of this process—with better assets, higher stakes, and a clearer understanding of what actually works.

If you win, go back to Chapter 5 Position Yourself to Win and rinse-and-repeat this book, from there till here. If you lose, go back to Chapter 4 Analyze District Options and pick a different office with potentially better odds of victory (for you, personally).

POST-CAMPAIGN PLAN: ACTION STEPS (48 HOURS BEFORE THE ELECTION)

1. Pre-commit to your posture. Write down exactly how you will speak and behave if you win and if you lose. Don't improvise it on adrenaline.
2. Prepare your three thank-you messages now: press statement, email, and social post—two versions each (win/lose).
3. Create a "retain data" checklist and assign one person to own it the moment the campaign ends (donors, volunteers, emails, IDs, scripts, templates, login credentials).

> **If you win**: Plan a simple victory gathering that cannot distract from turnout work (back room or backyard) and make "personal thanks" part of the evening.

If you lose: Be gracious, go quiet, and go grateful. Thank people directly and privately before you say anything online.

4. Schedule a post-mortem meeting within seven days (win or lose): what worked, what didn't, and what gets rebuilt first for the next run or the next candidate.

In the event of victory, proceed to the next chapter. Otherwise, back to Chapter 4.

Part III

Aftermath, Integrity, and the Future of Elected MAGA

CHAPTER 21

HOW TO STAY PRINCIPLED (ONCE ELECTED)

> ***There's something you should know.***
> Registered lobbyists have as high as a 4:1 success rate over and above citizens in securing meetings with elected officials.[58]

Back in 2013, I attended a Real Nature of Politics lecture from Mike Rothfeld in Arlington, Virginia, and Mike cracked a naïve assumption I had.

"How many of you think that if we could just get politicians to read the Constitution, we'd save the republic?" Mike asked. "Raise your hand."

Many of us raised our hands, myself included. That's what I'd always believed. America's Founding Fathers were geniuses and had roughly 5,000 years of recorded history to draw from to design a system of representative government that painstakingly incentivizes what does work to maintain law and order and promote citizens' prosperity—and punishes or otherwise prohibits that which works against it all. Since I knew all this as basically a kid, having come up in the TEA Party era in which we all read our founding documents to educate our activism, I assumed an acting-out politician was simply ignorant and hasn't seen the light.

Mike looked out at us all. With a subtle headshake, he said the four little words every Southerner knows by heart.

"Well, bless your heart."

Translation not needed. You already know. Mike wasn't done.

"We don't have an issue with educating politicians. We have an issue with controlling the environment, the incentives, and what motivates politicians. And that's how you impact the system. Not by trying to educate politicians."

That's the game. And now that you've won, that game is going to be played on *you*.

HOW POLITICIANS LOSE PRINCIPLES (WITHOUT EVER CALLING IT COMPROMISE)

An optimistic idealist loses sight of what brought them political victory in small, socially rewarded decisions that feel harmless, such as:

- letting other people "help" us staff our office
- letting leadership set our calendar
- letting lobbyists define what's "reasonable"
- letting charming colleagues pull us into their orbit
- letting reelection become the central goal

We don't get conquered by argument and blackmail; we get our frog boiled. You've no doubt heard the metaphor that a frog will launch itself out of a container of hot water, but left in a lukewarm space with the heat slowly rising will remain—until it's boiled alive. Such is the fate of many statesmen and women's integrity.

The game of politics is now being played; we need our counters, or the environment will turn us into the very thing we swore to destroy.

THE FIRST TRAP: LETTING THE LEADER PICK YOUR STAFF

One of the fastest ways to get captured is also one of the most common, letting party leadership pick your staff. It will never be presented that way. It will sound like genuine helpfulness.

- "We have people who know how things work."
- "We'll get you someone experienced."
- "You don't want to hire the wrong person."
- "This person can help you navigate."

But staffing is not an HR detail; staff are your gatekeepers and sensemakers and truthtellers. They control what information reaches you, which meetings get scheduled, which relationships deepen, and what "normal" feels like inside the building.

If your staff answers to leadership—culturally or politically—more than they answer to you, we will boil.

THE SECOND TRAP: LETTING LOBBYISTS FRAME REALITY

Lobbyists rarely need to lie. Their real power is **framing**. And so they show up with:

- the "reasonable" compromise
- the "grown-up" perspective
- the "everybody agrees" pitch
- the "this won't matter" vote that somehow always matters

It must be left up to you. You alone must decide what you work on. You alone must be your primary source. You alone must choose to actively engage with aligned colleagues. Your principles are the signal; the lobbyists are the noise. It's all up to you.

THE THIRD TRAP: CHARM AND BELONGING

Some politicians will try to push and pressure you. Most will do it by charm. They'll flatter. Include you when they otherwise wouldn't. Call you "refreshing." Invite you to dinners. Offer you good committee talk. Give you the feeling we belong. Then, behold, comes the favor-back ask: "Just one vote."

But then another. And another. Another. Then you're told you're "effective" now, a "rising star," becoming a "real power player." Because you're "flexible." It's the lobbyists' frame game by another name. And it works.

So decide ahead of time—that you'd rather be respected for integrity than liked for compliance.

YOUR STRONGEST DEFENSE: IDENTIFY ALLIES EARLY AND STAY CONNECTED

If you want to stay principled, you cannot do it alone. The system isolates people it wants to soften. It labels aligned reformers as "difficult," "crazy," "not serious," or "unable to govern." Isolation is how conversion happens. So do the opposite:

- identify allies immediately
- coordinate
- share intel
- back each other up when pressure comes

When you're not alone, you're harder to turn. Work with aligned colleagues and support networks that share your commitments. Because principled legislators are always looking for other principled legislators. That's how you win and keep winning.

THE BIGGEST LONG-TERM THREAT: REELECTION AND "NEXT OFFICE UP"

Once you win, the reelection clock starts immediately. The conversations begin:

- "What's next?"
- "How do you move up?"
- "How do we protect your future?"
- "How do we keep you safe?"

Some of that is practical. But it becomes poisonous the moment you let the next race become the reason you're here. That's how principles become negotiable, now that you have power. Everything then gets reframed through fear:

- Will leadership punish me?
- Will donors get mad?
- Will the press attack?
- Will this cost committee assignments?

Keep the hierarchy straight. You are here to serve the mission. Reelection is a consequence of serving it well, not the purpose of the job.

STAY PRINCIPLED: ACTION STEPS

1. Write your non-negotiables now (three to seven lines) and keep them visible. Don't redefine yourself under political pressure.

2. Hire staff deliberately and refuse any arrangement where leadership effectively installs your gatekeepers.

3. Build your ally map in week one. Identify aligned legislators, meet early, and coordinate so you're not operating alone.

4. Set meeting rules for lobbyists and power brokers. Never let them set the agenda; always require independent verification before you support anything.

5. Lock calendar boundaries. Reserve time for constituents and mission work, cap "access" meetings, and don't let the building consume your week.

6. Treat reelection talk as background noise until you've governed with integrity. Don't trade principles today for a promise about tomorrow.

Action step number three is, in our view, the one that enables you to complete all others with relative ease. Because if you've gotten this far, you might go further. But go together, and you surely will.

Running a campaign is a lot. Balancing work, family, church, and the rest of life with a campaign is tough. But you need to be tough. There is no perfect campaign. It's an art, not a science; with this book, we've given you a brush-stroke tutorial. Your specific situation is now the canvas, and you'll need supplies in the form of donor and volunteer resources (and more). But now you know what to do. As American master Bob Ross advised, reframe any mistakes as happy accidents. Useful lessons. Powerful insights. Don't let what goes down get you down. Execute on the important work—paint the damn canvas—and you will get the votes you need to get a picture-perfect win. It doesn't matter if you win by ten votes or 10,000; a win is a win.

Run Right; win Right.

CHAPTER 22

MAKE ELECTIONS GREAT AGAIN (A FEW VERY IMPORTANT WORDS ON ELECTION INTEGRITY REFORM)

There's something you should know.

In 2020, Joe Biden is said to have received approximately 37.7 million votes total from the fourteen states (and Washington, DC) that did not require any form of identification for in-person voting.[59]

Every campaign we've discussed in this book—from building your voter universe to working your targeted list—assumes something basic: the rules are knowable, the ballots are countable, and the system is credible enough that persuading and turning out real humans still matters.

Unfortunately, confidence in elections has become its own battlefield. And whether you're running in a deep-red rural district or a deep-blue metro seat with hope and data to back it up that you have a real shot at change, there are reforms we can support—measured, mainstream, and broadly popular—that make it easier to vote once and harder to game the system (or claim it was gamed).

VOTER ID: A NATIONAL BASELINE, NOT A PARTISAN PATCHWORK

Right now, voter ID policy is a state-by-state collage. Some states require strict photo ID. Others ask for identification but offer alternatives (like signing an affidavit) if you don't have it. Others don't request ID documents at the polls at all. Americans can live under totally different confidence standards depending on their ZIP code. That's why the solution we advise isn't "red-state rules versus blue-state rules." It's a national baseline which means **voter ID required for in-person voting, no exceptions.** You need an ID to drink and to drive (not at the same time). You need an ID to vote; this is only fair.

THE NEW ENGLAND EFFECT: REPRESENTATION LOOKS "OFF" BECAUSE IT IS

In the 2024 presidential election, the Republican ticket's share across the six New England states totaled to about 40 percent (with state GOP shares ranging roughly from the low 30s to the high 40s).[60] Yet, at the same time, New England currently has **zero** Republicans in the U.S. House delegation—Massachusetts, Connecticut, Rhode Island, Vermont, Maine, and New Hampshire are all represented in the House by Democrats.

Millions of voters look up and feel like their preferences never translate into representation. If we want a stable republic, we want fewer situations where big minorities feel permanently locked out—even when the outcomes were gerrymanderingly legitimate.

OK, so then what? Well, the problem doesn't require us to reinvent the voting system with something like ranked-choice voting (RCV). From our perspective, RCV is the wrong fix anyway. It adds complexity for normal voters, makes outcomes feel less intuitive (e.g., *Wait, how did my first choice lose but my ballot helped elect someone else?*), and can reduce confidence because the counting and transfers are harder to explain in a sentence. We generally prefer election rules that are simple, transparent, and easy to audit—where the public can understand the process without needing a tutorial.

So instead of changing how people vote, our suggested approach is to change what *we* control, which actually drives whether votes translate into seats, like district lines, candidate fit, and year-round organization. Let's dig into these three now.

First, let's collectively push for districting rules that emphasize compactness and real communities of interest, so maps are less likely to "pack" one side into a few districts and dilute it everywhere else. Now, that doesn't guarantee Republicans seats in say, New Hampshire, but it can create more genuinely competitive districts where a real campaign can win.

Second, an organized GOP can recruit candidates who fit the region. New England is full of independents and ticket-splitters who respond to competence, local credibility, fiscal seriousness, and cultural restraint more than national drama. Here, the candidate matters more there than in a base-driven red district where the right letter behind your name all but guarantees a win in the general.

Third, we can run an always-on ground game (not a six-week sprint) that steadily identifies supporters, builds relationships, and turns a consistent minority into actual majorities in specific winnable places over multiple cycles. In other words . . . send this book to every Republican you know in those six states who want things to be different. No taxation without representation; no representation without *Run Right*.

NO MORE BLACK BOX: PAPER BALLOTS AND REAL AUDITS

No vote-counting system should require blind trust in software. The clean, defensible standard is thus twofold:

- **Voter-verifiable paper ballots** as the ballot of record (hand-marked wherever possible, with accessible options for voters with disabilities).
- **Routine post-election audits**, ideally risk-limiting audits, which are widely described as the gold standard because they use statistical methods and hand-counted samples of paper ballots to confirm outcomes.

No, this is not us being "anti-tech" luddites. Optical scanners can still count paper ballots quickly. But the point is that when there's a dispute—real or manufactured—the paper is the truth. Let adults settle our differences with real, physical evidence and not conspiracies.

THE HARD PART: GETTING IT DONE (AKA, NUKE THE FILIBUSTER)

If we're serious about a national baseline for ID, paper ballots, and meaningful audits, we have to face the legislative reality. Big election reforms usually die in the U.S. Senate. That's why some Republicans—including our president, Donald J. Trump—have argued the Senate should stop letting the filibuster function as a permanent veto on major priorities (while Senate leadership has often defended keeping it).

We can debate the wisdom of ending the filibuster; yes, whatever you do today can be used against you tomorrow. But if we keep living under a system where federal election standards are impossible to pass, then we're choosing permanent patchwork and permanent distrust.

In closing . . .

Make voting simple. Make cheating hard. Make counting provable. Make the rules uniform enough that Americans stop feeling like the process depends on which party runs their state capitol. Make elections great again.

CHAPTER 23

KEEP AMERICA GREAT FOREVER (AND THE VISION TO WIN IN THE POST-TRUMP ERA)

There's something you should know.

As of 2025, 71 percent of Republican voters identify more with President Donald Trump and MAGA broadly speaking than with the GOP itself.[61] Among the young, Generation Z Republicans are "much more likely than older generations . . . to desire an increased government role in solving problems."[62] Meanwhile, three in ten previous Trump voters overall want a president who is "willing to break rules and laws."[63]

The future of the Right is not conservative-libertarian; it's America First.

We both own *Trump 2028* hats, and these hats, in turn, own the libs. How serious are we? Not at all. Obviously. The forty-seventh U.S. presidency officially ends on January 20, 2029.

The reason these hats in particular have a lingering residence amid Trump's presidency—as we wrote this chapter in December 2025—is predictive nostalgia. We're already beginning to reflect fondly on that which has not yet ended but we recognize inevitably will. *Trump 2028*.

Because what happens next? What is *Make America Great Again* without Trump? What will MAGA do beginning in '29? What about the MAGA coalition that includes MAHA (*Make America Healthy Again*) among numerous other parallel Right- and center-Right-wing groups, organizations, and coalitions?

We gaze into our crystal ball and see that the post-Trump era will tempt us into believing one of two comforting lies.

THE TWO LIES: AFTER TRUMP

The **first** lie is that everything depends on one man—so that when he's gone from the stage, the mission goes with him. The **second** lie is the opposite, that we never needed a leader at all—so we can go back to purity, commentary, and "being Right" while the other side keeps taking power. Both lies end the same way—we lose.

Keeping America great forever means building a movement that outlives any single election, any single personality, and any single news cycle. It means we stop acting like politics is a presidential hobby every four years and start treating it like what it is, a permanent contest for power, waged locally, statewide, and federally. Every cycle. Every day. And to do that, we have to hold two ideas at once without flinching. As Jack Posobiec puts it:

> For too long, conservatives have cared only about principles but not about power. When you have power but no principles, you are a tyrant. When you have principles but no power you are delusional.[64]

Neither extreme is acceptable if we're serious about governing. And we are. But the Left has consistently mastered winning power first, then hashing out internal differences later. We can moralize about that—or we can learn from the tactic without surrendering our values. The only way to preserve liberty is to be strong enough to defend it.

So, how do we keep the cause alive and winning after Trump? We see leading indicators already—building aligned candidates, protecting them once elected, replacing those who sabotage the mission, and rejecting the grifters who feed on movements like parasites. Let's dig into these and more, starting with a very special tribute.

CHARLIE KIRK: A DREAM, A SPINE, AND THE COST OF BUILDING TO WIN

Charlie Kirk started Turning Point USA in 2012 when he was just eighteen years old. There was no dynasty or inherited machine, just a conviction and the willingness to act. The man built a pipeline that trained and organized young conservatives at scale, which is exactly the kind of permanent infrastructure the Right has historically lacked.

He paid a price for choosing visibility and confrontation over comfort. After his assassination on September 10, 2025, even political opponents acknowledged how important to America he truly was, is, and forever shall be.

There is a sobering lesson from his life: If and when we the Right build real power to enforce our principles, the resistance will be real. Courage is the prerequisite. Death may be the price.

The living legacy that is Turning Point Action, Turning Point's sister political organization group, already shows us what this courage is all for—to build a system to win long term.

FROM CAUSE TO SYSTEM

A movement that depends on a single national figure is not a movement. It's a mood. Moods pass laws. The next one gets them undone. We don't want that. Lasting power, instead, requires a system. Such as:

- candidates who are recruited on purpose, not discovered by accident
- donors who give consistently, not emotionally
- volunteers who work in off-years, not just crisis years
- elected officials who remain aligned after they get the title

The Left has treated politics like an always-on operation for decades—local boards, prosecutors, school committees, state houses, federal seats, agencies, nonprofits, media, and culture. They move as a coalition to win power, then they fight internally once the power is secured.

We don't have to imitate their ideology to imitate their effectiveness. We do, however, have to stop treating power like it's somehow "beneath" us.

ALIGNED, YES; PERFECT, NO

In the real world, we will never build a majority out of perfectly matching America First clones. That's fantasy. What we need is something more practical: **reliability**. Aligned means that when it's hard—such as when leadership pressures, when donors threaten, when media attacks, when lobbyists dangle favors—our people still vote and act in the direction of the mission. So we should define alignment as **behavior** we can actually observe. Ask these loyalty questions of any of our rising leaders and future leaders:

- Do they hire staff who share the agenda—or staff who share the building?
- Do they show up for the tough procedural fights—or hide behind speeches?
- Do they vote with the coalition when it matters—or disappear at the moment of truth?
- Do they build constituents and volunteers—or build personal brand?

The post-Trump era will be won by people who are boring in the best way. That means to be consistent, disciplined, and hard to move. As Posobiec always says, "Stay frosty." If you have ice in your veins, you take the reins.

HUNTING RINOS (WITHOUT CIRCULAR FIRING SQUADS)

We all know the RINO type—the elected Republican who is neutral to the cause at best, quietly opposed at worst. The person who enjoys the *R* next to her name but treats the agenda as an embarrassment to manage.

But it's a balance. If we make a living RINO-hunting, we'll be leaderless, organizationless, and winless. But if we ignore sabotage from within—or worse, open collaboration with the enemy—we end up the same way. So we must go forward with wisdom. Here's how.

Judge by Receipts, Not Rumors

No guilt by association. No "I heard." No personality feuds dressed up as principle. We track:

- votes
- committee behavior
- procedural moves
- staffing choices
- coalition commitments

That is all.

Prioritize Strategically

Not every betrayal deserves a crusade. We conserve ammunition for the seats that matter and the fights that shape the rules. We need say no more on this. That's how much this hurts. Tough.

Use Lawful Replacement Mechanisms

Remember pleasure versus pain in politician persuasion? If the latter fails to move a RINO, we know what we need to do. Which will be:

- recruit challengers
- fund them
- train them and win primaries

This is not vengeance. Rather, it's maintenance. Movements decay when they tolerate internal obstruction indefinitely. No hard feelings.

REJECTING GRIFTERS: THE PEOPLE WHO FEED ON OUR FRUSTRATION

Another problem facing the present and future of the American Right is the "grifter," who may or may not be an elected individual but nonetheless establishes themselves as an influencer. Every movement attracts parasites—people who aren't here to win, govern, or build. They're here to extract attention, money, and status. This is what they do. And in the post-Trump era, grifters will try to derail us in predictable ways. You will know the kind:

- Late arrivals who show up when it's profitable and disappear when it's costly.

- Engagement-bait merchants who keep us permanently angry because anger is monetizable.
- Gatekeepers who weaponize "No True Scotsman" purity tests to fracture coalitions for clout.
- Factional hijackers who demand the movement serve a narrow identity, brand, or personal obsession above the mission.
- Professional doomers who sell "blackpill" despair as wisdom because hopeless people are easier to control and easier to harvest.

Is the new, powerful voice legitimate? Is she building power locally and supporting candidates in tight but winnable races where it counts? Or is he selling commentary about why nothing matters, voting never changes anything, and we should have voted for Kamala?

We don't have time to subsidize demoralization. Forever requires builders, not spectators.

BLACKPILLMAIL: WHY WE MUST BE RUTHLESSLY TRANSPARENT

If the post-Trump MAGA coalition can be compromised, we will be. And if we already have such a compromise buried in our past—maybe something we're hiding, something we're still tangled in perhaps—then someone else will eventually pull that string at the worst possible time.

Call it blackmail. Call it opposition research. Call it destruction. We're calling it **blackpillmail**, because that's what it creates—demoralization, disgust, division, and despair. Exactly the emotions that fracture a coalition. And it's coming for MAGA.

It won't even have to be illegal or illicit behavior. It just has to be shameful, hypocritical, or disqualifying to the voters we need. So our rule in the post-Trump era is this: **If you're hiding something, you're not ready to lead anything.**

Ruthless transparency, internal clarity, and strategic preemption. Trusted allies know our vulnerabilities before the enemy does, we don't live double lives, we don't preach what we privately reject, and we don't put the movement at risk because we're afraid of consequences.

When voters discover hypocrisy, they don't lose trust in the candidate *and* in the cause. With Trump off the ballot in all future presidential elections, each of us will rise and fall by our own merits in support of the cause. It's going to get dicey. But let's leave the dicing to our side.

THE BENCH: HOW WE WIN FOREVER (NOT JUST TWICE)

If we want a post-Trump era that wins, we need a pipeline—local to state to federal—running continuously. The Left understands this. That's why they rarely "start" a movement in a presidential year. They grow it in the quiet years. Consider how . . .

- School boards and city councils shape culture and budgets.
- County offices shape enforcement, administration, and local institutions.
- State legislatures shape election law, redistricting, taxes, and the policy engine.
- Congress shapes national policy—but it's downstream of everything above it.

So our standard must change. We must not wonder, *Who's our next presidential savior?* But rather, *How many candidates are we recruiting this quarter?*

Forever is a bench. Forever is a farm system. Depth. Understand this and win.

THE VISION: PRINCIPLES, POWER, PERMANENT VICTORY

To tie it all together now, here's what we do post-Trump.

We build a coalition strong enough to win.

We protect it from sabotage and grift.

We demand integrity to prevent morale-killing and blackpilling.

We replace obstructionists strategically.

And we keep recruiting candidates every single year, not just during the four-year presidential cycle.

Because power without principles is tyranny; principles without power are delusions. We keep America great forever by building what lasts.

For Charlie.

APPENDIX A

CASE STUDIES AND WAR STORIES

This book works if you work this book. The eighteen steps to run Right and win are based on lessons learned and hypotheses proven out by more than 400 winning campaigns that we—specifically Cliff Maloney and Justin Greiss—have managed, consulted on, worked for, and ran the door-knocking, GOTV, and ground game initiatives. We have curated here for your reading edutainment a collection of select campaigns from local, state, and federal races to give you a sense of what happens when you follow the playbook. Most are written from Cliff's first-person perspective (i.e., *I*, *me*, *mine*, etc.); some include Justin Greiss' perspective (i.e., *we*, *us*, *our*). Some of these will read like short anecdotes (because they are) while others will be fuller case studies in the classic sense of a rundown of what worked, why it worked, and how you can do the same. Enjoy.

RANDSLIDE 2016: DOORS WIN WARS

For Republican Senator Rand Paul's 2016 Senate race, I was coming off what felt like my big break. Earlier that cycle, I served as the National Youth Director of "Rand for President." We launched "Students for Rand" and formed 507 nationwide campus chapters. We were the only Republican campaign that was actually—really—targeting young people. When Senator Paul dropped out of the presidential race, I began working for a grassroots organization in support of liberty-aligned candidates (such as Senator Paul, and my eventual partner at Citizens Alliance, Justin Greiss, went to work directly on Paul's Senate reelection campaign. And *that* race taught us a few things fast. The greatest takeaway was this: Democrats and Republicans spend money on all the same categories—TV, radio, mail, digital, texting. Both sides have volunteers. But the one difference we kept seeing, over and over, was that Democrats pay for door-knockers. And for us, that was a genuine epiphany. We built a volunteer program called "Operation Randslide."

Looking back, the numbers still stick out. We had more than one hundred people come out for a week. And it wasn't just one kind of activity; they were knocking doors and making calls. That was the first time we ran something that felt large-scale, and it shaped how I thought about field operations from that point forward.

WESLEY MORGAN'S SIX, SIX-WEEK DOOR-KNOCKERS

Wesley Morgan ran for the Kentucky statehouse in 2016 in what was a Democratic-leaning district. We sent six people to the district for six weeks. And we flipped it by only seventy-six votes . . . beating the incumbent Democrat in a district that had not elected a Republican ever.[65] That same night, the Kentucky statehouse flipped from Democrat to Republican for the foreseeable future.

We flipped the seat by ten points when you compare the identical 2014 versus 2016 match up.

The key to Morgan's victory was unmistakable—doors win wars. We'd put six paid people on the ground for six weeks and we were able to flip the district. And there was another dynamic, too—it wasn't just door-knocker-driven turnout. We were pulling blue-collar Democrats to vote Republican during the Trump realignment. This is why I advised understanding your district and what's happening up-ballot and down-ballot. It very well could be that one of your own Top 3 issues has nothing to do with local goings-on and everything to do with what's happening federally. If so, make that part of your campaign messaging. We did for Morgan, and it worked.

(MIS)ADVENTURES IN THE LIBERTARIAN PARTY

In 2019, a special election popped up in Rhode Island—one of those rare situations where the normal party math gets scrambled. There were four candidates: a former incumbent running as an independent, a progressive Democrat, a more moderate Democrat, and a Libertarian. No Republican.

So the first thing we did was the basic district analysis question: What do Republicans typically get in that area?

The answer was consistent—about 35 percent in presidential races, U.S. Senate races, Congress, and even the overlapping state House district. And the math was obvious: If you can pull something like 35 percent in a one-round "jungle-style" special election, with the Democrats splitting the vote in different lanes, there's at least a plausible path to winning. No runoff. No second round. Everybody on one ballot. It's rare, but it happens.

So we sent a small team. The district was so small we were knocking every Republican-leaning and independent-leaning door—some of them twice in the same day, morning and afternoon. We were doing the work.

And then we saw something that was honestly shocking. The candidate was handing out reusable grocery bags outside a store instead of knocking doors and talking to voters. It was like watching someone refuse the easiest version of campaigning you'll ever get. In a district that small, a candidate can talk to nearly everyone multiple times. But instead, he's doing an untargeted, symbolic gimmick.

And now this is the part that says more about the Libertarian party than any campaign memo ever could. When the race first popped up, we called the Libertarian party headquarters in D.C. They have a small staff. We finally got someone on the phone and asked about the special election.

Their response was, "What election?" But that was the whole point, no? They exist to elect people. There was one winnable race in the entire country with a Libertarian on the ballot, and they didn't even know it was happening—despite it being public, on the ballot.

It got worse. This candidate, William Hunt, had just run the year before and done relatively well. They were bragging about him as one of their higher-performing candidates. He didn't win, but he pulled a surprisingly strong share against the Democrat who later left the seat. Then the special election comes—more winnable than the prior cycle—and the party doesn't even have situational awareness.

We did not win that race, but we performed far better than what you'd expect given the organizational negligence and the candidate behavior. That's the takeaway. It wasn't just "hard to win." It was an example of what happens when a political organization isn't built to win.

Now compare that to Marshall Burt in Wyoming in 2020. This one will jump off the page because it almost never happens. Burt was running in a district that voted nearly 90 percent for Donald Trump in 2016, against a Democrat incumbent. In a district like that, the theory is simple. If you can get Republicans to line up against the Democrat, it should be a straight shot. And it was—he wins and takes out the incumbent.

Wyoming matters here because it reinforces one of the core lessons in this book. The smaller the race, the less expensive it is, and the easier it is to knock doors and speak to a meaningful percentage of the electorate. You don't need to raise insane money if you can physically work the district. In a place like that, you can check the voter universe and realistically hit nearly all of it.

Marshall Burt won his election in 2020 becoming the highest elected Libertarian in America.

In his first session, right after taking office in early 2021, he voted for vaccine mandates—taking the position that businesses should be able to mandate vaccines if they want to, despite the pressure governments were putting on businesses. Even when the Libertarian party manages to win something, it often fails the very voters it needs because the ideological and institutional incentives aren't aligned with the coalition required to govern in a way that matches the movement's priorities.

Conclusion: if you want to be a Libertarian, you'd better hope it's a nonpartisan race. Our experience with this party was weak infrastructure and weak situational awareness, candidates who refuse the most effective tactics (doors), and officeholders who often don't act in alignment with the coalition that elected them. In partisan politics, non-mainstream baggage beyond the duopoly becomes a problem you don't need, and it costs you power you cannot afford to waste.

21,145 DOORS, DISTRICT 82, WIN BY 37

In 2018, there was a guy I'd known for a while—Jeff Shipley, a Ron Paul–style activist with a hardcore liberty bent. He was (and still is) extremely well-liked in his district, and he even survived an attempt to take him out through redistricting later on. I had donated to him years earlier, back in 2014. But in 2018, Jeff had been thinking about running and didn't file. Then something crazy happened—nobody filed against the Democrat incumbent by the primary deadline, meaning the Republicans had no primary at all—no candidate, period. The Democrat was going to win by default in a district that Trump had carried.

Jeff decided to do it anyway. He went through the process to petition his way onto the ballot. But the party's posture was basically, "We don't really like you. We think you're crazy. But we'd rather have a candidate on the ballot than no candidate at all." That tells you a lot. Contrast that strategic response with the Libertarians.

Anyway, we deployed heavily for Jeff. I ran the independent expenditure operation from September into October and through the first week of November. I put a team of seven on the ground, who subsequently knocked on roughly 21,145 doors. And Jeff Shipley pulled it off by a stupid-small margin; he defeated Democratic incumbent Phil Miller in the general election for Iowa House of Representatives District 82 on November 6th, 2018, by only thirty-seven votes.

As for takeaways, look for opportunities where the political parties fail because they are far from omnipotent. At the state level, especially, they often have way less staff and fewer resources than you think. This isn't always a smoke-filled room deciding who the next state rep is going to be. When you're dealing with hundreds of seats, sometimes it's just a guy working a spreadsheet and hoping for the best. (And for the record, Representative Shipley's district number changed after redistricting; he's in District 87 now.)

THE THREE JOBS OF STEWART JONES

Many of my victories have been in what are called "pivot counties"—counties Obama won and then Trump won—so they "pivoted" and became real battleground opportunities. Between that and the margins, a lot of our general elections have either been within five points or centered in these pivot-county environments.

We also have evidence of our progression in door numbers by year, which would make a really compelling graphic. We started out at something like a million doors, then it jumps to 2.5 million, and it keeps growing—almost exponentially from there.

Now, one of the best stories to illustrate why doors matter isn't purely anecdotal; it's backed by post-election polling data. In 2019, we wanted to make sure we weren't just knocking doors for the sake of knocking doors. We already knew turnout operations were effective, but we wanted to run our own tests—our own GOTV-style validation so we could point to proof, not just instinct.

One of the two major tests we ran that year was basically a qualitative test. There was a special election in South Carolina for a righteous man—Stewart Jones—who was known to me and my team through solid leaders in the state. He was running in April. We were very focused because there weren't many other races going on yet in 2019.

We deployed a team, and we avoided a runoff, thereby winning the primary election outright, by just thirty-nine votes. It was a tiny turnout. In a special election, you're not only persuading people who to vote for, but you also have to educate voters on when the election even is. Everybody knows "first week of November" in a presidential year or even roughly in a midterm, but a random special election is different. Mobilization becomes part of the persuasion problem.

At the end of it, we did a post-election poll. We asked voters how they made their determination on who to vote for, and what methods of contact influenced them. Far and away, the top two reasons were these:

1. Either they knew the candidate personally or the candidate knocked on their door.
2. Someone who was not the candidate knocked on their door—meaning our team.

Everything else—digital ads, TV, radio, and the rest—added up to just 10 percent. The door-related categories were in the 40s and when you make it a pie chart, it pops off the page. All of the other spending, all of the other stuff, only accounted for about 10 percent. Almost everything else came down to the candidate meeting them or knocking their door, or our team knocking their door.

That's why, when we coach candidates, we often say the candidate's job is threefold:

1. Raise money—because you have to pay for door-knockers, materials, branding, the website, the lead flow, all of it.
2. Work the district—chicken dinners, city council meetings, whatever is appropriate, being active in the community.
3. Knock doors yourself as the candidate—when that time comes. People think they need to raise tons of money to run TV ads and do all the usual stuff. But for statehouse, a lot of the time, it doesn't matter nearly as much as people assume—because you can win by putting in the shoe leather. You're trading time for dollars and knocking a ton of doors.

Now, you can only get away with that in places where the numbers are small enough that you can actually work the whole universe. In states where districts are larger—like Texas—maybe you can't pull that off, and you're going to have to run a much more expensive race to compete with your opponent. That's why, "How much money do you need to raise?" isn't really answerable in the specific, only in the abstract. You have to be able to compete with what your opponent is doing.

Door-knocking won't magically win every race regardless of circumstance. But in small districts where nobody is raising massive money and TV doesn't even make sense, you can win by knocking doors.

PA IS THE PLAY: HOW WE GOT OUR REPUBLIC BACK

In 2021 when I launched Citizens Alliance, my focus was to get back to the original idea: take over one state with liberty policies—prove it works—then let that success force the rest of the country to ask, "Why aren't we doing it like that?" When people ask me what it is that I do, I usually describe it as two projects I'm committed to.

The first is building what I call a Liberty State. The goal is simple and measurable—I want 25 percent of a statehouse, 25 percent of a state senate, and then the governorship. Those are the checkmarks. If we can get all three in one state, I believe we'll be able to pass serious America First and liberty-aligned policies that improve quality of life, attract businesses, and create a visible model other states can't ignore. Right now, New Hampshire and Idaho are my top two states for reaching those goals, and I'm seeing real progress in both. A lot of it isn't glamorous, and people don't pay attention to state-level policy the way they should.

The second is building a "Red Wall." One state that does have national attention is Pennsylvania, where we are dedicated to building a Red Wall for America First Republicans. PA in 2024 became the proving ground for that.

Charlie Kirk and Tyler Bowyer strongly encouraged me that if I was going to do Pennsylvania the right way, I needed to run a full ballot-chase program—something I had never done at that scale. I'd always done door-to-door advocacy, persuasion, and turnout. But I hadn't built a true chase operation.

The reason was simple: the rules now allow fifty days of mail voting in Pennsylvania, compared to the single Election Day I grew up with. That's not some minor tweak. It changes the battlefield. If voting stretches across nearly two months, then turnout can't be a one-day push. It has to become a process. So instead of Election Day . . . we now refer to the process as "Election Season."

A lot of people think campaigns are mainly about winning the "middle"—getting independents in a swing state to break your way, or carving out some share of this or that demographic vote. Sure. Messaging and coalitions matter. You saw that with the coalition Donald Trump built—everything from Robert F. Kennedy Jr.'s MAHA to the Tulsi Gabbard anti-war types and the rest. But my job—especially as an outside group—was turnout. In a swing state, if Democrats turn out at 75 percent and your people turn out at 78 percent, that margin can decide the entire election.

Then 2020 hit, and the mail-voting rules exploded. Previously, in Pennsylvania at least, voting by mail had been limited—often used by the military, required a request, and was a small share of total votes. In 2020, everything got liberalized. Ballots everywhere. Chaos. I don't need to litigate every detail of that here. But I do need to say the practical consequence: Republicans got crushed in the mail vote, and late-arriving mail ballots became a huge part of why results appeared to "flip" after Election Day.

What shocked me even more was that it wasn't just 2020. In 2021,

Republicans failed by mail again. 2022, again. 2023, somehow it got worse. Republicans' mail-vote share didn't improve—it kept sliding in the wrong direction. The system wasn't self-correcting. The "grownups in the smoke-filled room" were not solving it. So by 2024, it was time to get serious and build an actual plan—because the party either wasn't concerned about it or didn't understand it. To boot, we had a low-propensity voter problem.

When I talk about low-propensity voters, people imagine someone who doesn't know who they support. That's not what I mean. These are often people who are 95 percent likely to vote Trump—registered Republican, consistent in preferences—but they're inconsistent in behavior. They intend to vote . . . yet missed elections in the past. They're what you might call couch-potato voters: not dumb, not undecided—just not reliable.

What do you do? You make voting as easy as possible. That said, I don't advocate mail voting. I wish it didn't exist. I wish I didn't have to compete on that battlefield. But while the rules are the rules, I have to compete there until I can elect enough people to change the rules back to what they should be—ideally a tighter, simpler window of one-day voting with paper ballots.

Pennsylvania made the choice even sharper because it doesn't have "normal" early voting in the way many other states do. In practice, you have two options—vote by mail up to fifty days out, or vote on Election Day. And when one side votes early and the other side insists on Election Day only, you introduce risk on purpose.

Arizona in 2022 is a cautionary example of what happens when Republicans overwhelmingly vote on Election Day: Polling places get switched, lines stretch two hours, parking becomes impossible, polling places run out of ballots, people walk away. In a tight statewide race, that can be the margin.

Going into 2024, I built the program around a clear sequence that had to happen in real time. But, before you can chase anything, you have to know who matters. I built a targeted universe—people worth talking to, mapped down to household level. In Pennsylvania, we identified roughly a million low-propensity Republican or lean-Trump voters.

Then our door teams went to the voters' houses to educate them that voting by mail was an option, that it was easy, and—critically—that Trump himself had given permission to do it. He'd said variations of "vote by any method possible" and "bank your vote early." I used that language deliberately.

We weren't trying to change minds about who to vote for; we were trying to change behavior about when and how to vote.

Remember . . . the people we are talking to are registered to vote and support Donald Trump . . . but they don't show up to vote.

If you bank your vote early, life can't steal Election Day from you. Car accident. Sick kid. You get sick. A family funeral out of town. Endless possibilities. A vote banked early can't be taken away. In Pennsylvania, vote-by-mail is a two-step process:

1. You have to request your ballot.
2. Then you have to fill it out and return it.

People don't always understand step one. If you don't request it, it won't show up.

Pennsylvania was especially workable because it's one of the states where you can request a ballot online. My program used a website that linked into the state system, with QR codes, and NFC key chains (tap to open the website) so a voter could complete it from a phone in under two minutes.

Our teams also carried paper request forms. A voter could fill out the paper and hand it back. Our team leaders would then turn forms in to the county for them—because ultimately the request has to reach the county office. Whether someone submitted online, mailed it, or handed it to us, the goal was the same—get the request in.

When ballots hit doorsteps, chase returns relentlessly. This is what we do. Once ballots go out—around that fifty-day mark, with county timing varying—I shifted from "request" to "return." And this is where the word chase becomes literal.

Our data team received daily updates from the state, ingested them into the data system, and I could see who had returned a ballot and who still had it sitting on the kitchen counter.

That matters because of the 2020 election lesson in Pennsylvania: Joe Biden won the state by 80,000 votes (allegedly), and 141,000 Republicans had requested a mail ballot and did not return it. That is a shocking number. Even a minimal chase—maybe even texts alone—could have plausibly changed the outcome. But nobody did it at scale.

So we did, and it became such a central talking point that other groups started using it too. I was flattered. They were sending mailers with our exact headline logic: "In 2020, 141,000 Republicans left their ballots sitting on their kitchen counter."

My operating principle was straightforward: annoy the voter into turning the ballot in until it's received and verified. And once it's verified, we stop contacting them. We don't waste resources. As blunt as it sounds, once someone returns their ballot and it's recorded, they're "dead to us" in the best way, meaning I can move on to the next person who still needs to act.

Let the door program begin.

When a paid door-knocker went out, they had two main things in hand:

1. A piece of literature with our general message—why voting by mail was a viable option, why it was OK, that Trump endorsed it, and why patriots should bank votes early
2. The vote-by-mail request form a voter could fill out and hand back immediately

At the door, I used a short script—four questions—recorded in a smartphone app and fed into our data system in real time. People memorized it. The key questions were about voting habit and willingness to request/return by mail, plus whether the interaction was positive, neutral, or negative.

If someone said, "Yes, I'll vote by mail—I'll be out of town," door-knockers marked it accordingly. Then we tracked whether the voter actually requested a mail ballot. If they didn't, we followed up—texting a simple reminder with the link, or returning to the door and offering the paper form again.

If they already had a ballot, the job got even easier: "Just a friendly reminder—turn it in." And I was honest about the upside. Once you turn it in, it's over. No more texts. No more door-knocks. You did your job.

If nobody was home, door-knockers left the literature on the door and left a request form for each target voter in the household—two forms for two targets, three for three, and so on. The app made it clear who those targets were.

There was also some practical tech—QR codes on the literature and a keychain that could tap a phone using near-field communication and pull up the website instantly.

One more operational note: because I ran this as a nonprofit, I had limits on the exact wording I could use. The literature was obviously patriotic in tone and intent, but legally neutral in wording. I have examples and visuals of all of this.

The logistics nobody thinks about are those that you have to, from legal policy to the people you train to do this stuff for and with you. Let's dig into that next.

To run a door and chase operation, I needed people—and I had to manage them like a real program.

We recruit in three main ways:

1. Recurring—We've been doing this for about ten years. People return.
2. Referrals—People who enjoyed it refer to others.
3. Influencers—*Charlie Kirk Show* appearances, viral social media posts, influencers like Jack Posobiec and Nick Freitas amplifying, and more.

2024 was transformational. I saw people show back up who'd worked with us in 2016 and 2017. They'd message saying they felt compelled to come back—take time off, quit jobs, whatever—because it felt like the most important election of their lifetime. And I think it was.

Once someone applies, our team does a thirty-minute interview. Part of that is setting expectations—how the program works, what the job actually is. We screen for competence and run quick checks, and we screen for ideology on the application while staying within legal requirements. But truthfully, we give most people a shot if they're motivated.

Then we book travel, fly them out, and have them picked up by a field director. Field directors are key. Each Airbnb has a field director or team leader in charge. Houses typically have five to ten people depending on size and location.

During the Pennsylvania Chase, we maintained a minimum of ten Airbnbs at all times. Teams might rotate monthly to hit new territory, but the baseline was constant.

Airbnbs matter because they create a team culture. After eight hours of work, people come home, have a beer, debate, play board games—whatever. Their free time is their free time, and the house becomes a camaraderie engine.

Our public work hours were typically 10:00 a.m. to 7:00 p.m. We start later because you reach more people after work. And yes, people ask, "Is anyone home during the day?" The answer is yes. Older people, people not in the workforce, work-from-home folks. The "take rate"—actually talking to someone at the door—averages about 25 percent, roughly one in four doors. In primaries it can be higher, closer to one in three.

Every morning, teams have a quick meeting: review results, set goals, make sure everyone has supplies. The supplies matter more than people think:

- literature (half sheet cardstock folded hot-dog style)
- the mail ballot request forms
- a double-sided clipboard (blank forms on one side, completed forms on the other)
- battery pack and charger (phone screen on all day)
- pens (never lose a vote because you didn't have a pen)
- poncho
- backpack and water

Then teams select neighborhoods in the app—think Google Maps with house icons. You click on a house, see who lives there and their basic info. You ring, then knock. If someone answers, you run the short script, then enter the result as you walk away so it's logged and trackable.

It's all fun and games and campaigning to win until your people get hit with distractions. That's what happened during the PA CHASE.

I had an Airbnb in Philadelphia where the host watched our team through a Ring doorbell camera. He seemed like an obvious Democrat and started reacting to our guys going out in MAGA hats. After a few days he escalated, inventing complaints—too many people, too loud, "BS" allegations. It became obvious he wanted us out. He filed a complaint with Airbnb.

We decided to move out because we didn't want our people living in a hostile environment. Airbnb refunded the unused days and closed the case like normal. Then a news article got published framing it as political bias and removal. We documented the condition of the house to show nothing was damaged—claims about broken doors and weird stuff were nonsense. After the article, Airbnb contacted Justin and refunded the money for the entire week we'd already used.

And then there are the weird voter interactions. Someone's cat goes missing, and one of my guys—maybe because he has a good heart—spends two hours helping look for the cat. On the other end of the spectrum, you run into crazy accusations: a woman accusing us of stealing her dog because she saw our literature on the door and assumed anything that happened that day must have been "the door-knocker."

I recall a separate time in Wyoming where a voter accused my field director there on a state-level race of smashing all her pumpkins on her porch. The candidate got "candidate brain" and worried about rumors. *What if it spreads that we're smashing pumpkins?* And I had to say the obvious—this is a straitlaced kid about to go into the army, doesn't even drink. You think he's kicking in pumpkins in the middle of the day and then knocking doors for six more hours?

Give your people the benefit of the doubt. Door-to-door work puts you in weird situations, and voters sometimes attach their unrelated chaos to whoever they happened to see.

We had our misadventures, but in PA, we knew how to play. And we were getting closer. Once you're inside the fifty-day window, the state releases data daily. That lets you compare requests and returns by party—Republicans versus Democrats. You don't know where independents break, but you can see the ratio and whether you're closing the gap.

My public goal for Pennsylvania was not to "win mail." It was to raise the Republican mail-vote share from where it had been—roughly 20 percent against Biden—to 33 percent against Harris.

Every day, the data team tracked requests and returns in a line-graph style dashboard. I knew we were close to being on track. Then on election night, it broke—Republicans hit 34.5 percent of the mail-vote share. The downstream impact was measurable: Trump received 139,324 net GOP mail-in votes he did not receive in 2020, and he won Pennsylvania by about 120,266 votes.

The celebration of Trump's victory brings me two key moments. First was the media gaslighting. I did an interview the morning of Election Day, and a clip played of someone on MSNBC essentially saying, "The Left is on the ground in Philadelphia, and nobody from Trump world is on the ground." Meanwhile, I had forty full-time people in Philly at that point. It was just Left-wing bullshitting. The only response that made sense was, in as many words, *Enough of the deception; let's look at the scoreboard tonight when the election is complete.*

Second was the moment I called the election on Charlie Kirk's livestream. That's when Erika Kirk came in and hugged Charlie, and Charlie began crying. I gave a brief monologue at that moment. That short clip went viral—hundreds of millions of views by some counts—and it became its own cultural artifact. You'll remember that from the Preface.

And we'll remember Charlie Kirk for pulling together teams of titans to make the 2024 U.S. presidential election the year we all ran Right.

JARRETT COLEMAN AND THE FEW DOZEN DOORS

Jarret Coleman represented an area Justin Greiss grew up in, so that race was personal from the start. One of the things you learn pretty quickly—if you ever want a weird, depressing rabbit hole—is to Google "politician" and "DUI." Politicians and local elected officials rack up DUIs at a rate that feels wildly out of proportion to the general population. It's wild.

One of those multiple DUI recipients (four to be exact) was Senator Pat Browne, elected to legislative office since 1995 and chairman of the extremely powerful Appropriations Committee.

What drew my attention to Jarrett Coleman wasn't gossip; it was COVID-19. He was on the school board, and he was excellent during that period. While too many people were going along to get along, he was fighting the mandate like masks on little kids, closed schools, all of it. He was willing to take heat for it, and he started building a real name for himself in the community as someone who would fight when it mattered.

So, Jarrett Coleman ran for state senate in 2022, and it was the kind of contest that proves how thin the margins can be even when more than 34,000 primary votes are cast. He won by just twenty-four votes. Just think about that. A state senate race. Tens of thousands of ballots. And the entire outcome swung on what amounts to a handful of people showing up—or not showing up.

That's the lesson. These races aren't always won by grand speeches, viral ads, or national narratives. They're often won—or lost—by the smallest, most controllable things, like who got contacted, who actually turned their vote in, and whether you were willing to do the unglamorous work long enough to move a close election over the line. But don't cry for Senator Browne. After his historic loss he was appointed by incoming Democratic Governor Josh Shapiro to serve as Pennsylvania Secretary of Revenue. And yes . . . I expect an audit of our organization soon.

NO SEAT IS SAFE (AND THAT'S A GOOD THING)

Wendy Fink beating Pennsylvania State Representative Stan Saylor was one of those moments that made the entire Capitol sit up straighter. Saylor was the House Appropriations chairman, which means he sat on one of the biggest levers of real power in Harrisburg—the budget. He'd been in the Pennsylvania House since the early 1990s, and by the time that primary hit, he was essentially a three-decade incumbent who most people assumed was untouchable. And then Wendy Fink beat him in the Republican primary of 2022.

What made that night feel even bigger is that it wasn't just the House. That same primary cycle, we also watched the Senate Appropriations chairman, Senator Pat Browne, get knocked off in his own Republican primary—another entrenched power center, another budgeting gatekeeper, another "this guy isn't going anywhere" type of incumbent. Browne had chaired Senate Appropriations for years and had spent decades in the legislature overall, and he still lost—by a razor-thin margin. If you are keeping track, both the House and Senate Appropriations chairmen went to an early political retirement that night.

When you beat the people who control the money—especially after they've been there forever—you're not just winning a seat. You're changing the incentive structure. You're sending a message that even the most "safe" leaders can be replaced by young, up-and-coming patriots if the ground game is real and the base is activated. Excellent.

IDAHO'S NIGHT OF RECKONING, 2022

In Idaho in 2022, something happened that almost never happens in state politics—the center of gravity shifted in a single night. It wasn't just that a few incumbents lost. It was that the people who normally don't lose—the ones in leadership, the ones with the titles and the institutional power—started going down, one after another. By the end of the night, you were looking at a cascade: seven state senators and four state house members, all leadership-aligned figures, defeated in their own primaries. Eleven. In one night. That kind of sweep is so rare it barely feels real when you're living through it.

The context mattered. It was the COVID-backlash election—voters were finally getting their first real chance to push back on the COVID-19 tyranny and the broader wokeness they'd watched creep into schools, institutions, and everyday life. People were hungry for someone authentic, someone who wasn't going to manage decline with polite speeches. They wanted fighters.

So how did we support candidates in that environment and actually convert that disgruntlement into wins?

You already know the answer—door-knocking. But almost nobody knocks doors in Idaho—because it's Idaho. It's hard. The primary is in May, and for much of the work there's still snow on the ground. It's a big state, with rough roads, bad weather. Door-knocking in Idaho is physically miserable, logistically complicated, and easy to talk yourself out of. Which is exactly why it works. The terrain itself creates a moat, and most campaigns never cross it.

We did.

That cycle, we knocked 65,763 doors. And because the districts are quite small, we were able to talk to an enormous share of Republican primary voters—effectively saturating the universes we were working. That matters more than people realize; it's not "we made contact." It's "we made enough contact to change outcomes."

The message timing helped too—Idaho is an early state. For a lot of voters, it felt like their first real chance to register "No" in a way that actually counts. People assume Idaho is ruby-red and therefore immune to cultural fights, but it has the same problems everywhere else: schools, bathrooms, mandates, and bureaucratic creep. Calling those things out, locally and specifically, moved voters.

Now, you don't win by parachuting in with national talking points and assuming you're smarter than local knowledge. We don't assume that. We talk to local people and learn what actually matters in that district. Some races turn on issues that will never appear on cable news. And Idaho is the perfect example. In parts of the state, water rights are a top issue. Mining and industry compete for water, and people know what that means. If water access gets restricted, property values collapse. And for most families, their house is their biggest asset. If you get run out of where you live, your life is over.

JAMIE WALSH AND THE FOUR-VOTE VICTORY

Our guy Jamie Walsh won by four votes in a primary election with 9,466 votes cast, which tells you everything you need to know about how thin the margins can get in state-level fights.

Walsh was running for state representative in Pennsylvania, and the whole thing dragged out because of the new rules. It wasn't a clean "election night, declare the winner, move on" situation. It dragged on for more than five months after Election Day before he was finally declared the winner.

Another key detail about that race is the incumbent. He was arrogant, nasty, and voting far Left—so far Left it was honestly unbelievable he was representing what was supposed to be a conservative district.

An additional noteworthy aspect of this race was the timing. Usually, people only start telling the story three months out, when the candidate is already "the candidate," and the district is already in election-season mode. We don't do it that way. We went in way before the election, before we even had our candidate, Jamie Walsh. We were already sending mailers and text messages that exposed the incumbent's voting record.

We do that often; we start creating a lane for a primary well before primary season. There's nothing politicians hate more than being held accountable for their actual voting record. During legislative season, they get to be down at the Capitol—making law, having cocktails, sitting in their offices, living the comfortable version of politics. During election season, they fight for their political lives.

And if you get to run against an incumbent, the real blessing is that you can go on offense. People hear that and think "negative campaigning," like scandals or personal smears. That's not what this is. This isn't "this guy's a scumbag" or personal gossip. It's much simpler and cleaner to tell voters what the incumbent actually voted for, and show how it's out of lockstep with what he campaigns on and out of lockstep with what the district believes.

That ties in to the very beginning of this book, with pain and pleasure in politics. At the state level, most candidates campaign for the last three to four months. At the congressional level, maybe the last six months. What we try to do is different—we try to never leave. We don't want to pull out of the field. We're trying to be on the ground knocking doors 365 days a year.

What we're knocking for can change. Sometimes we're educating voters about how bad an incumbent is. Sometimes we're defending a good incumbent who's about to be challenged. Sometimes it's pushing legislation and building support for it. But the constant is the infrastructure, the permanence.

That's the goal: A permanent infrastructure, strong enough to raise the negatives of the bad Republicans or the bad Democrats we're trying to remove, strong enough to reward the good ones, and strong enough to keep the pressure on long before "campaign season" even officially begins.

THE WINNING ONE-LINER OF TJ ROBERTS

TJ Roberts is one of my favorite stories because it shows what happens when you combine relentless field work with a single, unforgettable message.

We helped elect TJ when he was in his mere mid-twenties. He ran in a Republican primary in very conservative northern Kentucky against a former incumbent and absolutely obliterated him 76 to 24 percent. Yes, door-knocking was a huge part of it. But the most shocking part wasn't the doors. It was the discipline—we tied the entire race to one issue and refused to let go.

That incumbent Republican—again, in a deep-red primary—had once donated $500 to Hillary Rodham Clinton. And the campaign basically became: *This guy gave money to Hillary Clinto*n. That was it. Over and over and over again.

People inside campaigns get bored because they're surrounded by their own messaging. They read every mailer. They see every text. They know every line of the script. So they start thinking, *We need something fresh this week—let's switch to pro-life, let's switch to guns, let's switch to taxes.* But normal voters aren't consuming your content like you are. They're not seeing everything. They're not paying that much attention. Which means repetition is not a flaw—it's the strategy.

The old rule of thumb is seven times: people need to hear something repeatedly before it sticks. The question becomes: When a voter walks into the booth and looks at that state House race, what's the one thing you want in their mind?

Not, *TJ is great.*

Not, *TJ is conservative.*

Not, *TJ has good values.*

It's, *that guy donated $500 to Hillary Clinton.*

We even made polling-day yard signs that hammered it in plain English, something like, "Don't vote for Hillary Clinton's donor." And when you can get a district to remember one simple indictment like that at the exact moment they're marking a ballot, you can crush a former incumbent.

In your own election, try to find a wedge issue that cleanly separates you from the opponent, make it memorable, and hit it so many times that even low-information voters can't not remember it.

PERSUASION AND TURNOUT

In the appendix story of Stewart Jones, we outlined the power of persuasion by door-knocking. But the other benefit to door-knocking is increasing turnout. Giving voters a reason to care.

For the PA CHASE program we targeted low-propensity voters. In our post-election analysis, we looked at the turnout data of these voters. For those low-propensity voters we spoke to at their door, the voter turned out at a 7 percent higher rate than if we attempted to speak to the voter, but they were not home. 7 percent. That number flips elections. It changes the entire makeup of the electorate.

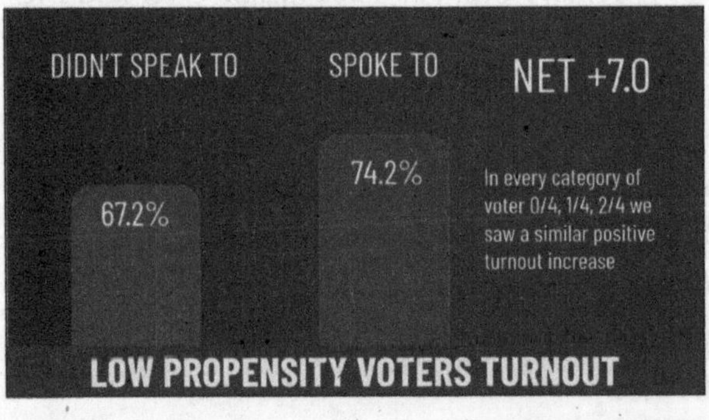

And it wasn't just the Trump 2024 election. We've been studying this.

Our friends at i360 have pegged door-knocking programs as leading to a net turnout increase of 1 percent–3 percent increase. But our programs (due to size and scale) have exceeded those averages.

In 2019, i360 ran our post-election numbers after knocking in six districts in the primary election. Our program increased overall turnout versus comparable competitive districts by 6.8 percent. But more impressively, by 11.6 percent amongst low-propensity voters. WE GAVE PEOPLE A REASON TO CARE. We talked to them. Explained the differences in the primary election candidates.

Similar results in 2019 in Virginia. This time analyzing rural turnout (the hardest doors to knock). By taking the time to visit rural homes we saw a 10.9 percent turnout increase among the primary electorate. No one knocks these folks. We often hear "you're the first person to knock my door." Winning every vote. People remember that.

And lastly, it's not just odd years. In the Missouri 2020 primary, we ran similar tests. We saw another increase in the entire electorate over comparable district and this time, even saw a 6.1 percent increase of high-propensity voters . . . again, talking to voters at their doorstep gives them a reason to care!

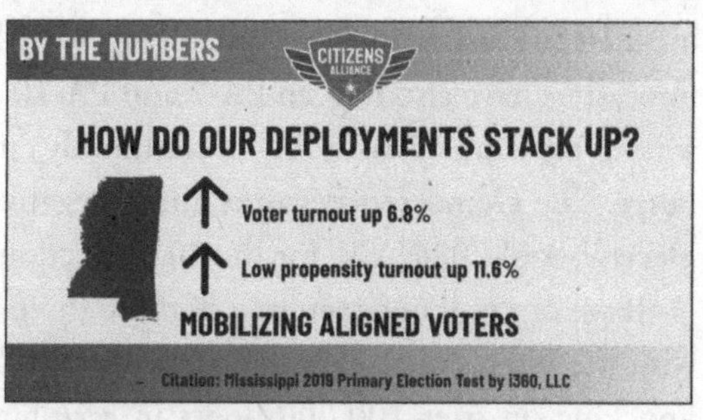

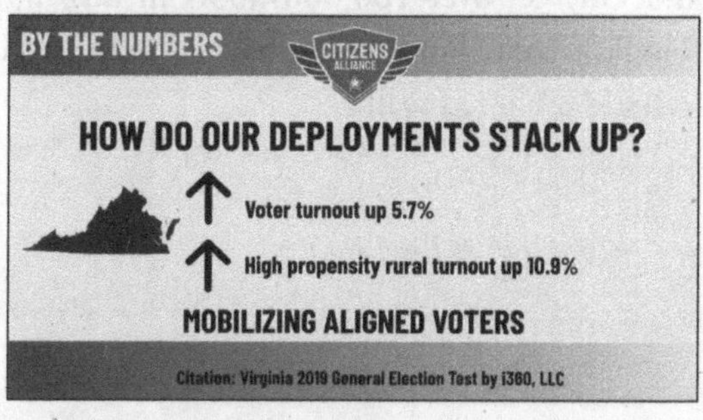

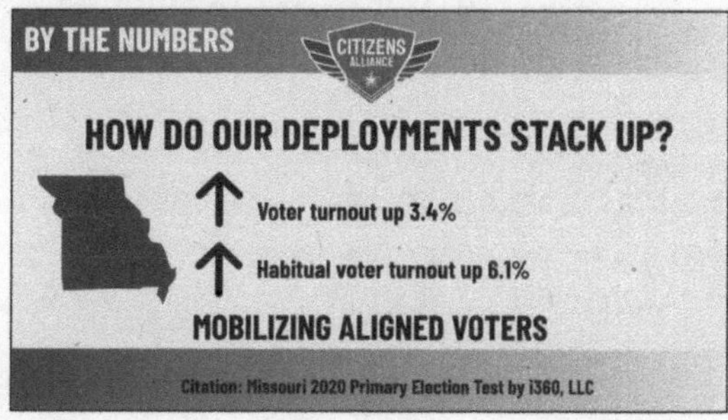

EXPECTATIONS AND PREDICTIONS FOR 2026

If you want to judge whether our work is real, don't judge it by the hype; judge it by what happens next.

In 2024, we helped flip

two congressional seats in Pennsylvania—PA-07 and PA-08—from Democrat to Republican. PA-10 also held, with Scott Perry winning reelection in a race that became increasingly competitive. That 2024 cycle marked yet another proof-of-concept in the election model this book teaches.

When people ask me what we're doing now, or what our "current battles" are, I point to the next scoreboard: Pennsylvania's 7th, 8th, and 10th U.S. House districts in 2026. As of this writing in December 2025, those are going to be the big races we're part of, and they're not going to be easy. Midterms often swing against the party holding the White House, and we should assume headwinds instead of excuses.

Those districts are three of the top Democrat targets nationally. We aren't guessing out of thin air—Democrats publicly put PA-07, PA-08, and PA-10 on their "Districts in Play" list (along with PA-01) for 2026. Nonpartisan forecasters have also flagged PA-7 and PA-10 as among the most competitive seats in the country, with PA-08 commonly rated in the "lean/tilt Republican" range. The Democrats began running negative TV ads against Scott Perry in December of 2024. Yes, for the 2026 elections.

If we can pull out even two of those three in 2026, it's a huge win. That's why the operational expectation is simple. We're preparing even now for knocking on over 100,000 doors in *each* target district. We may have our Republic back, but now we have to keep it. To defend it, we're going to need to build a big red wall.

APPENDIX B

18 STEPS TO WIN, SUMMARY

This appendix summarizes the core material of this book, Part II (Chapters 3 through 20), and eighteen steps we recommend you follow in the year leading up to your election.

Your 18-Step Plan to Win

Election date: ________________

Filing deadline: ________________

1. Decide You Will Run (and Why)

   a. Do this immediately after reading Part I, Chapters 1 and 2 and Part II, Chapter 3

2. Analyze District Options and Determine Where to Run

   a. Do this week

   b. Due date: ________________

3. Position Yourself to Win

   a. Due date: ________________

4. Determine Your Why and Refine Your Message

   a. 6 months before filing

   b. Due date: ________________

5. File to Run for Office

a. 12–6 months from election or when legal
b. Due date: ________________

6. Determine Your Budget

a. 12 months before election
b. Due date: ________________

7. Raise Money

a. 12 months before election or when legal
b. Start date: ________________
c. Deadline to raise budget: ________________

8. Have a Media Strategy

a. 6 months from election
b. Announcement press release submission date: ______________
c. Letters to the editor submission dates: ________________________

9. Gain Allies and Endorsements

a. Minimum: 6 months from election. Start now.
b. Deadline to find and contact 10 potential allies: ________________

10. Recruit Volunteers

a. 6 months from election
b. Due date: ________________

11. Design and Print Literature

a. 6 months from election
b. Due date: ________________
c. Amount of literature: ________________

12. Have Announcement and Door-Knocking Party

a. 6 months from election
b. Date: ________________

13. Build and Manage Your Team

a. 6 months from election
b. Start date: ________________

14. Purchase Data and Software for All Voters in District

a. 5 months from election
b. Due date: ________________

15. Create Your Target Universe

a. 5 months from election
b. Due date: ________________

16. Work Your Targeted List
    a. 5 months from election
    b. Start date: ________________
17. Get Out the Vote
    a. 48 hours before election
18. Have a Post-Campaign Plan
    a. 48 hours before election

APPENDIX C

THE RIGHT-WING ORGANIZER'S HANDBOOK: ORGANIZING PATRIOTS, POWER, CHANGE

Run Right is a Right-wing organizing handbook for a specific purpose—to empower American patriots to win local, state, and federal elections. That said, the original Left-wing organizing handbook by Dr. Marshall Ganz—*Organizing: People, Power, Change*—is **not** exclusive to elections. It's all-encompassing of sociopolitics and has been deployed not just to get a little-known, oddly named candidate into the White House—Barack Hussein Obama—but Ganz's work has also equipped homosexual community leaders and transvestite activists with the messaging frameworks, leadership principles, and step-by-step processes to form coalitions-of-the-fringes, agitate the citizenry, and force otherwise unpopular change upon all. Ironically, the *Organizing* handbook legacy is *anti*-democratic, where the motivated minority turn the will of the few into the law for all. And so when less than 5 percent of the country learns to run the playbook, they can govern the other 95 percent. That's power; the Right could use some, and not just politically but culturally.

Successes we've seen from the Right have of course included Turning Point USA on the college campus, Moms for Liberty within the public school system, and individuals like James O'Keefe and Robby Starbuck for corporate

America. But there are multiple fronts on which culture war is waged by the extreme Left against the normal-peopled Right and everyone else in between. **The seven culture-war battlegrounds are:**

- Organized **religion** (conservative faiths, specifically)
- The **family** (from traditional heterosexual marriage to multigenerational values)
- **Education** (pre-school through postgraduate)
- **Government** (local, state, federal, and the bureaucracies in between them all)
- **Media** (including the news business)
- The **arts** (and the entertainment industries more broadly)
- **Business** (including entrepreneurship, publicly traded companies, venture capital, and private equity)

As detailed in the *Unhumans* book by Jack Posobiec and Joshua Lisec, Cultural Marxists have engaged in both full-frontal assault and bitterly protracted siege warfare against all American institutions of the above. Many have fallen; many more may yet will. Unless we the people of the Right do something about it. Something legal. But something reciprocal. Something organized.

To this end, if you picked up this book to learn about Right-wing victory measures beyond four-year election cycles, this appendix is for you. What's to come next is a commentary-meets-repurposing of the seminal Left-wing organizing methodology of Dr. Marshall Ganz. We will follow that up with a reframing of radical Leftist Saul Alinsky's *Rules for Radicals* for a positive, patriotic audience who desires sociopolitical power not for its own sake but for the capacity to protect, preserve, and promote our most cherished and sacred American values. To quote again Posobiec, "For too long, conservatives have cared only about principles but not about power. When you have power but no principles, you are a tyrant. When you have principles but no power, you are delusional."[66]

Power. Let's get some. Let's beat the Left at their own game and by their own rules. Feckless "bipartisan" Republicans need not apply.

BEAT THEM AT THEIR OWN GAME: A COMMENTARY ON LEFT-WING ORGANIZING

The short, little book by Dr. Marshall Ganz goes by a number of different titles depending on where you stumble upon it. They include:

- *People, Power, and Change: Organizing for Democratic Renewal*
- *Organizing Guide: People, Power, Change*
- *Organizing: People, Power, Change*
- *People, Power, Change*
- *The Organizer's Handbook*

There also exist lectures, papers, and other media in which Dr. Ganz teaches his uniquely effective organizing methodology. That's not to say it's exclusively meant for Leftists; anyone anywhere with any cause can deploy his teachings. It just so happens that over the decades, it's been predominantly Leftists who've done so.

Here's what makes Dr. Marshall Ganz's organizing model, frankly, exceptional: He redefines organizing as **leadership**. Specifically, organizing is recast as the leadership practice of enabling people to turn their resources into the power needed for change through five core practices: **storytelling**, **relationship-building**, **structuring**, **strategizing**, and **acting**, rooted in developing collective capacity from the ground up, not just top-down directives.[67] You're creating a **constituency** of people who stand together with these shared narratives and commitment to achieve a shared purpose. And that purpose is more like, metaphorically, an "arrow of time" and not like a clock . . . which is a cycle . . . like, say, an election cycle.[68]

> Thinking of time as an "arrow" focuses on making change, on achieving specific outcomes, on focusing our efforts.[69]

Notice how, on a cultural issue, Left-wing activists on behalf of gays and lesbians had an arrowlike purpose—to legalize homosexual marriage nationwide. Contrast with the cyclic counter of conservative Christians who opposed this; their religious activism was more akin to campaigning for Republican politicians every two to four years who vowed to—somehow—push back.

Just before the U.S. Supreme Court's landmark ruling in *Obergefell v. Hodges* to legalize gay marriage, public support had finally reached a majority, at 57 percent.[70] Consider that just seven years prior in 2008, 52 percent of California voters brought forth Proposition 8, a state constitutional amendment banning same-sex marriage statewide.[71] But organizers followed the handbook, and significant LGBT interest group lobbying produced federal judicial overruling. And so, the will of the few became the law for the many. That's power. Let's get some. Here are the five core practices.

Organizing For Power: Storytelling

> Through public narrative, social movement leaders – and participants – can move to action by mobilizing sources of motivation, constructing new shared individual and collective identities, and finding the courage to act.[72]

Dr. Ganz is referring to the storytelling structure he developed known as **Public Narrative**, and it has three components:

- The Story of Self
- The Story of Us
- The Story of Now

Joshua Lisec, also a trained and certified professional hypnotist, uniquely understands how stories drive behavioral change. Hypnosis and its clinical twin, hypnotherapy, use storytelling tools like metaphor, simile, and analogy, all dense with potent meaning, to alter the patient's perception of themselves, their problems, their desires, and their world. And it all happens unconsciously, in the hypnosis session. A skilled hypnotist will draft the exact-right personal parable for the patient and tell a story of how they create a new identity for themselves in which their problem is solved, their pain is gone, and/or their purpose is achieved. And because the conscious mind's guard is down during the hypnotic trance, the subconscious mind more often than not accepts these suggestions. Through story, a new mind is formed. As we think, so we be. This is how hypnosis success stories cover fields as broad as stress and insomnia relief to smoking cessation to weight loss to long-awaited fertility and pain-free childbirth. That's hypnosis; that's story.

For the purposes of the Public Narrative, the primary organizer—in the case of someone leading an America First–aligned social change movement, that's going to be you—tells these three specific stories.

> Simply put, Public Narrative says, "Here's who I am, this is what we have in common, and here's what we're going to do about it."[73]

Let's dig a little bit deeper now.

Writing Your Story of Self

> We construct our stories of self around "**choice points**" – moments when we faced a challenge, made a choice, experienced an outcome, and learned a lesson. Ask yourself: *When did I first care about being heard? When did I first experience injustice? When did I feel I had to act and what did I do?*[74]

What are your choice points that ultimately resulted in you deciding that you had to "do something" and "get involved" and "make change happen" because "if not now then when and if not me then who"?

That's your story. For example:

- When did you first care that your voice as a straight white conservative Christian male was suppressed and silenced despite all your measurable merits and the content of your character?
- When did you first experience an illegal immigrant doing you wrong only to receive protection and even promotion?
- When did you feel you had to act upon a burly, bearded transvestite barging into the girl's room where your daughter had just gone in alone?

That's your story. Tell it.

Crafting Your Story of Us

> Hope is one of the most precious gifts we can give each other and the people we work with to make change.[75]

And that is the purpose of a Story of Us; you're telling *individuals* who may be without hope that they are, perhaps unbeknownst to them, members of a *collective* with a shared identity, united purpose, and yes . . . the gift of hope. "If you want to go far, go together," the old proverb goes. The Story of Us issues this call-to-action through a call to shared identity. From the handbook:

> In developing your Story of Us, reflect on these questions
> 1. What values do you share with this community? (Note: community here is the "us" in your story.)
> 2. What experiences have had the greatest impact on this community? What challenges has it faced?
> 3. What change does this community hope for and why?[76]

The more clearly you state this for your Right-wing cause, the more easily more people will see themselves in it—and feel motivated to join and act.

Note that the "**community**" here is defined as the set of shared **demographics** (e.g., age, race, vocation, location, etc.) and the **psychographics** (e.g., opinions, beliefs, preferences, etc.) that make up the community's identity. For example, the gay community is gay men who do gay things. It's not complicated. Your story needn't be either. Your Story of Us is about the Heritage-American value you share in common with your specific niche of MAGA and what experiences and challenges this specific demographic-psychographic has had as it pertains to what they do and don't want. There may be grievances unveiled here. Good. The more motivation, the better. That's leadership. That's the Story of Us. Tell yours.

Telling Your Story of Now

> Story of Now makes the bridge from story, *why* we should act, to strategy, *how* we can act. Specifically, your Story of Now should end with a "hard ask."[77]

Continuing from the Story of Us to the Story of Now, the transition is clear; *because* the community to which you belong wants what it wants, how are you all going to get it? Step by step with no step skipped? Who is needed to do what? And what happens if you fail?

That last question allows the terror of urgency to reframe your cause from optional to essential. Internal monologue becomes, *I HAVE to get involved RIGHT NOW.* Again, leadership.

> In developing your Story of Now, reflect on these questions:
> 1. What is the urgent challenge your "us" faces?
> 2. What change does this community hope for and why? What would the future look like if this change is made? What would the future look like if the change isn't made? (Note: here, you're trying to paint a picture of the "dream" of the future if the change is made, and the "nightmare" of the future if it isn't.)
> 3. What choice are you asking people to make and why now?
> 4. What action are you asking them to take and what impact will this have on the bigger picture? What's the risk, or again, what would the future look like if we fail to act?[78]

The questions are self-explanatory as ought be your answers.

In Summary:
You will weave your Story of Self, Story of Us, and Story of Now into a coherent narrative, one which checks every box and can be told in as few seconds as an "elevator pitch"—and be expanded all the way into a TED Talk . . . or campaign announcement speech . . . or statement to Congress . . . or to your inaugural address. In short, it's:

1. This is how I became this way.
2. This is how I'm just like you.
3. This is how we're going to get what we want—right now—or else.

That's your organizing story, and you're sticking to it.

Organizing for Power: Relationship-Building

> Organizing is based on relationships and creating mutual commitments to work together. It is the process of association—not simply aggregation—that makes a whole greater than the sum of its parts.
>
> Through association we can learn to recast our individual interests as common interests, identify values we share, and envision objectives that we can use our combined resources to achieve.
>
> And because it makes us more likely to act to assert those interests, relationship building goes far beyond delivering a message, extracting a contribution, or soliciting a vote.
>
> Relationships built as a result of one-on-one meetings create the foundation of local campaign teams, and they are rooted in commitments people make to each other, not simply commitment to an idea, task, or issue.[79]

Notice how relationship-building is effectively the Public Narrative but for each member of the group. The organizer sets this trend with their Stories of Self, Us, and Now, and in turn, models that behavior for all others to follow as they get to know and begin working alongside each other.

Remember the Snowflake Model from Chapter 12? This is saying the same, slightly differently. Unfortunately, it's why a well-funded establishment Republican will, for example, always be at risk of losing big to a grassroots socialist nobody who follows the handbook. In short, it's top-down versus reach-out; institution versus network.

In an institution, the lower levels only act when the top demands it, and collective morale and self-generated initiative are always concerns, as its feedback mechanism. The bottom reports to the top what's going on. The top sensemakes what to do about it amongst themselves. Then the top calls back to the trenches what ought be done. This is so slow. In a network, every node is a spokesperson, a deputy, a leader. In relationship-building, that means everyone knows, likes, and trusts everyone else. They're in it to win it—for the "right" reasons—not grift and self-promote and ladder-climb so they can be king or queen at the top of the institution. The Left is skilled at the former; the Right is prone to the latter (ladder).

Organizing for Power: Structuring

> Effective leadership teams must be bounded, stable, and diverse. They must agree on a shared purpose, clear norms, and specific roles.[80]

That's what is meant by structure. Everyone knows *why* they're here, *how* they're expected to act, and *what* their job is to do. It's company by-laws, standard operating procedures, and job descriptions. That's how the Left treats what is otherwise Human Resources afterthoughts; it's also how they organize and win with deeply unpopular ideas in highly opposed places. This is what they do. We can, too—except most people like us.

> The path from interested supporter to organizer does not happen overnight. Rather, it involves a supporter being recruited, tested, and escalated into roles that require progressively more commitment and skills. In order to grow and take on more leadership, our people must demonstrate that they have the ability to perform the roles of each position.[81]

Dr. Ganz calls it the "ladder of engagement" where the more an individual proves themselves trustworthy to and competent within the community, the more responsibility and thus authority they earn within the organization until finally they reach the center of the network (where the people doing the initial Structuring are to be found). A sample engagement ladder from the handbook is:

1. Supporter (e.g., petition-signer)
2. Volunteer Prospect (e.g., supporter who completes a volunteer sign-up form)

3. Team Member (e.g., a prospect who shows up, helps out, and meets with the primary organizer one-on-one; receives lower-level task responsibility)
4. Leadership Prospect (e.g., a team member who receives higher and higher levels of task responsibility)
5. Organizer (e.g., a prospect who passed the tests)

That's how you structure an effective, nimble network to self-organize and win.

Organizing for Power: Strategizing

> [E]ffective organizing campaigns focus on a clear strategic objective, a way to turn those values into action; e.g., desegregate buses in Montgomery, Alabama; getting to 100% clean electricity; etc.
>
> Trans-local campaigns locate responsibility for strategy at the top (or at the center), but are able to "chunk out" strategic objectives in time (deadlines) and space (local areas) as a campaign, allowing significant local responsibility for figuring out how to achieve those objectives.[82]

In Strategizing, the Story of Now gets broken down into measurable, doable steps. And of course, it's the Structure of the network center—you as the organizer and thus you consider your trusted advisors and co-leaders—who will do this "chunk out." From the handbook:

> A theory of change statement uses this format:
> **If** we do (TACTICS)
> **then** (STRATEGIC GOAL or CHANGE)
> Because (REASON)
>
> In the Montgomery Bus Boycott example from earlier in this section, the theory of change could be written like this:
> **If** African Americans in Montgomery boycott the bus system
> **then** the bus company will desegregate the buses
> **because** the decrease in ridership will significantly impact their profits.[83]

In our view, the best first few strategic objectives are realistic for your scale. For example, perhaps your concern is the transvestites in women's restrooms issue. "Ban all trans from all locker rooms nationwide" may be too grand a goal for you and three other people. But what if it's in one specific building of some local significance to you? That's a start. One after another. Let it build and cascade. Lead. Win.

Organizing for Power: Acting

Here, we transition from the thinking about the doing to the actual doing.

> Organizing outcomes must be clear, measurable, and specific if progress is to be evaluated, accountability practiced, and strategy adapted based on experience.[84]

It's all about **feedback**, i.e., measuring and reporting. *Are we getting done what we said we wanted to by when and how do we know?* A network has a key advantage as we said earlier because they can move relatively permissionlessly, acting and responding as needed in real time, where those closest to the situation are calling the shots.

Besides feedback, the other two essentials of Acting are **meaning** and **autonomy**. From the handbook:

1. Meaningful: the person can see that the action is significant and makes a difference towards achieving a meaningful goal.
2. Autonomy: people are given levels of responsibility according to their skills and
3. abilities to achieve a particular outcome.[85]

That's it. That's organizing. Not mystery nor magic. Not "what the Left does somehow, somewhere." Just five repeatable practices that turn scattered frustration into disciplined power:

1. You tell the right **stories**.
2. You build the right **relationships**.
3. You **structure** the right teams.
4. You choose the right **strategy**.
5. You take the right **actions**, again and again.

The Left has run this play for sixty years—with ideas most Americans hate—and still managed to capture institutions, write the rules, and turn their niche obsessions into everyone else's "new normal." They did it by organizing.

Now you know the blueprint. Your job is now to follow it. Take these tools, translate them into your church, your veterans club, your homeschool group, your business network, your county party, your parallel economy project. Tell your Story of Self, rally your Story of Us, and make your Story of Now impossible to ignore. Then build the relationships, structure, strategy, and action to back it up.

If we don't, they will keep winning. If we do, we can, too. But before you close this appendix, open your notebook, and start organizing, we need to rewrite some of the rules you'll be following along the way. If we want to beat the Left in all seven domains, we have to face them in the game *they* are playing—not the old one where conservatives existed to conserve the liberal agenda from ten years ago. Those days are over.

Dr. Marshall Ganz gives us the architecture of power—how to turn scattered, frustrated individuals into a disciplined force that can actually win. His five practices explain how the Left built lasting movements that outlive any single candidate or campaign. We would be foolish *not* to steal that architecture and build our own.

That said, architecture alone is not enough. Movements also run on rules of engagement—the street-level maxims that tell you what to do when you're under attack, outnumbered, ignored, or smeared. On the Left, that tactical playbook is, naturally, Saul Alinsky's *Rules for Radicals*. For decades, his rules have served as the unofficial operating system for every pressure campaign, boycott, media pile-on, and "spontaneous" protest that somehow always seems to break their way.

Building on the Left's organizing model (Ganz), we're next going to raid the Left's tactical rulebook (Alinsky). And we're going to do it using a mental technology from one of the most beloved American thinkers and creatives of all time to convert integrity-free rules for radicals into principle-driven rules for patriots.

So now, we turn from how they build power . . . to how they wield it . . . and how we can, too, without doing the very things we hate and becoming what we swore to destroy.

RULES FOR RIGHT: OUR PRINCIPLES, THEIR RULES

In 2023, the late great Scott Adams published *Reframe Your Brain: The User Interface for Happiness and Success*. Joshua Lisec served as contributing editor for this and other projects of Scott's, but it's this one in particular that is widely credited with empowering the most people to make the most positive changes they ever have in the most areas of their lives. One of the hypnotic techniques deployed in the book is called **reframing**, and it's where a short, simple redesign of a belief completely changes everything else that comes afterward, from our behavior to the identity we hold around it. Pretty incredible, if you ask us.

Throughout the book, a reframe template reoccurs, and it goes like this: *Usual frame* versus *Reframe*. For example:

Usual Frame: Success depends on who you know.
Reframe: Success depends on how many people you know.[86]

The purpose of Scott's system is what it does; it's to replace unhelpful, disempowering, dare we say even depressing beliefs with useful, motivating, and success-driving alternatives. And when we consider in the political activism realm Saul Alinsky's *Rules for Radicals*, we can get a bit . . . depressed. Most rub conservatives the wrong way because they demand principle-free deception; others turn off our libertarian friends because their impact is the accrual of power to the regime. So we leave the radical changemaker's rulebook off our shelves, abandoning all copies to Leftists whose primary principle—really, their only principle—is **power**. How to keep it, wield it, get more of it. This is what they do. Every single time.

We need some reframing, if we the good and normal people who happen to appreciate Western civilization are going to win the long game against the radical Left whose explicit and stated agenda is to subvert, weaken, and otherwise destroy our values and our heritage. Therefore, we will repurpose Scott Adams's reframing technique to sanitize and sanctify Alinsky's original integrity-free rules to give ourselves a new rulebook for a new game—the zero-sum, winner-take-all affair that the Left is playing, unbeknownst to the vast majority of elected establishment Republicans and their staff.

We want to play to win. Here's how.

Reframing Saul Alinsky's 13 Rules for Radicals

Repurposing the reframing technique, we now have superior rules to play by as we organize, advocate, and campaign to win. Below is the original rule of Alinsky followed by our principle-meets-power reframe.[87]

Rule #1

Usual Frame:

"Power is not only what you have but what the enemy thinks you have."

Reframe:

Real power is what you can actually do together and how clearly you demonstrate it.

An honorable movement doesn't rely on bluffing or massaging numbers; it builds real capacity—people, money, skills, attention—and then communicates that capacity clearly. A parents' coalition, for example, might have 800 people on their email list and 150 who consistently show up to meetings. Instead of pretending they have "thousands in the streets," they show school board members a documented record: packed meetings, signed petitions, disciplined public comment, and local media coverage. Decision-makers are under no illusions; they can see it in attendance, votes, and earned media.

In a campaign, this looks like a candidate running a visible, disciplined field program—volunteers at doors, phone banks, yard signs in key precincts, and a transparent fundraising report with many small donors. Rather than inflating polls or inventing momentum, the campaign uses real data—doors knocked, IDs gained, ballots requested—to show that they have built a serious machine. Opponents see that and adjust accordingly; donors and volunteers see it and lean in harder. No bluff required.

Rule #2

Usual Frame:

"Never go outside the expertise of your people."

Reframe:

Organize around what your people already know how to do and grow their skills on purpose.

A community group that's full of teachers, nurses, small-business owners, and parents shouldn't try to act like a think tank or a legal shop overnight. Instead, it can lean into its existing strength—teachers leading curriculum reviews and messaging about education, small-business owners speaking about local regulations and taxes, parents telling stories about safety or content in schools. As the group matures, it can deliberately bring in or train people in new areas—media, legal research, public records—without overextending.

Similarly, a campaign that's strong at door-to-door contact should not abruptly divert all attention to high-production TV ads it doesn't understand. It can double down on the field, where volunteers and staff are competent, while gradually building in other channels—simple social media, clean email outreach, basic press relationships. Expertise then is the starting point from which you add new skills intentionally, step by step.

Rule #3

Usual Frame:

"Whenever possible, go outside the expertise of the enemy."

Reframe:

Compete where the other side is weak, but do it transparently and on merits.

If a local establishment is used to winning through glossy mail and insider endorsements, a citizens' group can shift the contest onto a terrain those insiders rarely touch: direct, personal contact. When neighbors host house meetings, organize town halls, and show up at committee hearings with well-prepared questions, they move the fight into a realm where an entrenched opponent is often clumsy or slow to respond. The point isn't to trick anyone; rather, emphasize forms of civic engagement the other side has neglected.

In a campaign, this can look like emphasizing high-quality door-knocking and relational organizing in a district where the opponent is obsessed with television and consultant-driven messaging. By training volunteers to talk issues, listen, and record real feedback at the door, the campaign gains a live, granular map of voter concerns and intentions—while the opponent is flying blind off stale polls. You're not going "outside their expertise" to confuse them; you're choosing more citizen-driven methods where consultant-heavy operations tend to underperform.

Rule #4

Usual Frame:

"Make the enemy live up to its own book of rules."

Reframe:

Hold everyone—especially powerful people—to the standards they publicly claim to uphold.

When an institution loudly proclaims transparency, fairness, or "following the science," a principled movement has every right to ask them to actually do so. A citizen group can respectfully demand that a school district that champions "parent partnership" release curricula, hold accessible forums, and respond promptly to public records requests. The goal here is not some naked *gotcha*; it's to line up stated values with real behavior. When they match, trust rises. When they don't, the public has a legitimate basis for demanding change.

In a campaign, this means contrasting a candidate's voting record or public statements with their slogans but sticking to verifiable facts. If an incumbent promises "no new taxes" and then presents years' worth of votes for tax increases, it is fair and honest and just for a challenger to pound hard that contrast in mail, speeches, and debates. The key is accuracy and restraint—no exaggeration, no invented scandals. Just a clear comparison between what was promised and what was done so the voters can judge for themselves. You're just . . . helping them out with that. A lot.

Rule #5

Usual Frame:

"Ridicule is man's most potent weapon. There is no defense. It is almost impossible to counteract ridicule. Also it infuriates the opposition, who then react to your advantage."

Reframe:

Use humor to expose absurdity. The funniest always wins.

Carefully crafted humor that highlights obvious contradictions or absurd policies can be powerful and legitimate. A community group might use a light-hearted meme, cartoon, or skit to show the ridiculousness of a bureaucracy that requires five forms to change a lightbulb or a policy that bans ordinary snacks but allows truly unsafe materials.

In campaigns, smart satire can clarify stakes for voters without turning politics into pure cruelty. We don't want you to risk galvanizing your top supporters but then lose 40 percent of the electorate because you objectively went "way too far." So you as a candidate might run a short video or mail piece that playfully contrasts an opponent's promises with their record using biting sarcasm with rhymes to make the inconsistency unforgettable. The lines not to cross are mocking genuine disabilities or family tragedies. Humor that punches up at power and hypocrisy can energize supporters; humor that punches down at ordinary people with ordinary problems—just like the voters—erodes legitimacy.

Rule #6

Usual Frame:

"A good tactic is one your people enjoy."

Reframe:

A good tactic is one your people can sustain because it fits their values and they don't hate doing it.

If a tactic feels miserable, degrading, or pointless to the people carrying it out, they won't stick with it. A neighborhood group that enjoys potluck meetings, small group discussions, and well-organized canvasses will do far more over a year than a group that constantly guilt-trips people into grim, chaotic "actions" that never seem to go anywhere. Leaders should pay attention to what energizes their members—door-to-door outreach, community clean-ups, petitions, public comment—and build tactics around those strengths.

For your campaign, this might mean discovering that volunteers love knocking doors together on Saturdays, rotating through precincts with friendly competition, but burn out quickly if forced into scripted phone calls they dislike. Your campaign can lean into canvassing, give people clear goals and recognition, and make the work social and meaningful. Enjoyment simply means that the people doing the work feel they're using their time well and in a way that matches who they are. Alignment. Sustainable.

Rule #7

Usual Frame:

"A tactic that drags on too long becomes a drag."

Reframe:

Rotate your tactics and celebrate milestones so your people feel progress and not fatigue.

Even the best tactic loses energy if it becomes monotonous and aimless. A citizens' campaign to change a local policy might start with petitions and testimonies, then shift to targeted meetings with decision-makers, then to a visible rally when the time is ripe. Between phases, leaders can share wins—signatures collected, meetings held, endorsements earned—so that participants sense forward motion rather than endless slog.

In electoral politics, a campaign might plan distinct phases of field work—early identification, persuasion, then turnout, each with its own scripts, goals, and internal rewards. Volunteers who spent weeks identifying supporters at the door can later shift to reminder calls and "chase" efforts when ballots are out, with updated messaging and different metrics. The work is still hard, but it doesn't feel like the same day repeated forever. People can see the story unfolding. You got this.

Rule #8

Usual Frame:

"Keep the pressure on."

Reframe:

If it's working, do it more; the moment it stops working, stop it forever.

Pressure doesn't have to mean, for example, being annoying and shouting; it can simply mean persistence coupled with the discipline to roll it back at the first sign of overuse. A community group that calmly follows up after every meeting, submits follow-up questions, tracks promises made by officials, and keeps showing up month after month creates a kind of soft but real pressure. Decision-makers learn that they can't simply wait out the latest controversy; the citizens will still be there, watching and asking.

In a campaign, upping the pressure might look like regularly updated contrasts on key issues, consistent door-knocking in target precincts, and disciplined communication, even when the news cycle is chaotic. Rather than chasing every outrage, your campaign returns again and again to your Top 3 issues, showing with new examples why change is needed. This form of increasing pressure respects voters' time and intelligence while making it harder for an opponent to hide behind a single good news week.

Rule #9

Usual Frame:

"The threat is usually more terrifying than the thing itself."

Reframe:

Tell the truth about the stakes—the whole truth and nothing but the truth.

Fear of what might happen often outruns reality. An ethical movement doesn't invent dire consequences; it describes real ones clearly and then follows through on lawful actions it is truly willing to take. A neighborhood group might say, "If this zoning change passes, we will work to elect new council members who oppose it," and then actually do the hard work of recruiting candidates and turning out voters. No need to hint at chaos or unrest. The "threat" is simply credible civic engagement.

In campaigns, candidates sometimes warn of what will happen if certain policies continue. The honorable version is to base these warnings on solid evidence and to pair them with specific, realistic remedies. For example, rather than vaguely suggesting "disaster" if an opponent wins, a candidate can explain, "If this tax increase goes into effect, here is how it has played out in similar communities, and here is the legislation I will sponsor instead." The goal is to replace nebulous dread with informed seriousness.

Rule #10

Usual Frame:

"The major premise for tactics is the development of operations that will maintain a constant pressure upon the opposition."

Reframe:

Build operations that keep issues on the agenda, not that harass people into silence.

Constant, mindless attack wears everyone down and can turn the public against you. But consistent, organized attention to a set of issues keeps them from being buried. A citizens' coalition might maintain a simple cadence: monthly public reports on an agency's performance, regular op-eds, periodic public forums, and standing invitations for officials to respond. The "pressure" comes from visibility and accountability, not from mobbing or personal vendettas.

A campaign can do something similar by maintaining a steady contrast on policy and performance, not personality. Regularly publishing side-by-side comparisons on taxes, schools, public safety, and ethics keeps those topics alive in voters' minds. The other campaign feels "pressure" in the sense that they cannot escape their record, but they are not being personally hounded or demonized. Voters get the chance to weigh competing visions under clear light.

Rule #11

Usual Frame:

"If you push a negative hard and deep enough, it will break through into its counterside; this is based on the principle that every positive has its negative."

Reframe:

Expose real harm clearly, then pivot to constructive solutions so the people don't associate you with dread.

If all a movement ever does is complain, people eventually tune it out, even if the complaints are justified. A community group trying to reform a failing institution must sink real effort into documenting harm—wasted money, poor outcomes, broken promises—but then quickly push toward concrete alternatives, like better policies, new leadership, or different models. The "counterside" then is built by offering a credible way forward.

In a campaign, emphasizing an opponent's weaknesses is inevitable. Now, you'll want to connect each criticism with a "counterside" that is more than just "vote for me instead." If you hammer an incumbent's absenteeism, for example, you follow it with your own attendance record and a plan for constituent service. If you highlight broken promises, you lay out a transparent pledge and how voters can verify you kept it. Got it? The negative opens people's ears; the positive gives them something better to choose. Go and do likewise.

Rule #12

Usual Frame:

"The price of a successful attack is a constructive alternative."

Reframe:

You haven't won an argument until you've shown a better way that works.

This one barely needs reframing, yet still it does. A citizens' group that fights to overturn a harmful policy must be ready with a replacement that addresses the original problem without the unintended consequences. That might mean drafting model policies, working with experts, or pointing to successful examples from other communities. Simply tearing something down and walking away leaves a vacuum that will usually be filled by something worse.

In campaign terms, this means that "throw the bums out" is not enough. If you criticize an opponent's spending priorities, you must show your own budget framework. If you attack mismanagement in a department, you should explain how you would measure improvement and hold leadership accountable. Voters are more likely to trust criticism that comes paired with a plausible path forward, not simply outrage.

Rule #13

Usual Frame:

"Pick the target, freeze it, personalize it, and polarize it."

Reframe:

Define the issue, name who is responsible, and show how you're different."

Turning a human being into a caricature to be "frozen and destroyed" crosses an ethical line. Obviously. That's why the Left has been doing it since

1971 when *Rules for Radicals* first appeared. But naming specific decision-makers and holding them accountable for specific actions is both legitimate and necessary in a free society. A community group might say, "The school board majority voted for this curriculum; here's how each member voted; here are the consequences we see; here are the candidates we support instead." The "target" is not their humanity; it is their public role and record. After all, the Left is the side that unhumans their enemies. We grant them the dignity due them by God. That doesn't mean we won't proceed to metaphorically crush them.

In campaigns, personalization can mean clearly explaining, for example, "In this race, the choice is between Candidate A, who voted this way and supports these policies, and Candidate B, who will do this other thing instead." Polarization, in an honorable sense, simply means clarifying differences so that voters understand the stakes and cannot be lulled into thinking "they're all the same." What must be avoided is demonization, which might include attacking family with baseless accusations (especially minors).

You now have a choice. Either you learn to organize and act with principle and power, or you will be governed—culturally and politically—by those who have power and no principles at all. There is no third option where you stay "above it all" and somehow still win.

As for us—Cliff Maloney and Joshua Lisec—we aim to get power and keep it. But that's only the half of it. Marshall Ganz explained how to generate power from the ground up. Saul Alinsky taught how they wield it in the street and in the news, by hook and by crook. And Scott Adams's reframing gave us a way to decontaminate the effective methods without importing the unhuman malice. Which brings us back to Jack Posobiec.

Power without principles is tyrannical; principles without power are delusional.

But power and principles together, will make America great forever.

Thank you for your attention to this matter.

ACKNOWLEDGMENTS

Cliff Maloney: I would like to acknowledge and thank my family, my friends, and all the patriots who support my work to advance the principles of liberty. God bless you all.

Joshua Lisec: Thank you to my children, whose presence gave me vision beyond my own lifetime to a world you will one day inhabit. I will do what I must to help make American great again, for you, dear ones. My gratitude also goes to the late great Scott Adams, who introduced me to Jack Posobiec, who introduced me to Cliff Maloney, who believes in the message—and necessity—of this book as much as if not more than I do.

ABOUT THE AUTHORS

Cliff Maloney is a blue-collar activist from the Philadelphia suburbs who now serves as the CEO of Citizens Alliance. By age thirty-four, Cliff and his teams of door-knockers have knocked on more than 9 million doors across the United States to deliver confirmed victories in 418 federal, state, and local elections. Roger Stone nicknamed Cliff "the Godfather of Door-Knocking."

In 2024, Maloney was recruited by the late Charlie Kirk to launch *PA CHASE*, hiring 124 full-time ballot-chasers to knock on 510,000 doors across Pennsylvania. The historic program helped to increase now-President Donald J. Trump's share of the Pennsylvania mail-in vote from roughly 20 percent against incumbent Joe Biden to 34.5 percent against candidate Kamala Harris. Cliff has committed to chasing ballots every election to make Pennsylvania a permanent "Red Wall" for Republicans.

Cliff is also a political strategist and commentator regularly seen on Newsmax, Fox News, and Real America's Voice. He can be found on X @Maloney and at www.cliffmaloney.com.

Joshua Lisec writes books of consequence. He is author alongside Jack Posobiec of the *New York Times* bestseller *UnhumanXs: The Secret History of Communist Revolutions (And How to Crush Them)* and the *Newsmax* bestseller *Bulletproof: The Truth about the Assassination Attempts on Donald Trump*, endorsed by Vice President JD Vance and President Donald J. Trump, respectively.

Lisec is best known for his literary collaborations with controversial public figures, capturing their authentic voice and conveying the whole story. He is a *New York Times*, #1 *Publishers Weekly*, and *USA Today* bestselling coauthor and has ghostwritten more than 110 nonfiction books on politics, business, and more that have been translated into a dozen languages. He has been featured in *The New York Times*, *Publishers Weekly*, *Newsweek*, *The Observer*, *Forbes*, BBC, TEDx, and TMZ. He is the world's only Certified Ghostwriter and Certified Hypnotist.

Follow Joshua on X @joshualisec and at www.lisecghostwriting.com.

ENDNOTES

Preface

1 Mastrangelo, Dominick. "When News Organizations Called the Race for Trump." The Hill, November 6, 2024, https://thehill.com/media/4976368-trump-wins-2024-election/.

2 Cliff Maloney, "The PA CHASE: Official Behind the Scenes Documentary," February 26, 2025, YouTube video, https://www.youtube.com/watch?v=2WcxJ1h-iXw.

Introduction

3 Joshua Lisec (@JoshuaLisec), "The most influential book of the last 30 years, bar none: The Organizer's Handbook by Marshall Ganz There is a good reason you've never heard of it: It works.," Twitter (now X), October 12, 2021, https://x.com/JoshuaLisec/status/1447964339407835138.

Chapter 1

4 Ballotpedia Staff, "95% of Incumbents Won Re-election," Ballotpedia, November 25, 2024, https://news.ballotpedia.org/2024/11/25/95-of-incumbents-won-re-election/.

5 Samuel Wonacott, "94% of incumbents won re-election in 2022," Ballotpedia, January 5, 2023, https://news.ballotpedia.org/2023/01/05/94-of-incumbents-won-re-election-in-2022/.

6 Gallup, "Congress and the Public," Gallup, accessed February 3, 2026, https://news.gallup.com/poll/1600/congress-public.aspx.

Chapter 2

7 Brent Ferguson, "Congressional Disclosure of Time Spent Fundraising," *Cornell Journal of Law and Public Policy* 23, no. 1 (2013): 13.

Chapter 3

8 Sara Suzuki, "Supporting Young People on their Path to Running for Office," Tufts University, September 8, 2022, https://circle.tufts.edu/index.php/latest-research/running-for-office.

9 Seth Motel, "Who Runs for Office? A Profile of the 2%," Pew Research Center, September 3, 2014, https://www.pewresearch.org/short-reads/2014/09/03/who-runs-for-office-a-profile-of-the-2/.

10 Donald J. Trump, "Follow the money. Remarks as prepared for delivery: Thank you, it's so great to be in...," Facebook, September 28, 2016, https://www.facebook.com/DonaldTrump/posts/follow-the-moneyremarks-as-prepared-for-delivery-thank-you-its-so-great-to-be-in/10157785869445725/.

11 "6 Books to Help Understand Trump's Win," *The New York Times,* November 10, 2016, https://www.nytimes.com/2016/11/10/books/6-books-to-help-understand-trumps-win.html.

12 John London, "Ohio US Senate Race Gains National Attention," WLWT (Cincinnati, OH), May 2, 2022, https://www.wlwt.com/article/ohio-us-senate-race-gains-national-attention/39886178.

13 Michael Moline, "DeSantis Vows to 'Stand Our Ground' Against 'Woke' in Launching Second Term," Florida Phoenix, January 3, 2023, https://floridaphoenix.com/2023/01/03/desantis-vows-to-stand-our-ground-against-woke-in-launching-second-term/.

14 Lauren Boebert for Congress, "Lauren Boebert Announces Run for Congress," December 9, 2019, https://laurenforcolorado.com/news/lauren-boebert-announces-run-for-congress/.

15 Annie Karmi, "Weeks Before Prison, a Defiant Bannon Is Still Rallying MAGA World," *The New York Times,* June 7, 2024, https://www.nytimes.com/2024/06/07/us/politics/steve-bannon-bob-good-trump-prison.html.

16 Georgia's 14th Congressional District Election, 2020 (June 9 Republican Primary)," Ballotpedia, accessed February 4, 2026, https://ballotpedia.org/Georgia%27s_14th_Congressional_District_election,_2020_(June_9_Republican_primary).

17 Pew Research Center, "10. Financial Well-Being, Personal Characteristics and Lifestyles of the Political Typology," Pew Research Center, October 24, 2017, https://www.pewresearch.org/politics/2017/10/24/10-financial-well-being-personal-characteristics-and-lifestyles-of-the-political-typology.

18 Byron Donalds (@ByronDonalds), "I'm running for Congress not only because SWFL needs a proven Conservative, but because together we can make a difference. With the political culture war, we need a member of Congress who'll represent our cause for liberty, expand our base, and spread our message of Conservatism." Twitter (now X), August 12, 2020, https://x.com/ByronDonalds/status/1293686804173000704.

19 Donalds, "I'm running for Congress."

20 Anna Paulina Luna for Congress, "Anna Paulina Luna Ad: 'Ditch,'" June 14, 2021, YouTube video, https://www.youtube.com/watch?v=QKSWxB-sQts.

21 massie4congress, "Thomas Massie Commercial," April 10, 2012, YouTube video, https://www.youtube.com/watch?v=Tns9_fMEX-g.

22 "About Mike," Mike Lee U.S. Senator for Utah, accessed February 4, 2026, https://www.lee.senate.gov/about-mike.

23 Senator Rand Paul. "About." Accessed February 4, 2026, https://www.paul.senate.gov/about/.
24 Ron DeSantis, "I'm running for Governor because I want Florida to be a place where my children will want to live when they grow up—a state of prosperity and promise...," Facebook, October 5, 2018, https://www.facebook.com/photo.php?fbid=1939401646126592&id=318196171580489&set=a.319978888068884.

Chapter 4

25 Cook Political Report, "2026 CPR House Race Ratings," Cook Political Report, accessed February 4, 2026, https://www.cookpolitical.com/ratings/house-race-ratings.
26 OpenSecrets, "Incumbent Advantage," OpenSecrets, accessed February 4, 2026, https://www.opensecrets.org/elections-overview/incumbent-advantage.
27 "State-by-State Comparison of Campaign Finance Requirements," Ballotpedia, accessed February 4, 2026, https://ballotpedia.org/State-by-state_comparison_of_campaign_finance_requirements.

Chapter 5

28 Guosong Xu, "Political Donations from Mega-Donors Affect Political Representation in US Politicians," Rotterdam School of Management, Erasmus University, December 16, 2024, https://www.rsm.nl/discovery/2024/political-donations-from-mega-donors/.
29 Bryan Metzger, "Montana GOP Senate Candidate's Old Facebook Includes Lewd Photos of Women, Racist Costumes, and Homoerotic Jokes," Business Insider, July 2023, https://www.businessinsider.com/tim-sheehy-senate-montana-facebook-lewd-photos-racist-homoerotic-2023-7.

Chapter 6

30 Chad Boutin, "To Determine Election Outcomes, Study Says Snap Judgments Are Sufficient," Princeton University, October 22, 2007, https://www.princeton.edu/news/2007/10/22/determine-election-outcomes-study-says-snap-judgments-are-sufficient.
31 "An Introduction to the Leesburg Grid," Majority Strategies (blog), July 25, 2024, https://www.majoritystrategies.com/uncategorized/an-introduction-to-the-leesburg-grid/.

Chapter 7

32 Team BallotReady, "5 Things to Know about Candidate Filing Deadlines," BallotReady for Organizations, August 21, 2024, https://organizations.ballotready.org/research/5-things-to-know-candidate-filing-deadlines.

Chapter 8

33 OpenSecrets, "Winning vs. Spending," OpenSecrets, accessed February 4, 2026, https://www.opensecrets.org/elections-overview/winning-vs-spending.

Chapter 9

34 Bridget Bowman, "Poll Highlights Democrats' Grassroots Donor Advantage," NBC News, July 3, 2023, https://www.nbcnews.com/meet-the-press/meetthepressblog/poll-highlights-democrats-grassroots-donor-advantage-rcna92059.

Chapter 10

35 National Newspaper Association Foundation, "Newspaper Readers Are Voters; Voters 'Hungry' for 'Professional Integrity,'" March 28, 2022, https://www.nna.org/newspaper-readers-are-voters-voters-hungry-for-professional-integrity.

36 FairVote, "Voter Turnout," accessed February 4, 2026, https://fairvote.org/resources/voter-turnout/?section=turnout-in-the-united-states.

Chapter 11

37 Marcy Shieh, Hayley Munir, Michael Catalano, and Nathan Henceroth, "Campaign Endorsements and Election Outcomes in Judicial Elections," *American Politics Research* 53, no. 2 (2025): 151–166, https://doi.org/10.1177/1532673X241295681.

Chapter 12

38 Maryland Today Staff, "Value of Volunteer Time Rose in 2024, Do Good Institute and Nonprofit Organization Find," University of Maryland School of Public Policy - Do Good Institute, April 25, 2025, https://dogood.umd.edu/news/value-volunteer-time-rose-2024-do-good-institute-and-nonprofit-organization-find.

39 Obama for America, *2012 Obama Campaign Legacy Report* (2012), https://time.com/wp-content/uploads/2015/02/legacy-report.pdf.

40 Obama for America, *Legacy Report.*

Chapter 13

41 Billerud, "Election Advertising: Print Moves and Motivates Voters," October 2024, https://www.billerud.com/globalassets/billerud/insights/power-of-print/billerud_maximizing-political-advertising.pdf.

Chapter 14

42 Jared Barton, Marco Castillo, and Ragan Petrie, "What Persuades Voters? A Field Experiment on Political Campaigning," Interdisciplinary Center for Economic Science Working Paper No. 12-31 (Fairfax, VA: George Mason University, June 2012), https://ssrn.com/abstract=2087135.

Chapter 15

43 Sadie Bograd, "Campaign Managers in State and Local Races Are Often Recent College Graduates," *Teen Vogue*, October 28, 2020, https://www.teenvogue.com/story/campaign-managers-state-local-elections.

Chapter 16

44 Kobi Hackenburg and Helen Margetts, "Evaluating the Persuasive Influence of Political Microtargeting with Large Language Models," *Proceedings of the National Academy of Sciences* 121, no. 24 (2024): e2403116121, https://doi.org/10.1073/pnas.2403116121.

Chapter 17

45 Jennifer Ruff, "Nearly 80% of Eligible Voters Don't Participate in Primaries," Bipartisan Policy Center, March 3, 2023, https://bipartisanpolicy.org/press-release/voters-dont-participate-primaries.

Chapter 18

46 Alan S. Gerber and Donald P. Green, "The Effects of Canvassing, Telephone Calls, and Direct Mail on Voter Turnout: A Field Experiment," *American Political Science Review* 94, no. 3 (September 2000): 653–63.

47 Stephen Despin, Medium, https://medium.com/@sdespin/why-door-to-door-canvassing-wins-campaigns-and-how-to-power-it-with-digital-2262c4f5ad37.

48 Alan S. Gerber and Donald P. Green, "Does Canvassing Increase Voter Turnout? A Field Experiment," *Proceedings of the National Academy of Sciences* 96, no. 19 (1999): 10939–42, https://doi.org/10.1073/pnas.96.19.10939.

49 Donald P. Green and Alan S. Gerber, *Get Out the Vote: How to Increase Voter Turnout, 5th ed.* (Bloomsbury Academic, 2023).

50 Stephen G. Greene, "Cost of Door-to-Door Canvassing Is $19 Per Vote, Research Finds," The Chronicle of Philanthropy, July 22, 2004, https://www.philanthropy.com/news/cost-of-door-to-door-canvassing-is-19-per-vote-research-finds/.

Chapter 19

51 Hannah Hartig et al., "Voting Patterns in the 2024 Election," Pew Research Center, June 26, 2025, https://www.pewresearch.org/politics/2025/06/26/voting-patterns-in-the-2024-election/.

52 Kiana Cox, "An Early Look at Black Voters' Views on Biden, Trump and Election 2024," Pew Research Center, May 20, 2024, https://www.pewresearch.org/race-and-ethnicity/2024/05/20/an-early-look-at-black-voters-views-on-biden-trump-and-election-2024/.

53 Jens Manuel Krogstad and Mohamad Moslimani, "Key Facts About Black Eligible Voters in 2024," Pew Research Center, January 10, 2024, https://www.pewresearch.org/short-reads/2024/01/10/key-facts-about-black-eligible-voters-in-2024/.

54 Peter M. Gollwitzer et al., "When Intentions Go Public: Does Social Reality Widen the Intention-Behavior Gap?" *Psychological Science* 20, no. 5 (2009): 612–618, https://doi.org/10.1111/j.1467-9280.2009.02336.x.

55 Marwa Azab, "Why Sharing Your Goals Makes Them Less Achievable," Neuroscience in Everyday Life (blog), Psychology Today, January 1, 2018, https://www.psychologytoday.com/us/blog/neuroscience-in-everyday-life/201801/why-sharing-your-goals-makes-them-less-achievable.

56 National Conference of State Legislatures, "Electioneering Prohibitions Near Polling Places," NCSL, accessed February 4, 2026, https://www.ncsl.org/elections-and-campaigns/electioneering-prohibitions.

Chapter 20

57 Rachel Bernhard and Justin de Benedictis-Kessner, "Men and Women Candidates Are Similarly Persistent After Losing Elections," *Proceedings of the National Academy of Sciences* 118, no. 26 (2021): e2026726118, https://doi.org/10.1073/pnas.2026726118.

Chapter 21

58 Josh Brodbeck, Matthew Harrigan, and Daniel Smith, "Citizen and Lobbyist Access to Members of Congress: Who Gets and Who Gives?" *Interest Groups & Advocacy* 2 (2013), https://doi.org/10.1057/iga.2013.11.

Chapter 22

59 National Conference of State Legislatures, "Voter ID Laws," accessed February 4, 2026, https://www.ncsl.org/elections-and-campaigns/voter-id.

60 John Woolley and Gerhard Peters, "2024," The American Presidency Project, last modified December 31, 2024, https://www.presidency.ucsb.edu/statistics/elections/2024.

Chapter 23

61 Ben Kamisar, "Polling Shows Growing Number of Republicans Identify with the MAGA Movement," NBC News, April 14, 2025, https://www.nbcnews.com/politics/trump-administration/polling-shows-growing-number-republicans-identify-maga-movement-rcna201071.

62 Kim Parker and Ruth Igielnik, "On the Cusp of Adulthood and Facing an Uncertain Future: What We Know About Gen Z So Far," Pew Research Center, May 14, 2020, https://www.pewresearch.org/social-trends/2020/05/14/on-the-cusp-of-adulthood-and-facing-an-uncertain-future-what-we-know-about-gen-z-so-far/.

63 Aaron Blake, "3 in 10 Trump Voters Want a President Willing to Break 'Rules and Laws,'" The Washington Post, December 18, 2023, https://www.washingtonpost.com/politics/2023/12/18/3-10-trump-voters-want-president-willing-break-rules-laws/.

64 Human Events Staff, "Jack Posobiec at NatCon: 'When You Have Principles but No Power You Are Delusional,'" *Human Events,* July 10, 2024, https://humanevents.com/2024/07/10/jack-posobiec-at-natcon-when-you-have-principles-but-no-power-you-are-delusional.

Appendix A

65 Bill Robinson, "Morgan Beats Smart by 76 Votes," *Richmond Register* (Richmond, KY), November 8, 2016, https://www.richmondregister.com/news/morgan-beats-smart-by-76-votes/article_d5efe77e-a631-11e6-b772-eb28598fd1d7.html.

Appendix C

66 Human Events Staff, "Jack Posobiec at NatCon."

67 Leading Change Network, Marshall Ganz, New Organizing Institute, Peter Gibbs, and Shea Sinnott, "Organizing Guide: People, Power, Change," The Commons, 2014, https://commonslibrary.org/organizing-people-power-change/.

68 Leading Change Network et al., "Organizing Guide."

69 Leading Change Network et al., "Organizing Guide."

70 Pew Research Center, "Support for Same-Sex Marriage at Record High, but Key Segments Remain Opposed," June 8, 2015, https://www.pewresearch.org/politics/2015/06/08/support-for-same-sex-marriage-at-record-high-but-key-segments-remain-opposed/.

71 SIECUS, "California's Proposition 8 Overturned by Federal Judge," SIECUS, August 2010. https://siecus.org/california%C2%92s-proposition-8-overturned-by-federal-judge.

72 Ganz, M. (2010). "Leading Change: Leadership, Organization, Social Movements" (p. 526).

73 Shea Sinnott and Peter Gibbs, *Organizing: People, Power, Change* (October 2014), https://commonslibrary.org/wp-content/uploads/Organizers_Handbook.pdf.

74 Sinnott and Gibbs, *Organizing,* 12.

75 Ganz, M. (2009). *Why Stories Matter: The Art and Craft of Social Change. Sojourners.* Retrieved from http://www.sojo.net/magazine/2009/03/why-stories-matter.

76 Sinnott and Gibbs, *Organizing,* 13.

77 Sinnott and Gibbs, *Organizing,* 13.

78 Sinnott and Gibbs, *Organizing,* 14.

79 Leading Change Network, Marshall Ganz, and New Organizing Institute, "What Is Organizing? An Introduction Based on the Work of Marshall Ganz," Commons Library, 2021, https://commonslibrary.org/what-is-organizing-an-introduction-based-on-the-work-of-marshall-ganz.

80 Leading Change Network, Ganz, and New Organizing Institute, "What Is Organizing?"

81 Sinnott and Gibbs, *Organizing,* 28.

82 Leading Change Network, Ganz, and New Organizing Institute, "What Is Organizing?"

83 Sinnott and Gibbs, *Organizing,* 35.

84 Leading Change Network, Ganz, and New Organizing Institute, "What Is Organizing?"

85 Sinnott and Gibbs, *Organizing*, 37.

86 Scott Adams, *Reframe Your Brain: The User Interface for Happiness and Success* (Scott Adams, Inc., 2023).

87 The Commons, "Rules for Radicals by Saul Alinsky," The Commons, accessed February 4, 2026, https://commonslibrary.org/rules-for-radicals-by-saul-alinsky/.